LANGUAGE: CONTEXT AND CONSEQUENCES

MAPPING SOCIAL PSYCHOLOGY

Series Editor: Tony Manstead

Current titles:

Icek Ajzen: Attitudes, Personality and Behavior
Steve Duck: Relating to Others
J. Richard Eiser: Social Judgment
Russell G. Geen: Human Aggression
Howard Giles and Nikolas Coupland: Language: Contexts and
    Consequences
John Turner: Social Influence
Leslie A. Zebrowitz: Social Perception

Forthcoming titles include:

Robert S. Baron, Norman Miller and Norbert L. Kerr: Group Processes
Marilyn B. Brewer and Norman Miller: Intergroup Relations
Richard Petty and John Cacioppo: Attitude Change
Dean G. Pruitt and Peter J. Carnevale: Bargaining and Third Party
    Intervention
Wolfgang Stroebe and Margaret Stroebe: Social Psychology and Health

LANGUAGE: CONTEXTS AND CONSEQUENCES

Howard Giles and
Nikolas Coupland

OPEN UNIVERSITY PRESS
MILTON KEYNES

Open University Press
Celtic Court
22 Ballmoor
Buckingham
MK18 1XW

First published 1991

British Library Cataloguing in Publication Data

Giles, Howard
  Language: contexts and consequences.—(Mapping social
  psychology).
  1. Sociolinguistics
  I. Title   II. Coupland, Nikolas   III. Series
  306.44
  ISBN 0-335-09873-8
  ISBN 0-335-09872-X pbk

Typeset by Rowland Phototypesetting Ltd
Bury St Edmunds, Suffolk
Printed and bound in Great Britain by
Woolnough Bookbinding Ltd
Irthlingborough, Northampton

CONTENTS

FOREWORD

There has long been a need for a carefully tailored series of reasonably short and inexpensive books on major topics in social
psychology, written primarily for students by authors who enjoy
a reputation for the excellence of their research and their ability to
communicate clearly and comprehensibly their knowledge of, and
enthusiasm for, the discipline. My hope is that the *Mapping Social
Psychology* series will meet that need.

The rationale for this series is twofold. First, conventional textbooks are too low-level and uninformative for use with senior
undergraduates or graduate students. Books in this series address
this problem partly by dealing with topics at book length, rather than
chapter length, and partly by the excellence of the scholarship and
clarity of the writing. Each volume is written by an acknowledged
authority on the topic in question, and offers the reader a concise and
up-to-date overview of the principal concepts, theories, methods and
findings relating to that topic. Although the intention has been to
produce books that will be used by senior level undergraduates and
graduate students, the fact that the books are written in a straightforward style should make them accessible to students with relatively
little previous experience of social psychology. At the same time, the
books are sufficiently informative to earn the respect of researchers
and instructors.

A second problem with traditional textbooks is that they are too
dependent on research conducted in or examples drawn from North
American society. This fosters the mistaken impression that social
psychology is a uniquely North American discipline and can also be
baffling for readers unfamiliar with North American culture. To

combat this problem, authors of books in this series have been encouraged to adopt a broader perspective, giving examples or citing research from outside North America wherever this helps to make a point. Our aim has been to produce books for a world market, introducing readers to an international discipline.

In this volume, Howard Giles and Nikolas Coupland provide the reader with a thorough introduction to the social psychology of language. This is a large field, ranging from the study of the cognitive factors that mediate language production and language reception to the role played by language in social interaction both as an independent variable, helping to construct social reality, and as a dependent variable, reflecting that reality. In writing an introduction to such a broad area, the authors have inevitably had to be selective, and they have chosen to focus on a number of interrelated topics. This, together with the fact that the book builds from theoretical issues to practical applications, gives the book a satisfying structural integrity. The book begins with a consideration of the relationship between language and social context, showing how speakers choose language forms to suit their immediate circumstances, and also how language can shape our perception and understanding of social phenomena. The authors go on to discuss the classic research on language attitudes, showing how the way someone speaks has important implications for how others react to him or her. This is followed by an analysis of speech accommodation theory, which addresses the processes underlying convergence and divergence between speakers' language. These three theoretical chapters provide an essential backdrop for the more applied chapters that follow: on ethnicity, on bilingualism, and on ageing and health. Here we learn about the crucial role played by language in establishing and threatening a speaker's sense of identity and well-being.

The approach adopted by the authors is noteworthy for the emphasis it places on an *intergroup* level of analysis. As they themselves note, this shifts the focus away from the adaptive and cooperative aspects of language that are often stressed in this literature, to a consideration of the problems that can arise in the course of communication between speakers who belong to different linguistic, ethnic, or generational groups. It also helps to remind us that linguistic phenomena in social interaction are shaped by forces that are 'macro' (political and cultural) in nature, as well as more 'micro' factors such as communicative competence. Another distinctive quality of the book is that it has a social constructionist flavour, according as much attention to the role played by language in constructing and reconstructing social life as to the way in which it reflects other social psychological constructs and processes. This takes the authors beyond research methods that are conventional for social psychologists, with a discourse analytic perspective being used to shed light on certain issues. In summary, the authors have accomplished the difficult task of providing a well-integrated and superbly up-to-date introduction to a disparate and fast-growing literature, while at the same time maintaining an epistemological balance between established and more novel approaches to the study of language in social life. The result makes for very interesting reading, and this book should prove to be invaluable to students and researchers alike.

Tony Manstead
Series Editor

PREFACE

Although sociopsychological work in language goes back a number of decades to the pioneering work of Michael Argyle, Jerome Bruner, Wallace Lambert, Roger Brown, Ragnar Rommetveit, Susan Ervin-Tripp and others, it is only because of an outpouring of research and theory in recent years such that we can now talk of a robust and definable 'social psychology of language' (SPL). As many have commented, this is in fact very surprising given that much of our social behaviour is essentially communicative and surfaces as language use. On the other hand, there is an enormous range of work, some of it long-standing, that has crucial *implications* for a sociopsychological understanding of language. That is to say, there is much in sociolinguistics, the sociology of language, communication science, the ethnography of speaking, discourse analysis and so forth which is of relevance to social psychologists, but which has yet to enter the mainstream of social psychology courses and texts.

For us and our colleagues, SPL has been characterized as the investigation of how cognitive factors mediate language reception and production, how language functions as a dependent as well as an independent variable in social contexts, both reflecting and determining our social reality. These priorities, together with an emphasis on experimental methods, have to date been the most distinctive features of the SPL approach relative to other language sciences (see Smith *et al.* 1980, for a more detailed discussion). But at this point, as our selection of topics and research contexts in the following chapters shows, we would wish to bring the mediating function of *affective* processes into sharper focus. At the same time, we would want to endorse the important claim that an SPL also needs to be centrally concerned with the ways in which sociopsychological constructs (attitudes, attributions, norms, identities) are constructed and reconstructed for individuals during interaction rather than immutable givens (Burgoon 1983; Antaki 1985; Potter and Wetherell 1987; Semin 1989). In later chapters, therefore, we reflect the growing impact of qualitative, discourse-analytic research designs in SPL which offer an important and traditionally untapped resource. This methodological realignment is not happening easily in SPL, and readers should be prepared for a bumpy ride when ideologies, and even epistemologies, collide. We do not set out to resolve the experimentalist–interpretivist conflict here, and in fact we doubt the need to frame a rather healthy process of reappraisal as 'conflict'. But quite starkly varying approaches to social explanation will appear, reflecting the ongoing debate within SPL about adequate methods.

This is, we think, only the second authored text devoted to the social psychology of language – the first being Robinson (1972). However, no book can now do real justice to the wide-ranging topics falling under the rubric of 'language' – even if we narrowly define the social psychological perspective. Inevitably, therefore, for some readers the book will not be cognitive enough, or child-developmental enough, will pay too little attention to non-verbal or other specific dimensions of discourse, or will underrepresent certain intra- and interpersonal processes, and so on. However, a very broad coverage of the area, with detailed reviews and analyses across a very range of topics, has been accomplished recently with the advent of the first *Handbook of language and social psychology* (Giles and Robinson 1990). Moreover, there are many excellent texts available in areas such as sociolinguistic development in children, language and gender, language and social class, discourse analysis, non-verbal communication and so forth. Our intention has been to focus on a manageable number of interrelated topics, and to introduce them in what we hope is a cumulative manner, beginning with more theoretical issues (in the first three chapters), then moving to specific 'applied' contexts where language and social forces and inequalities intersect. This spread of concerns, at least to our minds, builds on Lambert's (1980) vision for SPL in the 1980s. He argued that our most important role was and is to contribute to the dismantling of social discriminations, many of which are based, at least in part, on language or stylistic issues and/or are managed and reproduced through interaction and discourse. Relatedly, this book has a distinct *intergroup* flavour. Influenced by the late Henri Tajfel, we conceive of much so-called 'interpersonal' communication as being more appropriately and insightfully construed as intergroup in its dynamics, and this can be emancipating in at least three ways.

First, while there is a positivity bias in the study of language and communication towards understanding co-operation, communicative competence, satisfaction, efficiency and second language proficiency, an intergroup perspective implicitly instills in us the need to look at the other side of the coin – why speaker-hearers are in many respects, and perhaps inevitably, less than competent; why communication is often flawed, inefficient and partial; why the acquisition of skills and competencies (for example, in a second language) is often impaired. These 'miscommunicative' processes, as we shall see, may not be the simple converses of those success-orientated ones we tend to investigate, but are rather of a different order.

Second, when *individual* linguistic and communicative deficits are highlighted, as in the case of elderly people 'underaccommodating' to younger conversation partners, an intergroup approach encourages us to consider ways in which such language patterns derive from rational, positively valued, *group* identity needs.

Third, such an approach suggests that the factors which affect our production and reception of language behaviours need not be the micro-level ones *immediate in* that situation. Given that our interactions are sometimes based on group definitions, macro-level factors (for example, perceptions of social and political inequity), sometimes of hundreds of years' standing, can permeate the sociolinguistic here-and-now without our being aware of them. This in turn suggests that attempts to modify the local dynamics of interindividual communication (for example, patterns of doctor–patient exchange) address the problem at the wrong level – if the social structure and institutional (for example, health and medical) realities, norms, roles and images remain unchallenged.

Ultimately, we hope readers will recognize how language impinges in crucial and complex ways on *adult* social life that should not be sidestepped by mainstream social psychology. For example, we know that one of the few agreed causes of marital discontent and divorce is a breakdown in communication between spouses, sometimes resulting in severe clinical conditions, damage to the couple's social networks, and lowered productivity at work. Job satisfaction and productivity are also related to the exchange of open messages up and down the occupational hierarchy. The ability to adapt linguistically to one's listeners has also been positively related to effective leadership in organizational settings. A lack of satisfying and 'quality' experiences of communication can have serious consequences, with chronic loneliness leading to depression, alcoholism and drug abuse. On the other hand, 'effective' interaction can be a means of easing psychological suffering for those who have cancer or have been recently bereaved. A comprehensive listing of the important roles of language in psychological as well as material outcomes would be wellnigh endless. It shows how urgently we need to reach a better understanding of the sociolinguistic and relational factors that comprise these deceptively simple-sounding descriptions of talk in context.

In this book, we shall see that an understanding of language behaviours informs the micro-dynamics of everyday social interactions which in turn are the breeding ground for many of the identities we are continually evolving. So we shall attend to the old standards of language attitudes and second language learning (though with some fresh insights), but also highlight the roles of language in domains that either have been the traditional province of other language disciplines – such as the survival and death of languages – or have not figured prominently in some areas at all – such as ageing and health. We shall examine how and why our language patterns change as we move from one situation to another and as our social circumstances change through the life course. But we shall also be concerned about how and why, at the group level, a language evolves according to historical demands and can even disappear altogether. Overall, this book is an attempt to provide a coherent theoretical approach for the study of culturally relevant interpersonal and intergroup processes across a wide range of language situations. The analyses not only have relevance for cosy constructs such as interactional satisfaction but are also critical for our physical well-being across the lifespan.

We have tried to make the volume readily accessible to students and scholars whose knowledge of linguistic phenomena and analysis is minimal. Rather than immerse readers in the descriptive minutiae of language, we have on this occasion leapt straight into the interrelationships between language use and sociopsychological constructs. We fully acknowledge that the future development of SPL will hinge on a closer integration of descriptive sociolinguistic rigour and cognitive theorizing than has typically been achieved to date. On the other hand, our goals are to intrigue the language novice in social psychology, and to show the theoretical developments that sociolinguistics and other language-based approaches can already draw on to illuminate their own traditions of research. There is also the important consideration, implicit in the very origins of SPL as a distinctive discipline, that what is defined as language and what we hear and act on as language is subject to a host of cognitive biases which may contradict descriptive linguistic characterizations. Language and linguistic varieties are, after all, social constructs, and just as much sociopsychological (and political, and sociological) as linguistic. Relatedly, and as we shall see throughout this volume, to isolate language conceptually from other social constructs may be analytically appealing – yet it can blinker us from appreciating the very processes and issues that we set out to study. For example, we need to treat language as an inextricable component of situational and health definitions, expressed attitudes, and ethnic and ageing identities. Not surprisingly, then, all topics in this book are inter-meshed. We cannot reasonably talk, for instance, of second language acquisition without having recourse to ethnic identity, and ethnic identity cannot be adequately conceived without notions of context. When discussing context, we have to look ahead (in terms of the book's structure) to language attitudes, interpersonal influence pro-cesses and even bilingualism. Any starting point is somewhat arbit-rary and we have chosen context only as the traditionally conceived 'backdrop' for language behaviours, though recognizing that its separability may be illusory. We hope that the connections we are able to make, and need to make, to non-psychological traditions of research will foster some of the cross-disciplinary exchange we have argued for among the language sciences for many years now. After all, a true understanding of language and society *has*, ultimately, to be *inter*disciplinary. Disciplinary boundaries must be overcome, and by more than mere lip-service; it is our hope that this book will make some modest contribution towards this end, despite its principally sociopsychological focus.

No preface is complete without heartfelt acknowledgements, despite the interpersonal hazards of perceived unjustified omission. For its first author, this book is the cumulation of many years' research and teaching in SPL and as such is directly dependent on the influence of scores of students and colleagues at UC Cardiff, Bristol, McGill and Santa Barbara who have assisted immeasurably to its development. For its second author, it is the opportunity to set down ideas that have hovered for several years over a 'boundary' between sociolinguistics and social psychology that ultimately proved illusory. Again, gratitude needs to be expressed to students and colleagues at the University of Wales College of Cardiff (and formerly at UWIST) for allowing this interdisciplinary approach to foster. A year as a visiting professor at Santa Barbara, sponsored by the Fulbright Commission, gave the time to collaborate on this manuscript.

Several other venues, friends and associates rapidly and legitimately spring to mind and we trust they will understand contextual constraints and the need to avoid Oscarization. However, a few folk over the years have had considerable influence on our understanding of language and the writing of this book, including the aforementioned Wally Lambert and Henri Tajfel as well as Don Taylor, Klaus Scherer, Peter Powesland, Phil Smith, Jim Bradac, Richard Bourhis, Jitu Thakerar, and Peter Robinson. Moreover, a number of the sections of different chapters of the book arise from collaborative writing with Justine Coupland, Peter Garrett, Miles Hewstone, Pat Johnson, Laura Leets, Ellen Ryan, John Wiemann, and Angie Williams (who was also of invaluable assistance at the bibliographic stage). Our sincere appreciation also to Jim Bradac and Cindy Gallois who generously agreed to read a draft version and provided us with valuable feedback. Finally, this volume would not have emerged without the pulls, patience, and advice of Tony Manstead and the valued understanding of John Skelton on the one hand, and the tugs, understanding and love of Jane Byrne and Justine Coupland on the other, the first of whom was left literally 'holding the baby' during the entirety of far too many weekends. This book is for you all and for our families.

Howard Giles and Nikolas Coupland

1 / LANGUAGE IN CONTEXT

In the late 1950s and early 1960s, the study of language came to focus on explaining why it was that people could produce an endless stream of novel sentences, many of which had never been uttered by anyone else before, and yet were readily understood by others. The answer at that time (Chomsky 1965) was that there are a limited number of complex but finite grammatical rules from which an infinite number of sentences can be generated. This work stimulated research in the field of child language development and brought new life to the field of (cognitive) psycholinguistics. Nevertheless, the impact of this approach which we can term 'language *without* social context' seemed to draw most researchers away from considering language as a *social* instrument used for communicative purposes. Over the last two to three decades, other approaches to language have emerged that have revived the early British linguists' concern for meanings in context, and are therefore more communicative in essence. The two main perspectives we shall discuss in this chapter view language either as *determined by* or as itself *determining* the nature of a social context (Giles and Wiemann 1987; Pellowe 1990). Not every approach can be encapsulated in this neat dichotomy, and some span the two perspectives. Nevertheless, this conceptual net captures a large proportion of the existing literature.

The 'language builds upon context' approach

But first, we need to establish that, in a more general sense, language also needs to *build upon* the context in which it is encoded. In saying this, we suggest that interactants share an array of assumptions; in fact, while it is perennially difficult to capture what *is* actually shared, this must be the case otherwise meaningful communication could never get off the ground. As Hermann (1982) points out in articulating the *pars pro toto* principle, a basic problem facing speakers is how to construct messages which convey the essence of the necessarily larger set of assumptions and implications they hold, and in such a way that a reasonable proportion of this information can be accessed by receivers. The more shared assumptions we have between us, the greater 'intersubjectivity' there will be (see Rommet-veit 1979). Knapp's (1983) model of relationship development explores the way romantic partners 'intensify' their intimacy by developing so-called 'taken-for-granteds' (Hopper 1981). Similarly, Ragan and Hopper (1984) note that in novels, the last encounter depicted between lovers usually involves a 'suspension of the let-it-pass rule', a so-called 'consensus on dissensus'. One or other of the characters begins a process of exploring tacit relational nuances, with questions such as 'What do you mean?'. This indicates a sudden lack of intersubjectivity between them, thereby legitimizing (per-haps sometimes strategically) an exit from the relationship by the perpetrator.

Of course, in everyday conversations much is 'let pass' without meanings ever being made clear, either because it lacks immediate significance to the listener, or perhaps because the listener believes that 'all will be revealed in due course'. So interactants at times count on the fact that they will not be taken to task on each point, which can facilitate intentional misunderstandings, deceptions, and other similar less-than-truthful episodes. In this way, much of language use is built on shared presuppositions and shared knowledge about our social contexts; meanings by far outstrip the referents of the words themselves. What is achieved in an act of speaking (the so-called 'illocutionary force' of an utterance) is as much a function of contextual inferences as of the meanings of words and grammatical structures themselves. The more shared presuppositions of relative power in a relationship – say, between mother and child, doctor and patient, or employer and employee – the more tacitly the illocution-ary force of a command can be conveyed. In an example provided by Ervin-Tripp (1980) of a mother wanting her child to put on his new pair of shoes, the mother does not give him a forthright command, but achieves this implicitly:

MOTHER: Where are those nice new shoes I bought for you
yesterday, Johnny?
CHILD: In the closet (*said with a grin*)
MOTHER: Don't you get clever with me . . .

The powerful can thus use language to influence others when the
surface forms of their language appear polite, where explicit commands are unnecessary and talking 'off-record' gets the job done
(Brown and Levinson 1987).

The 'language reflects context' approach

Many approaches have recognized the importance of social context
even to the extent of claiming that language use is very largely
prescribed and proscribed by the situation in which it is spoken,
including the characteristics of the speakers involved (see for example, Gumperz 1972). This 'language reflects context' paradigm is
built on the well-established foundation that we have speech (and
also non-verbal) *repertoires* from which we can select to meet the
normative demands of situations. This allows speakers to select
(sometimes mindfully and othertimes as a matter of scripted behaviour) different languages or dialects for producing essentially the
same message, alternative variants of the same word-meaning (think
of the voluminous possibilities for referring to another or oneself as
'drunk'!), a range of syntactic forms varying in complexity, a modified accent, pitch range, speech rate and intonation pattern for the
same set of utterances, and so on. People will account for the same
action quite differently, depending on the context they find themselves in (Cody and McLaughlin 1990). And, on the receptive–
interpretive side, the same disclosive act has different interpretive
potential depending on timing and social location (Holtgraves
1990). As Hymes (1972: 38) stated:

> No normal person, and no normal community, is limited to a
> single way of speaking, to an unchanging monotony that
> would preclude indication of respect, insolence, mock serious-
> ness, humour, role distance, and intimacy by switching from
> one mode of speech to another.

An important issue arising from this is to appreciate that another's
speech style is not simply a static dispositional reflection of competences and personality but is rather, and in large measure, a

barometer of how they construe themselves in the situation as they define it (or have it defined for them). Indeed, when we perceive others to be consistent in their speech style on different occasions, this may well *not* be a cue as to what they sound like trans-situationally, but rather a reflection of how they respond socioling-uistically to *us* (and those like us) very specifically. Or perhaps it reflects how we have tacitly negotiated how talk between us should proceed. A lack of appreciation of contextual constraints on lan-guage use in everyday social life can lead to all sorts of misattribu-tions and misguided decisions, as was sorely evident in the study of the relationships between language and (socioeconomic) class. Too often, assessments and interpretations of the communicative incom-petence of certain ethnic minorities and working-class people were based (as they doubtless still are in some everyday settings) on analyses of their language sampled in very formal, anxiety-provoking situations on abstract, unfamiliar topics introduced to them by statusful elders (see Labov 1969).

One of the most influential concepts in the sociolinguistic litera-ture is 'diglossia', which relates to the use of two languages or dialects in bilingual or bidialectal societies, each serving different functions with different status connotations. The so-called low (L) variety of language or dialect is most often confined to such areas as the home, everyday activities, and friendship, while the high (H) variety is often acquired later in the socialization process and is reserved for use in more formal and public arenas. Rubin (1962) provided the vivid example of Paraguay, where at the time it was expected that courting couples should converse in Spanish until they had solemnized their vows. Thereafter, they were immediately free to converse in their local (and more intimate) language, Guarani. In his research, Fishman (1972) proposed five general situational domains: the family, the neighbourhood, religion, education and employment. He notes that for bilingual Mexican Americans, Spanish might be used in the context of the family, neighbourhood or religion but English would be used at work or in the classroom. An important feature of this analysis is that because the two varieties are fulfilling separated social functions in their different domains, their linguistic structures will represent this division and will not overlap. Thus, for instance, informal grammatical structures and the vocabulary of the kitchen would exist in Spanish for such Mexicans but not in English, which would be represented only through more formal structures and lexis. In many multilingual societies, such a simple dichotomy into H and L varieties is grossly insufficient, as indeed are the five situational categories. For this reason, Platt (1977) invoked the notion of 'polyglossia', illustrating it by the case of ethnic Chinese in Malaysia who have a speech repertoire that includes six varieties for use in particular sub-domains.

This general conceptual framework for characterizing speech diversity in multilingual societies has been adapted for describing similar processes in monolingual communities. To this end, a variety of taxonomies have emerged over the years that attempt to specify how objective characteristics of social situations affect particular speech patterns, including the fine details of socially significant vowel and consonant sounds. The first of these to receive widespread acceptance is that of Hymes (1972) who concentrated attention in the main on three components: *setting* (which physically locates the interaction); *participants* (characterisics of the interactants); and *ends* or *purposes* (the extended objectives). Subsequent taxonomies deserve mention regarding their special features. Ervin-Tripp (1969) and others provided situational taxonomies with a view to formulating *rules* for social grammars specifying the particular speech patterns appropriate for certain situations. Giles and Powesland (1975) stressed the salience of characteristics of the *person addressed* whereas Brown and Fraser (1979) and others have opted for the pre-eminence of the *purpose* of the interaction in determining the speech patterns produced (cf. Fielder *et al.* 1989; Semin and Fielder 1989). Brown and Fraser (1979: 34) suggested that 'purpose is the motor which sets the chassis of setting and participants going'. We shall dwell on this taxonomy not only because it is one of the most comprehensive and archetypal of the so-called 'objective taxonomy' approaches (Giles and Hewstone 1982) but also because, more than others, it goes some way towards considering speakers as actors in a dynamic social relationship rather than as static individuals.

Brown and Fraser's taxonomy

As Figure 1.1 shows, Brown and Fraser divide their taxonomy of situations initially into two components of *scene* and *participants*. Scene has been further subdivided into *setting* and *purpose*, each of which includes finer distinctions, while participants has been sub-divided into *individual* and *relationship* characteristics, each again having their finer discriminations. From the vast empirical literature on language and context, let us provide a flavour of the speech correlates found to be associated with these objective features of situation.

Within the scene category, Brown and Fraser (like many others) have noted that the dimension *formality–informality* is a core determinant of speech. Labov (1966) was one of the first to point out the linear relationship between formality and the prestige value of phonological variants. In his seminal work, which subsequently stimulated a tradition of such work in a wide array of Anglo- and Francophone communities, he showed that when different groups of New Yorkers were interviewed, their language patterns showed increasingly frequent use of prestigious forms as they moved from so-called 'casual' topics to the serious interview itself, through to reading and finally reading word-lists. Many facets of this work are important, though we shall outline only three of them here. First, Labov showed that all socioeconomic sectors of New York society shifted in this manner, though their starting and ending points differed. For example, the upper-middle class as classified by Labov used 69% of a high prestige pronunciation variant (postvocalic /r/) in casual speech and 96% in their reading style; working-class speakers used 0% and 14% respectively. Second, he demonstrated many between-group effects: for example, women shifted more than men, with lower-middle-class women shifting into sociolinguistic strata even beyond those of the upper-middle-class informants. This phenomenon, known as *hypercorrection*, was also found among some second-generation Italian, Jewish and Mexican Americans in the United States in their attempts to differentiate themselves from sub-stratum influences in their parents' English, and to over-compensate on certain vowel sounds. As Trudgill (1974: 63) stated:

> Native speakers of Italian tend to use an /a/ type vowel, more open than the English sound in English words of this type, and their children, in wishing to avoid this pronunciation, may have selected the highest variants of this vowel available to them, i.e. the ones most unlike the typically Italian vowel.

Such hypercorrections themselves soon become recognized, and often stigmatized as speech markers of the ethnic group involved. Third, Labov also showed that a speaker's social aspirations more accurately predicted the prestige value of their spoken language than their currently measured socioeconomic position.

Figure 1.1 shows that the specific componets of setting – the social

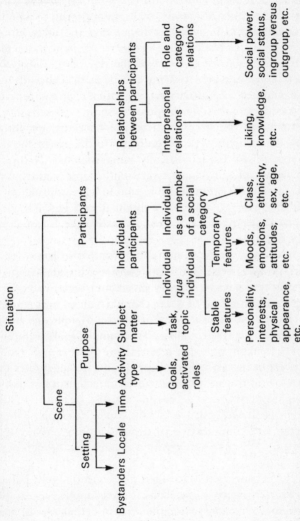

Figure 1.1 Components of situation

Source: Brown and Fraser (1979: 35)

composition of the interaction and its physical temporal locations –
all have potentially important consequences for linguistic usage. For
instance, in a particular Aboriginal language, a distinctive 'mother-
in-law' code is spoken whenever the implied relative is present (a
'bystander effect'). In some Polynesian societies, there is reportedly
avoidance of the king's name or anything approaching the sound of it
in the confines of his kingdom (a 'locale effect'). And in Morocco, a
different Arabic word denoting 'needle' is rendered in the morning
from the one used for the rest of the day. Regarding *purposes*,
different large-scale activity types can be associated with different
stylistic qualities. The activity type of casual chatting, for example,
has a more 'verbal' style, evident in short, syntactically simple
utterances, and the very frequent use of verbs, pronouns and
adverbs. The activity type of lecturing (to the extent there is uni-
formity there) is characteristically more nominal. Naturally, the
subject matter of the activity type itself has important speech correlates, so that, for example, more emotionally arousing topics will
predictably give rise to more colloquial and less standard pronunciation patterns, together with a faster speech rate and more
dysfluencies.

Regarding the second major component of situations in Figure
1.1, *participants*, speech has been found to correlate with speakers'
stable characteristics, transitory states and social category memberships. As an example of stable characteristics, Laver and Trudgill
(1979) have discussed the ways in which physique and height can
determine various vocal qualities (for example, a tall, well-built man
may for evident physiological reasons have a deeper and louder voice
than his smaller peers). Scherer (1979) has reviewed studies showing
that stable and transitory personality characteristics of individuals
such as extroversion and depression can also be indicated linguistically. For instance, extroverts talk louder and pause less than
introverts, and certain kinds of depressives are verbally less productive and talk more softly with a greater lack of high overtones
than 'normals'.

A fairly recent review of the literature concerning the influence of
individual difference dimensions (for example, levels of self-
monitoring and cognitive complexity) on verbal, vocal, and non-
verbal indices of communicative behaviours, however, failed to
produce many reliable main effects for these intra-individual parameters (Giles and Street 1985). Such factors do indeed have effects,
but usually only in interaction with other sociodemographic and

contextual variables. For instance, highly anxious individuals display a linguistic profile of distress (for example, speech disfluencies) but *only* when talking about or actually in an emotionally arousing situation.

The *relationships* existing between participants, whether they be interpersonal, role-based or category-based relationships, also affect patterns of speech and non-verbal behaviour. Participants who like each other display more verbal productivity and self-disclosures but less silent pausing than those who are not mutually attracted. In fact, the study of relationships and language is a burgeoning area of research (Wilmot and Shellen 1990). Berger (1979) has, from a cognitive perspective, characterized initial encounters between people as involving the reduction of uncertainty and has outlined the language behaviours used strategically to achieve this. For instance, mutual interrogation followed by self-disclosure not only allows participants to make their partner more predictable but delivers more certainty about how they themselves might respond 'appropriately' (see Chapter 6). Asymmetrical status and power roles are found cross-culturally in address terms, as in the case of a pupil calling his teacher 'Sir' and receiving last-name in return, and in non-verbal distancing patterns by differential use of interpersonal space, backward lean, and gaze patterns. Among the many contexts where status and/or power differences abound and have pragmatic significance are the doctor's consulting room and the courtroom. Table 1.1 summarizes some central findings from American studies in medical settings. The conversational imbalance displayed here (which obviously depends on a host of doctor styles and characteristics such as experience, age and gender) runs the risk of a physician

Table 1.1   A sociolinguistic profile of conversational imbalance in medical consultations

1	Doctor does most of the talking.
2	Doctor initiates 99 per cent of the utterances.
3	Patient poses only 9 per cent of questions raised.
4	Doctor keeps asking further questions before patient has answered last one.
5	Doctor interrupts patient more (except when doctor is female).
6	Doctor determines agenda and topic shifts.
7	Doctor determines encounter's termination.

Source: Wiemann and Giles (1988: 205)

'not getting to the bottom' of the problem by not letting patients frame it in their terms or allowing them their own interpretations of events.

Knapp (1983) has discussed eight dimensions of language and communicative behaviour that differentiate short- from long-term encounters (for example, breadth and depth of disclosures, and 'smoothness'). Moreover, he argues that relationships develop toward greater intimacy through five stages – initiating, experimenting, intensifying, integrating, and bonding – each of which has discernible language correlates. For instance, 'intensifying' is associated with increasing use of private codes and neologisms and more direct expressions of commitment. In his 'staircase' model, Knapp likewise argues that the dissolution of relationships is concomitant with a decrease in intimacy. Again with language correlates, he posits five phases that typify relationships as they tumble down to actual termination. Duck (1982) has criticized the notion that relationship decline is simply the converse of its development, claiming that there are distinct and unique features associated with dissolution, and Baxter (1984) agrees that the process of relationship breakdown can take many paths. She provides a trajectory model elucidating these various ends. Moreover, Baxter (1985) discusses the language behaviours associated with unilateral and bilateral disengagement in terms of two orthogonal dimensions – directness and other-orientedness. Thus the quadrant of high directness and other-orientedness would be marked communicationally by explicit 'state of the relationship talk' and 'negotiated farewells'. Baxter also discusses the individual and relational attributes that would increase the likelihood of linguistic directness (for example, androgyny, prior closeness).

Marital relationships have been the target of much research where language and communication variables are shown to reflect relational dissatisfaction or distress (Noller and Fitzpatrick 1988) and divorce, as mentioned in the Preface. This literature shows marital nonadjustment to be apparent in vocal, verbal and non-verbal channel inconsistencies, lowered informational exchange, fewer self-disclosures, and the like. Moreover, there often appears to be asymmetry in distressed couples, such that wives respond even to small affective changes in their spouses whereas husbands do not react to even significant changes in their wives' language patterns. Gottman (1982), sequentially exploring the nature of conflict situations in distressed and adjusted couples, suggests that a communication feature of adjusted couples is their ability to de-escalate, linguistically, potential negative affect when it emerges. Finally, Fitzpatrick (1990) has been able to discriminate polythetically and empirically three couple types – ('traditionals', 'independents' and 'separates', as well as various 'mixed' types) based on their subjective appraisals of their own interdependence, relational ideology and communicative expressiveness. She has been able to present a linguistic profile of these as well as the kinds of marital schema which mediate them.

There is a long and well-known tradition of research into the relationship between language and sex/gender, much of it triggered by Lakoff's (1973) claim that women use 'powerless' language to the extent they use, for example, more hedges ('sort of', 'kinda'), intensifiers ('so', 'very'), and tag questions ('isn't it?') and by the finding that men interrupt women more than vice versa (Zimmerman and West 1975). Such differences – and they have been far from unequivocal empirically and in any case more a matter of degree than kind – were claimed to be a reflection of the subservient role of women in society. However, the use of a powerless speech style is not confined to females, or even necessarily related to gender yet it seems to be downgraded in many contexts (see, however, Berk-Seligson 1988). Others such as Maltz and Borker (1982) have been pointing to cultural differences between men and women which may predispose communicative differences, such as different interpretations of the meaning of questions and different conventions for coherence in linking utterances. In terms of problem-sharing and advice-giving, Maltz and Borker (1982: 213) claim that:

> Women tend to discuss problems with one another, sharing experiences and offering reassurances. Men, in contrast, tend to hear women, and other men, who present them with problems as making explicit requests for solutions. They respond by giving advice, by acting as experts, lecturing to their audiences.

Indeed, a controversy has reigned over the years about whether differences do exist or not and, if so, in which contexts. At the same time, convincing evidence is emerging (West and Garcia 1988) across a wide array of ages, writing, speech and media contexts suggesting distinctive gender differences in language usage (see also Mulac and Lundell 1986). The findings indicate that what constitutes so-called male and female language styles differs across socioverbal contexts, and that the cues people use to evaluate these styles also vary somewhat depending on the domain. This 'gender-linked language effect' – which becomes apparent by women being upgraded on dimensions of sociointellectual status and aesthetics but down-graded relative to men on dynamism – is less evident in mixed-sex dyads where members of each sex possibly accommodate linguisti-cally to their stereotypes of the other sex's behaviour (see Chapter 3).

Of course, differences *within* the sex categories have also been examined, although the more general tendency has been to study inter-gender differences as though they were homogeneous entities. However, Trudgill (1974) has pointed to the interaction of social class and gender, and Giles *et al.* (1980) produced data suggesting that ideologies concerning the role of women in society can them-selves be marked vocally. In relation to gender identity, for example, Smith (1980) showed that listeners could identify masculine, femi-nine, and androgynous individuals from voice features alone (as when reading the same passage of prose). Some commentators have recently been advocating abandoning the sex difference and cultural approaches in favour of a move towards a more dynamic framework which examines the relationships between power, abuse, sexism and language. For instance, Kramarae (1990) states that 'language main-tains the gender hierarchy by its power to "victimize" women in their relationships (friendly, loving and professional) with men'. In any case, people expect communicative differences to exist and these expectations may set up an evaluative template for the interpretation of power- or gender-salient language features (such as tag questions).

Other pertinent areas of concern in the literature include the relations between socioeconomic classes and between ethnic groups, which often cannot be separated empirically. In the class domain, while many linguistic and communication differences have been identified – and most of them tend to be evaluated in 'deficit' terms, with lower-class people seen to be less expressive non-verbally, to use less diverse vocabulary, more ungrammaticalities, and so on (Haslett 1990) – controversy has reigned about the origins and communicat-ive consequences of differences. The language of working-class people has been shown to be no less rule-based, logical or rich than middle-class language; it has been argued that working-class lan-guage should be considered 'different' rather than sub-standard (Labov 1969), a position often also relevant in situations relating to minority ethnic groups. But however they are labelled, these lin-guistic differences function as class or group 'markers' that provide the opportunity for easy ingroup–outgroup distinctions (both desired and undesired) for sustaining and expressing group identity.

An important point made by Brown and Fraser here is that the speaker's speech patterns may well not be a function of their individual or social group characteristics, whether they be sex-or class-linked (as above) or ethnic- and generationally-dependent (see Chapters 4 and 6), though this is often assumed to be the case. Rather, they can be a reflection of the *social relationship* existing between them and their interlocutors in different scenes (Brown and Levinson 1987). In other words, if the power or affective relationship between the two speakers is changed the ensuing speech patterns will, of necessity, be modified too.

Several further features of Brown and Fraser's analysis are worthy of note and have stimulated subsequent theoretical developments. First, they were aware that within a situation a speaker may act, and be seen to act, either as an individual *qua* individual or as an exemplar of a particular social category (see below). Second, like others, they point out (1979: 54) that 'an understanding of the nature of the scene, *as viewed by the participants,* is essential in order to detect and interpret many of the markers that appear in their speech' (emphasis added) and hence 'we would do well to pursue lines of research that could get at the actor's-eye-view of the situation' (1979: 56). Taking on board these issues, Giles and Hewstone (1982) devised a subjective approach to the study of language and situation which was intended as a complement to the foregoing and provides a clear programme for empirical research. But before considering this, it is necessary to provide a brief backdrop to the specifically social psychological study of situations and intergroup relations.

Perceived structure of social situations

We now focus upon the fundamental dimensions underlying people's perceptions of social situations. Wish and Kaplan (1977) asked subjects to evaluate a series of hypothetical communication episodes involving both role relationships (for example, bitter enemies) and situational contexts (for example, exchanging views about a politician both participants disliked). Multidimensional scaling analyses of the data revealed that subjects cognitively represented the episodes on five dimensions: co-operative–competitive; intense–superficial; formal–informal; dominant–equal; task-orientated–non-task-orientated. Even when the hypothetical episodes to be evaluated explicitly included the raters themselves (for example, you and your co-worker are attempting to work out a compromise when your goals are strongly opposed), the same five dimensions emerged. Interestingly, it was found in both studies that the nature of the role relationship affected formality and dominance, whereas the situational context affected more the dimensions of co-operation, intensity and task-relatedness. In another study, subjects were asked to view a series of short videotapes involving different scenes with husband and wife, lawyer and client, strangers, and so forth. Once again, even when naturally occurring communication episodes were observed, essentially the same dimensions accounted for subjects' definition of the situations.

One interesting feature of Wish and Kaplan's findings is that different sub-groups attach different emphases to the five dimensions. So, for instance, left-wing students placed more weight on the dominance–equality dimension than students of other political persuasions. The importance of sub-cultural differences emerges very strongly from the related research of Forgas (1979), who has asked different sections of the community to evaluate social episodes with which they were familiar. He, too, used multidimensional scaling techniques and found that different status-groups within an institution placed different weights on the same dimensions they used for defining the same social episodes. Thus, within an academic university department, the teaching faculty tended to judge situations more in terms of an involvement dimension, graduate students gave preference to a socioemotional dimension, while technical and other staff relied mostly on an anxiety dimension. Forgas also found that certain groups have more complex construals of episodes than others in the sense that undergraduate used three, while housewives used two dimensions for construing the same social situations. Forgas (1979: 282) commented that 'while "socializing with friends" for students appears to be natural, self-selected entertainment, for housewives it may be a more demanding, formal and organized affair, involving an element of self-presentation'. Social values are also likely to affect representations of episodes, and Forgas, together with Bond, focused upon the cross-cultural dimension by examining differences between Australian and Hong Kong students in this respect. Forgas (1988: 207) overviewed the findings as follows:

'Chinese subjects saw episodes in terms of communality, collectivism, and social usefulness. The episode characteristics that Australian subjects weighted most highly are competitiveness, self-confidence, and freedom as well as the hedonistic aspects of interactions'. For the Hong Kong students, 'equal–unequal power' was the prime dimension whereas it was 'competitiveness' for the Australians. As Forgas suggested, the greater the discrepancy between two interlocutors' episodic representations of the same conversational context, the greater the potential for problematic talk (see Chapter 4).

But we should be wary of asserting that individuals always perceive situations in these terms, or that such perceptions always guide their behaviour. As Langer (1978: 38) has claimed, 'most of the time people are not consciously seeking explanations or trying to assess their cognitive processes'. Indeed, in many routine interactions, people probably only need to process minimal cues in order to engage a script to interact successfully. Still, the point to be drawn out here is that different individuals *may* use different dimensions for construing the same situation. In addition, the dimensions used by different people may vary in complexity and even when different individuals do use common dimensions, different weights may be placed upon them, and the same episodes may be seen at opposite poles of the same dimension. Hence, no *objective* classification of situations, such as that provided by Brown and Fraser and others, is sufficient in itself for understanding individuals' subjective definitions of the same social episodes. Therefore, objectively describing a social situation as 'a formal interview on a serious topic with a 90-year-old Scottish woman' will be a poor predictor of her speech-patterns if *she* defines the interview herself informally, considers the subject matter irrelevant and trivial, feels her ethnic background is irrelevant to who and what she is, and feels 50 years of age! In other words, speech is far more likely to be dependent upon how speakers cognitively represent their characteristics and subjectively define the scene than any upon objective classification imposed from without. That said, given social consensus about particular normative ways of behaving in situations, there is often much homogeneity of episodic representations within a group of people in the same situation. This is why objective situational definitions have had some success in predicting linguistic variation. Perhaps we could add that because there are social sanctions against communicative deviance in many formal situations, it is possible that individuals' construals may be overriden by the prevailing norms and expectations, and communicative choices will after all follow normative predictions.

Intergroup relations

Research into the social psychology of intergroup relations has relied on notions such as authoritarianism, frustration-aggression, belief dissimilarity, and realistic group threat to account for social prejudices (Billig 1976). But Tajfel (1978, for example) has shown that such factors cannot account for intergroup discrimination when individuals are simply allocated membership of two distinct categories, and where resources are not scarce for either group. Rather, he contends that processes of a different order (such as social identification and identity) are operating at the intergroup level. In Chapter 4, intergroup theory will be discussed as a way of promoting our understanding of language discrimination and creativity. In the meantime, we need to introduce an important distinction made by Tajfel and Turner (1979) concerning two types of social interaction which were considered bipolar. At one extreme – the 'inter-individual' pole–speakers would conduct their discourse in terms of each others' idiosyncratic attributes, personalities, moods and temperaments. When this happens, individuals' *personal* identities are activated. Contrastively at the 'intergroup' pole, people tend to depersonalize themselves and treat those they are interacting with not as individuals but rather as representative members of social categories. Under these conditions, relevant aspects of a particular *social identity* are accessed. Tajfel and Turner (1979: 36) argued that the more members of a group conceived of an encounter to be 'located' towards the intergroup pole (and presumably, away from the interindividual pole),

> the more uniformity will they show in their behaviour towards members of the relevant outgroup . . . [and] . . . the more they tend to treat members of the outgroup as undifferentiated items in a unified social category rather than in terms of their individual characteristics.

That different processes are operative at either end of the continuum was well exemplified in an interview with Nabih Berri (the Lebanese Shiite Amal militia chief) who was reported in a London newspaper, *The Guardian* (26 September 1982) as saying that 'when we deal with each other individually, we can be civilized ... But when we deal with each other as groups, we are like savage tribes in the Middle Ages'. The unique drawing power of the intergroup end of the continuum was also apparent when the captain of the 1988 New Zealand Olympics team was interviewed in a local newspaper after the opening ceremony, where he surprised onlookers, as well as himself, by parading the national flag. Relating his excitement and sense of pride at representing his nation in this way, he commented that at that time 'I would have done anything they asked'.

Giles and Hewstone (1982), like others since, preferred to consider this bipolar dimension as essentially two separate and independent continua, each with extremes that can be labelled 'high' and 'low'. An advantage is that it allows us to conceive of some situations as simultaneously high on *both* intergroup and interindividual levels, such as participants in trade union–management negotiations who are trying to come to terms not only with the group stances of the other party but also the personal styles of their representatives.

Tajfel and his associates have been concerned with developing a theory for understanding social processes operating at the intergroup end of the continuum, much of which is concerned with specifying the conditions necessary, and strategies used, for achieving a positive ingroup identity (termed *'psychological distinctiveness'*), as we shall see in Chapter 4. Given that language can be an important dimension of identity for many social groupings (particularly class and ethnic categories), it has been argued that when a situation is defined as high in intergroup, (and low in interindividual) terms, then speaker-hearers will search for psycho*linguistic* distinctiveness on language dimensions they value and accentuate their ingroup speech and non-verbal markers. In terms of communication accommodation theory, which will be introduced in Chapter 3, they will diverge in their language patterns from outgroup speakers. However, should they define an interaction as high in interindividual (and low in intergroup) terms, then they are likely to attenuate their distinctive ingroup markers and converge towards the language behaviours of the other person. The admittedly gross linguistic contrasts that are allied to these intergroup cognitions are open to all sorts of situational (and other) caveats of course, and these will be entertained in Chapter 3 in due course. Yet this rudimentary classification will suffice for the early pages of this book, if it underscores the communicative value of a fundamental situational definition of many so-called 'interpersonal' settings (relations and communications) as being more properly and informatively construed in intergroup terms.

A model of speech as a reflection of situational representations

By integrating notions about interpersonal–intergroup social interactions with Wish and Kaplan's (1977) five subjective dimensions, we are now in a position to provide a more adequate model for understanding situational determinants of speech, along the lines of Table 1.2. For present purposes, four of the most typical ways of defining a social situation according to Wish and Kaplan's dimensions have been selected and appear as A1 to D1 in Table 1.2. Situations A to D, then, are examples of concrete, objectively described situations which would be likely to correspond to those subjective definitions for many people. Although there is as yet no empirical research following this conceptual framework, previous work following from the objective taxonomy approach does provide us with some useful clues, and these appear as A2 to D2 in Table 1.2. So when a situation is defined (as in A1) in terms of co-operation, informality, non-intensity, equality and non-task orientation, we would predict speech patterns similar to those appearing in A2, and so on. How often the objective and subjective characteristics of situations in fact coincide as predicted is an empirical question. Giles and Hewstone argued that enough *lack* of overlap exists for the objective taxonomy approach to be theoretically inadequate. Still, it would be short-sighted merely to replace an objective taxonomy with a subjective one. This is in part because of considerations of social norms, as we discussed them above, but also because part of a situation's subjective meaning can be based on an appraisal of its presumed objective characteristics for other participants present.

Language, then, not only reflects objective indices of context but is also a barometer of how individuals define the situation, as they see it, and their own identity at that time. Power enters the 'language reflects context' paradigm because it is usually 'the establishment' that dictates what is normatively appropriate language behaviour in formal public situations. For instance, in bilingual or even bidialectal situations, where ethnic majority and minority peoples coexist, second language learning tends quite dramatically to be uni-directional; it is very uncommon for the dominant group to acquire

Table 1.2 Towards a model of speech as a dependent variable of social situations

	A Friends chatting during coffee break	B Prosecuting and defence lawyers in law court	C Welsh and English rugby supporters in pub after international match with mutually satisfactory result	D Trade union and management negotiation crisis
Objective characteristics of certain typical social situation (e.g., A–D)				
Possible cognitive structures of social situations by participants	A1 Interindividual encounter Co-operative Informal Relaxed Equal Not task-related	B1 Interindividual encounter Competitive Formal Tense Not equal Task-related	C1 Intergroup encounter Co-operative Informal Relaxed Equal Not task-related	D1 Intergroup encounter Competitive Formal Tense Not equal Task-related
Potential speech patterns	A2 Low linguistic diversity 'Restricted' code Verbal style Non-standard pronunciations Imprecise enunciations First name and informal address forms	B2 High linguistic diversity 'Elaborated' code Nominal style Standard pronunciations Precise enunciations Title and or last name address forms	C2 Low linguistic diversity 'Restricted' code Verbal style Non-standard pronunciations Imprecise enunciations First name (and informal address forms) Attenuation of ingroup speech markers (speech convergence)	D2 High linguistic diversity 'Elaborated' code Nominal style standard pronunciations Precise enunciations Title and/or last address forms Accentuation of ingroup speech markers (speech divergence)

Source: Giles and Hewstone (1982: 200).

the linguistic habits of the minority. It is no accident that cross-culturally what is 'standard', 'correct', 'cultivated' language is that of the aristocracy, upper classes, elites and their institutions, the language of the most powerful – politically and economically. In Chapter 4 we examine the dynamics of such social situations.

The 'language determines context' approach

This next broad approach to the relationship between language and situation is built upon a sociology of knowledge perspective, and deals far more squarely, as we shall see, with the relationship between language and power. We might start with the observation that any utterance is the context for the utterances that follow it (Schegloff and Sacks 1973). Thus, a speaker can attempt to influence his or her interlocutor by strategic linguistic choices that effectively manipulate the context. The more powerful speakers are, the greater the conversational and relational control they can exert. There are very few *inherent social* laws; so each culture decides on norms of appropriacy and deviance and uses language to help construct its social reality. Numerous studies, from Whorf (1941) onwards, suggest that our language forms (for example, colour terms, terms for types of physical phenomenon such as different kinds of taste, snow, sand and so on) can greatly influence the perceptions and sociopsychological discriminations we make. But the relationship between language and cognition is more intricate and more active than merely perceptual socialization into the cultural 'stuff' that our languages provide for us. By our very mouths we can influence our own cognitions. The language forms we use to describe a specific event to a particular other will distinctly affect our memory of the original event, in a way that makes it consistent with our linguistic expressions (see, for example, Higgins and McCann 1984).

As already mentioned, there are other levels beyond the referential, propositional content of words and phrases and now we shall focus upon the *evaluative meaning* behind expressions and statements. In Eiser's (1980) studies, students were forced to write essays using adjectives that were biased either for or against the values inherent in topic they were to write about, for example in the case of capital punishment: 'starry-eyed', 'oversentimental' versus 'callous', 'sadistic'. Adjective usage had a predictable effect not only on the tenor of their products but on their own subsequently expressed attitudes on this social issue. In this light of this research, it might be interesting to note that there are few terms available in the English language for categorizing different phases of and/or feelings toward intimate relationships. Conceivably, this may contribute to our experience that many of our personal relations are steeped in uncertainty.

It is, then, virtually impossible to describe an event, issue, or person in an evaluatively neutral manner, since our linguistic choices betray, sometimes quite unwittingly, our feelings towards the social object being referenced. As Schiappa (1989: 254) commented, 'put crudely, one has the choice of whether to use language to damn something, praise it, or pseudo-neutrally describe it'. Perhaps more important, however, is the notion that the language we use to describe events and people influences the framework of our understanding of these phenomena. The media's and the government's choice of 'terrorists' versus 'guerillas' versus 'freedom fighters' to refer to similar kinds of actor in Nicaragua and El Salvador is not only a political-linguistic decision but also one which may well shape readers' and viewers' interpretations of them. In many everyday social situations, participants look to each other's speech as a means of social comparison to determine how the other is construing the interaction. In the language of the experimental tradition, language therefore not only acts as a dependent variable of situations but also can function actively as an independent variable by providing participants with cues on how to structure their definitions of those situations cognitively. As Giles et al. (1979: 355) commented:

> A meeting in an informal, unconstrained situation may become defined as an opportunity for idle chatter, ingratiation, a chance to engage in sensitive business matters, or as a means of appearing to others that one is socially active. Which one of these the situation evolves into may sometimes depend on the participants, the speech markers they employ, and the extent to which these are perceived, reciprocated and jointly acted upon.

Hence, if we return to Table 1.2, it can be argued that use of speech pattern A2 will induce one's interlocutor, in social comparative terms, to construe the situation as it is represented in A1. Similarly, if the speaker then shifts speech style to D2, there will be pressure on the recipient to recognize a redefinition of the situation more as an intergroup, formal one, and so on. Giles and Hewstone (1982) argued that language would most likely act as an independent variable, determining the nature of the situation, when initiated by the highest-status participant, as it is more likely to be accepted as a reasonable contextual definition. They also claimed that situational *re*definitions would occur under a number of specified conditions, as for example, when: (a) a high-status person's authority or competence has been unquestionably established and participants feel more comfortable and secure (that is, they would shift to A2-type speech, relaxing the situational climate); or (b) a high-status person's authority or status has been questioned and/or threatened, or the perceived goals of the interaction have been considered unfulfilled (that is, a dominance-related shift to B2 or D2 would be in order). Of course, lower-status people will also wish to change the nature of a situation – for example, when they consider their inferiority to be unfair and potentially changeable and use language so as to make the other's cognitive structuring of the situation unacceptable (by their use of D2 speech markers in the face of prevailing A2; see also Chapter 4). Bourhis (1979) pointed out that such speakers may also use language to expand the range of social situations in which their own choice of speech variety is perceived as being the prerogative. Ultimately, any newly acquired equality could be directed into higher status by changing the nature of the task to one in which the previously lower-status speaker was now the undisputed leader. Brown and Fraser (1979: 53–4) comment:

> Hierarchical social status is . . . contextually relative in certain respects, or at least the domains in which status expression is relevant vary contextually, so that a doctor consulting a lawyer on a legal question might well express deference in formulating her query, whereas the lawyer when consulting the doctor about his heart condition would be the one to express deference.

This is not to suggest that relative status is the only relational dimension negotiated through language. Good (1979) discussed speech strategies used to *maintain* casualness and equality during an interaction. These strategies include requests rather than commands and the use of contradictions or reassuring remarks rather than agreement when the other has made self-effacing statements. Both strategies facilitate what Good called the 'parity principle' in conversations. In other circumstances, language can function to *avoid* providing a situational definition, as was evident in the media reports of the Iraqi-invasion of Kuwait in the summer of 1990. Early on, the US administration was apparently deliberately avoiding public use of the word 'hostages' to refer to Americans detained by the Iraqis in the Middle East for fear of exacerbating intergroup definitions of the conflict in the minds of the Iraqi authorities and nearer at home. Scotton (1979) also pointed to such a situation in East Africa, as have others in other settings, where norms regarding the use of certain languages over others are unclear for multilingual speakers. Here, speakers often avoid committing themselves and refuse to define the situation sociolinguistically by repeatedly code-switching from one lingua franca (English) to another (Swahili) and back again. It seems that language choice and speech cues have inherent advantages as means of achieving redefinitions (Brown and Fraser 1979) because of their oblique and often ambiguous semiotic force. A Welsh person's broadening of his or her dialect could signal the desire to become more familiar with another, the desire to emphasize national or even class identity or to modify some more individual projected trait. This range of possibilities for attributing shifts in speech style allows speakers a more covert and subtle means of renegotiating situational definitions.

Linguistic construction is most pernicious when it is the prerogative of the privileged and powerful in society, whether they be news reporters, politicians, or authority figures who subtly determine our perceptions of events and 'truths' by the language they adopt. For example, Husband (1977) found that news reports concerning black immigrants to Britain were more often than not associated with adjectives which had unfavourable connotations – control, conflict, swamping, violence, and so on – even in so-called 'quality' newspapers. Such associative language can then shape our perceptions of ethnic groups. Language forms used by the news media can also neutralize the emotional loading of repugnant events. For example, one press release reporting the Vietnam War referred to massively destructive air raids as 'routine limited duration protective reactions' (Tromel-Plötz 1981: 75).

Ross (1984) undertook an examination of the writing of the US Departments of Defense and State with respect to preparedness for nuclear war. He argued that use of jargon, nominal style and depersonalizations gives the impression of 'everything being under control'. Hence, the use of the abbreviation '6559 MT' hardly conveys the true horror of an explosion equivalent to '6,559,000,000 tons of dynamite'! More recently, Schiappa (1989) has discussed the processes of 'domestication' and 'bureaucratization' in relation to the language of nuclear development (or 'nukespeak'). Through domestication, nuclear weapons are referred to by friendly, benign names, normalizing this warfare technology. As Kauffman (1989: 283) puts it, in an analysis which included President Reagan's rechristening of the MX intercontinental ballistic missile as 'Peacekeeper', 'in roundabout fashion, as our weapons have become more sophisticated, our names for them have become less threatening'. Similarly, Boyer (1984: 410) suggested that:

> Even the names given the various missile systems evoked not their actual doomsday potential but reassuring associations with the heavens, classical mythology, American history, and even popular slang: Polaris, Nike-Zeus, Poseidon, Tomahawk, Minuteman, Pershing, Davy Crockett, Bullpup, and Hound Dog.

The process of bureaucratization is to adopt supposedly technologically sophisticated language to mystify concepts and to remove them from the apparent concern of everyday people. As an illustration, 'if one lives through a "protracted period" or a "subholocaust engagement" [a nuclear war] and is not part of the "collateral damage" [unintended death and destruction], then one "operates" in a "post-attack environment" [like Hiroshima, August 6, 1945]' (Schiappa, 1989: 258). Schiappa argues that these dual processes work to make weapons appear beneficial, to lessen fear about the possibility of nuclear tragedies, and to engender a feeling of impotence. However, Kauffman (1989: 283) concludes:

> the dialectical possibilities inherent in symbols provide rhetorical opportunities for opponents, as well as for advocates of particular doctrines and weapons . . . Rather than reducing nuclear conflict to a problem of technology beyond human control, an orientation that stresses the centrality of symbols offers humanity a way to take responsibility for nuclear weapons.

Domestication and bureaucratization appear as elements of what Ng (1990) has called 'the linguistic depoliticization of control', through which language forms are used to mislead people and mask control. Ng (1990: 272) also writes of the 'routinization control'. Here, subtle yet pernicious meanings become habituated in language use to such an extent that users not only internalize them but 'participate in their own control'. Ng gives the example of research on the supposedly generic masculine pronoun, pointing out that using 'he'/'his' to refer to both or unspecified sexes has the psychological effect of restricting the apparent currency of females and hence their active participation in certain domains of the social life. Indeed, Ng has also demonstrated an androcentric coding of 'man' and 'his' in memory to the extent that these items are coded as part of the masculine but not the feminine category. Put another way, in a phrase often used in this literature, the psychological cost to females of being so routinely dismissed linguistically is nothing less than being a non-person in one's own language. Frye (1983: 34) sardonically expresses the same general point:

> For efficient subordination, what's wanted is that the structure not appear to be a cultural artifact kept in place by human decision or custom, but that it appear natural – that it appear to be quite a direct consequence of facts about the beast which are beyond the scope of human manipulation . . . We do become what we practice being.

The political implications of this perspective are clear, and we can begin to see how the context-determining power of language leads to critical analyses of propagandizing and sociolinguistic manipulation. But this chapter has repeatedly warned of possible contradictions and the risks of overgeneralizing particular lines of interpretation. One salutary final consideration is that linguistic power and powerlessness are attributions that need to be very carefully made in context. Power is a multi-level concept, and its relation to styles of behaviour can be highly complex. For instance, in a case study of three egalitarian couples, Fishman (1980) has shown that the wives evidence 'powerless' language to the extent that they use two and a half times as many tag questions and five times as many hedged utterances as their husbands. But closer examination showed that these did not simply occur randomly throughout conversations; they occurred in clusters at certain points in interaction. More specifically, they were used (and actually by females and males alike) when they were attempting to obtain their spouses' complete attention and detailed judgement. Rather than being a simple reflection of a lower power position within the family, women were using these devices actively and creatively to achieve their communication goals and solve interpersonal problems. At one level, then, the 'powerless' styles can be seen as strategic and powerful.

Further complexities and directions

This chapter has attempted to provide a more cognitive overview of language—context relations than is typically found. We have focused on the mediating role of speakers' own representations of social situations as one important set of forces determining language variation. We have also stressed the need to view language as an independent variable, not only in defining, maintaining and re-defining situations, but also in sometimes avoiding situational defini-tions. In this sense, language and situation are not conceptual autonomies but rather *interdependent*: they operate simultaneously, reflecting a speaker's construal of a situation and potentially defining it for other participants. How friends or spouses talk to one another not only reflects the status of their relationship but also quite clearly *constitutes* it, and this is generally the case with all manner of social definitions and classifications. As Smith *et al.* (1980: 285) write:

> our assignment of an interlocutor to a certain SES [socio-economic status] or ethnic category, or our definition of a social situation as informal or technical, can on many occa-sions be based exclusively on our interpretations of the other's speech. To exclude language *a priori* from a definition of social variables is to run the risk of employing concepts that are impoverished from the perspective of participants and obser-vers of interaction.

Thus, while we often wish to claim that a context can have language behaviours as one of its constituents, it is generally more appropriate to say that the essence of 'a context' is the language which constitutes it.

In this chapter, we have not tried to cover all approaches to the study of situation in social psychology and elsewhere or the rela-tionships between them. One interesting avenue to explore further would be Furnham's (1986) observation that we frequently choose the situation which best fits the message we wish to convey, thereby again exerting more control over our environments. In this way, people tend to opt for the written mode rather than verbal face-to-face encounters for delivering personally critical views or bad news. Three important issues need to be addressed in future work and thinking on the interrelationships between language and context. First, besides episodic representations, speakers' goals and norms, along with other mediating forces (such as affective processes), will dictate language output. Indeed, Giles and Street (1985) proposed that there were no fewer than 27 cognitive variables mediating language performance, such as construals of relational knowledge, identities, rules and so forth. They described their model as 'a self-perpetuating one with cognitive representations being activated, eliminated, and reactivated in different combinations, much like a departure-board at a busy international airport with its flashing lights and destination signs' (1985: 245). Certainly the nature and extent of speakers' multiple goals will have a strong bearing on linguistic outcomes. Indeed, some see speakers' perceptions of multiple goals and their hierarchies as fundamental to understanding communicative diversity (see, for example, Tracy and Coupland 1991). Argyle *et al.* (1981) have located, in Western societies at least, the three goal-driven schemata of task-orientation, relational or self-presentation concerns, and interaction management. Indeed, when the perceived goals of a situation change, doubtless its episodic representational structure will be modified accordingly.

Social norms also compete for salience (Bourhis 1985). Yet there is little research available which explores speakers' cognitive representations of the supposed prevailing communicative norms; usually the norms are taken for granted (see, however, Gallois and Callan, in press). McKirnan and Hamayan (1984) consider norms to be shared cognitions about the expected (communicative) behaviours of others which also provide the basis for guiding a speaker's own language patterns. They proposed a three-factor model which may be of enormous value in future work on language–context relationships. For them, social norms can be construed in terms of the specific language forms socially expected or not (their *contents*), the range and distinctiveness of behaviours so prescribed (their *clarity*), and the strength of affect associated with them (their *evaluation*). In an empirical investigation exploring some aspects of the social meanings of norms, McKirnan and Hamayan (1984: 30) found that:

The speech norms shared by . . . [an] Anglophone population are . . . most sensitive to the intrusion of Spanish lexical items, particularly when accompanied by phonemic intrusions within English words. By contrast, syntactic and/or phonemic intrusions themselves, while perceived as clearly 'non-normative', receive substantially less extreme ratings, falling around the midpoint of the scale.

Gallois and Callan (in press) speculated that these strong sanctions levied against lexical intrusions arose from listeners' attributions that they were deliberately encoded and not so much due to low competence in English. They examine Australian males' and females' views about what they considered verbally and non-verbally appropriate in situations where people of different ethnicities and statuses offer compliments or criticisms. Gallois and Callan found evidence that, in their specific interpersonal and interethnic contexts, norms more clearly specify what *not* to do, rather than what to say and how to say it.

This focus on cognitive representations must not overshadow the pressing need to explore *affective* representations (Scherer 1988) and interpretive processing. The potency of affect will become apparent in the light of research reviewed in the next chapter. In other words, situations trigger off not only episodic representations, goals, and communicative norms but also emotional construals (see Argyle and Crossland 1987) and states such as arousal and anxiety in both interpersonal situations and intergroup encounters (Gudykunst 1988). Collier and Thomas (1988) also argue that positive sentiments arising from the situation, the communicative event and other participants can be far more important than the accomplishing of specific, previously articulated goals. This suggestion points to a rich seam for both empirical and theoretical studies in the future. Also, in her review of language and gender research, Kramarae (1990) urges scholars to examine more closely the linguistic parameters involved in women's experiences of frustration, anger and abuse in many situations with men.

Second, we have discussed situations thus far at a rather micro level, largely within the bounds of the immediate encounter (see Figure 1.1). (This is in fact an emphasis characteristic of most sociopsychological research into interpersonal communication.) However, as was argued in the Preface, macro-contextual features also impinge on the dynamics of day-to-day interaction in ways that are not usually modelled in this area. Cultural patterns such as religious, philosophical traditions, cultural values and so-called 'low-context' and 'high-context' cultures, and ethnolinguistic vitality are fundamental here (see our brief discussion in Chapter 4). Bronfenbrenner's (1979) contextual framework in developmental psychology might offer some further discrimination here. He specifies four contextual dimensions: the micro, meso, exo and macro. The *macro* context of the interaction, as above, has a wide range of influence at the level of the sub-culture or culture as a whole, along with any consolidated belief systems or ideologies (Atkinson and Coupland 1988). For instance, in our analyses in Chapter 6, the macro system involves the age and health definitions of a society, such that in one culture it may be considered healthy to talk openly about one's feelings and somatic states while in another it may be frowned upon. The *meso* system refers to the relations between two or more settings in which persons participate (for example, family and work). Hence, support gained from family members at home may actually work against an individual venturing out into new situations beyond the home environment. The *exo* system refers to those settings in which persons are not actively involved, yet which do affect them. For instance, companions of an elderly woman at a social club will interact with her often in quite detailed knowledge of her own family networks, their satisfactions and difficulties. The *micro* context is then the set of environmental factors impinging on face-to-face interaction.

Therefore, in Bronfenbrenner's terms, contexts have a nested structure; an individual's relationship with the environment is trans-actional and contexts are conceptualized as evolving systems which are undergoing constant change and mutual influence. In this way, it shares much with Fisher and Todd's (1986: xiii) framework of

> a contextual web as a heuristic device for reintegrating lan-guage with context, social structure with social interaction. Picture communication between the participants of medical, legal, or educational events at the centre of this web. However, since neither medical interviews, classroom lessons, nor court-room scenes occur in a vacuum, the web extends from these micro-episodes of interaction to the organizational, structural, and cultural contexts in which they occur and folds back again to shape interactions and communication ... we envision macro-influences reflected in micro-episodes of interaction, rather than conceptualizing the macro as a layer of reality on top of these interactional events.

The advantage of a transactional view of contexts is that con-textual effects can be envisaged as an intricate and dynamic set of feedback events rather than as main effects *per se*. In this way, it can be shown that individuals are both products and producers of their environment (Lerner and Busch-Rossnagel 1981). Its disadvantages, however, lie in the difficulty of empirically operationalizing the myriad transactional effects in any one contextualized event. It also acknowledges that the full range of contextual influences and predispositions may be variably salient during face-to-face interaction, and that the sequential constraints of talk itself may play a part in determining which contextual dimensions are in fact accessed, when and why. This perspective generally appears to require qualitative and critical analyses of language and context, and challenges the simpler conceptualizations of context that tend to feed controlled experimental research.

Third and relatedly, we must be wary of tolerating too mechanistic an approach, given that interactional definitions, goals, social and personal identities often emerge through and are negotiated in language use rather than being always predetermined and 'templated on to' contexts. Notions such as gender, ethnicity or age should not simply be frozen as given variables in our objective taxonomies (see Figure 1.1) but should also be conceptualized – in the manner in which West and Zimmerman (1987: 126) cogently construe gender – as accomplishments and achieved properties of situated conduct (see also Chapters 4 and 6). And the categories we achieve (and that others achieve for us) are of course *simultaneously* many and varied.

Summary

We have seen in this chapter how speakers select from their repertoires particular language forms to meet the social demands of the moment. Moreover, we argued that it is speakers' cognitive representations of objective social situations which are particularly influential in terms of the myriad alternative language choices made. Of the episodic representations discussed, particular attention was given to the interindividual–intergroup continua as fundamental kinds of social context leading to qualitatively different language outcomes, and this will be a contextual parameter that will emerge again and again in this book from now on. Yet we also saw the power of language in shaping our understanding of events, and how those with influence – sometimes deliberately, other times non-consciously in the blinkered pursuit of 'telling it like it is' – can use language to mould our social realities in ways we can be frighteningly unaware of. But language and situation are really only convenient labels for a very complex set of interdependencies, such that the very ways we communicate can themselves construct the nature of the situation we are in and the identities that emerge in them. In this pursuit of richer definitions, we also noted that there is much left to discover in terms of, for example, the perceived structure of goals and the webbing of micro- and macro-contextual systems in which we participate. With this backdrop, we can proceed to examine how language reflects and manufactures different kinds of evolving social meaning and personal and social identity in context, and how these can in turn affect the very existence and health of languages over time.

Suggestions for further reading

Forgas, J. P. (1985). *Language and social situations*. New York: Springer-Verlag. A diverse and important collection of essays dealing with the relationships between situation and the production and reception of language in an array of contexts.

Hermann, T. (1985). *Speech and situation*. Berlin: Springer. An influential cognitive perspective and theory on the relationship between referential language and situation.

Labov, W. (1970). The study of language in its social context. *Studium Generale*, 23, 66–84. A seminal article in sociolinguistics, providing a comprehensive and extremely valuable set of insights and data relating to language and situation relationships.

Smith, P. M. (1985). *Language, the sexes, and society*. Blackwell: Oxford. For those interested in the relationships between gender and language, this is an excellent social psychological review and integration of the topic.

2 / LANGUAGE ATTITUDES

Having established the multiple interconnections of social situations and language choices, we now come on to consider how such choices are socially meaningful to others. In fact, even a single vowel or consonant sound, contrasting with others or with our expectations, can have evaluative repercussions for its utterer. Huspek (1986: 158) suggests that images evoked in response to someone saying 'he went jogg *in* last night after work' rather than 'he went jogg *ing* last night after work' differ to the extent that, even if the utterance is the same in all other respects, the speaker in the first case will be afforded less respect than the speaker of the second. Such slight and inherently trivial details of pronunciation can clearly take on crucial social significance, when they index differences in 'standard' versus 'non-standard' language use, with their echoes of prestige, class and competence. And how many times have we made guesses (who knows how accurately) about the relational status of a couple in a bar or restaurant (whether they are on a first or second date, newly or not so newly married), or guessed which of them is more 'into' the relationship, based on verbal and non-verbal cues? We clearly use others' speech and language to assess their level of affiliation too, and monitor our own projections of affiliation correspondingly. Most language behaviours are in fact socially diagnostic and vary cross-nationally, and space prevents us examining all of these, such as speech rate, pitch and many others (see Bradac 1990, for a review). In this chapter, we shall dwell specifically on language choice, dialect and accent, partly because these have been prominent in the literature, and partly because they are so salient to the intercultural issues we shall consider in Chapters 4 and 5. We shall overview the origins of this work, together with several of the recent empirical and theoretical advances that have been made. We shall end up with an analysis of how this research domain, which developed as a classic experimental paradigm, can profit from discourse-analytical approaches which can relate attitudes more directly to language in action.

Research in this area started in the 1930s with Pear's (1931) classic study inviting BBC audiences in the UK to provide personality profiles of certain voices heard on the radio. Much research followed over the decades to determine whether voice parameters were an external mirror of someone's actual dispositional states. At the end of the day, the research concluded that there was only a very modest overlap between listener-judges' ratings of 'the' vocal features of 'targets' and peer-ratings of those targets' personalities. There appeared little advantage in pursuing voice as a cue to actual personality. On the other hand, study after study has shown that there is a quite considerable social consensus among listener-judges about the *stereotypical* traits associated with voices (see Giles and Powesland, 1975; and also Chapter 4). These stereotype-based judgements of voice are none the less socially vital, and there has been an explosion of research since 1960, in different parts of the world, showing that people can express definite and consistent attitudes towards speakers who use particular styles of speaking. Encouragingly, the cultural diversity of speech communities studied is ever on the increase (for example, Morocco, Yugoslavia, Papua New Guinea, Nigeria and the People's Republic of China). Although a variety of methods have been fruitfully adopted, most of the research has been contained within the so-called 'speaker evaluation paradigm'. Its origins can in large part be found in the Lambert *et al.* (1960) study introducing the *matched-guise technique* (MGT). Indeed, many of the roots of the social psychology of language itself can be traced to this seminal investigation.

The matched-guise technique

Lambert was initially interested in inter-ethnic attitudes in Montreal; more specifically in how French and English Canadian people perceive each other. Distrusting people's overt and public ascriptions (as would be the case with direct questionnaire procedures) as a true reflection of their privately held views, he and his co-workers formulated the MGT as a means of eliciting attitudes to users of different speech and language varieties. (This area of study has tended to be referred to as 'language-attitudes' research.) The procedure is built on the assumption that speech style triggers certain social categorizations which will lead to a set of group-related trait inferences. In other words, hearing a voice which is classified as 'French Canadian' will predispose listeners (depending, of course, on their own group memberships) to infer a particular set of personality attributes. So, balanced bilinguals (people with roughly equal facility in two languages) were tape-recorded reading a standard passage of prose in both French and in English. These recordings could then be used as 'stimulus' materials for evaluation. Each speaker's (two or often more) versions were interspersed with other recordings to avoid their being identified as produced by the same speaker. Care was and is always taken to ensure that the 'guises' are perceived to be authentic; in other words, in the case we are currently considering, independent listeners must believe the English guise to derive from an English Canadian and not from a French Canadian speaking English. In this way, considerable care is expended on issues of stimulus control. Prosodic and paralinguistic features of voice (such as pitch, voice quality and speech rate), as well as other aspects of reading style and expressiveness, are kept constant as far as possible across the different recordings. By these means it is argued that reactions to the 'speakers' are dependent solely on social expectations, based in turn on language cues.

Listener-judges are asked to listen to a series of (supposedly) *different* speakers on audiotape, to form an impression of these speakers, and to frame these appraisals using a series of person-perception rating scales (for example, along dimensions to do with *competence* traits, such as intelligence, ambition or confidence, and *social attractiveness/integrity* traits, such as sincerity, friendliness or generosity) provided for them on a questionnaire. Judges are asked to undertake this task in the same way as people gaining first impressions about speakers they hear but cannot see – say, behind them in a bar or on the radio. In the original Lambert *et al.* study, the judges were French and English Canadian (FC and EC) students, matching the basic tape-recorded guises. Although there were many facets to this study, so that a variety of findings emerged, for our present purposes the main results were that: (a) EC listeners judged speakers of their own ethnic group more favourably on half of the 14 traits; while (b) the FC listeners not only went along in the same evaluative direction, but accentuated this in favouring the 'outgroup' over their own on ten out of 14 traits.

The value of this initial MGT study is at least fivefold. First, Lambert *et al.* invented a rigorous and elegant method for eliciting apparently private attitudes, which at least arguably controlled for extraneous variables. Second, the findings underscored the important role of language (and code and dialect choice) in impression formation. Third, the study laid the foundations for an interface between sociolinguistic and sociopsychological analyses of language and was an important factor in establishing the cross-disciplinary field of language attitudes. Indeed, Labov's (1966) exploration into this arena through his 'subjective reaction test' owes much to the innovations of Lambert. Fourth, the original study spawned an enormous number of studies world-wide, particularly in Wales, Australia and the United States, and more recently in the Netherlands. Indeed, an array of journal special issues, review chapters and collected essays and reports in this tradition have emerged since. Perhaps, too, the importance of the Lambert *et al.* paper can be gauged by the fact that Tajfel (1959) published a critique of it a year before the original was published! Fifth, the dependent variables used in the study gave rise to the now pervasively recognized (though relabelled) judgment clusters of *status* versus *solidarity* traits, as well as highlighting the notion of 'group denigration'.

The study was far from being a 'one-off' affair. Lambert and his colleagues were involved in a whole programme of research over the years, and nurtured its development in many ways. For instance, the important role of language in social evaluation was substantiated by introducing variants of the technique across a range of black, French, and Jewish communities in the United States, Israel and the Philippines. Moreover, they examined the roles of listener variables such as age, and also reported on interactions between speakers' and 'listeners' ethnicity and gender (see Lambert 1967). In this respect, Lambert discussed the unpublished thesis work of Preston, who investigated whether judges react similarly to male and female speakers in the FC and EC guises. In general, it was found that the EC listeners viewed the female speakers more favourably in their French guises, but the male speakers more favourably in their English guises. EC female listeners were not quite as resolute as male listeners in their upgrading of FC female listeners, but there was still a strong tendency in the same direction. As Lambert (1967: 97) commented:

Table 2.1   Relative favourableness of evaluations of French Canadian and
English Canadian speakers

Listeners	Speakers			
	Males		Females	
	FC	EC	FC	EC
FC males	−	+	−	+
FC females	+	−	−	+
EC males	−	+	+	−
EC females	−	+	+	−

Source: Giles and Powesland (1975: 59)

this prejudice [towards FCs] is selectively directed towards FC
males, possibly because they are better known than females as
power figures who control local and regional governments and
who thereby can be viewed as sources of threat or frustration
(or as the guardians of FC women), keeping them all to
themselves.

Regarding FC listeners, the findings indicated not only that judges
react differently to male and female speakers, but also that male and
female *listeners* differ in their reactions (see the summary of the
overall findings in Table 2.1, where a positive sign indicates a
relatively more favourable personality assessment accorded to a
given speaker by a particular group of listeners, in comparison with a
speaker of the same sex in the opposing language community). For
instance, the tendency found in the case of FC male listeners to prefer
both male and female representatives of the EC group is not found to
the same extent in the case of FC female listeners. According to their
judgements of the guises, the females appeared to view FC men as
more competent and socially attractive than EC men. Commenting
on this finding, Lambert (1967: 97–8) wrote:

the FC women, in contrast, appear to be guardians of FC
culture in the sense that they favoured male representatives of
their own cultural group . . . FC women may be particularly
anxious to preserve FC values and to pass these on in their own
families through language, religion and tradition.

Lambert and his associates also moved beyond 'static' varieties of speech style towards evaluations of language shifts, as in the case of language 'convergence' and 'divergence' – processes we shall examine in the next chapter – and showed how language could affect other forms of social decision-making in an educational context. In addition, the original empirical effects were monitored from time to time to appraise the influence of changing sociocultural and historical climates in quasi-replication studies (see, for example, Genesee and Holobow 1989). Interestingly, although the downgrading of Quebecois French was dissipating in the wake of laws to provide the language with better institutional support, widespread improvements on ratings of status have not really been forthcoming.

The empirical avalanche which followed

Work following through with the basic methodological paradigm, though modified in one way or another, continues avidly today. Much of it, as can be expected, is descriptive, to the extent that it generates valuable base-line data about intergroup attitudes in particular sociolinguistic communities, though in some cases it has clear applications in social settings. Before describing some of the findings from this research, it is pertinent to consider the general basis of the social evaluations that are being made here. Edwards (1982) points out that there are three broad possibilities for the underlying patterns of speech-style judgements: they may reflect (a) intrinsic linguistic superiorities or inferiorities; (b) intrinsic aesthetic differences; or (c) social convention and preference. It is, however, unlikely that languages and language varieties can reasonably be described, as (a) suggests, as being 'better/worse', 'correct/incorrect', or 'logical/illogical'. Similarly, with (b), aesthetic judgements of language varieties do not in fact seem to be based on inherent qualities of 'beauty', though they may be represented as such by members of speech communities. In a series of studies (see Trudgill and Giles 1978), it has been shown that listeners rating totally unfamiliar (foreign) varieties, which judges could not categorize as class- or status-related varieties, did not discriminate between them on the grounds of aesthetic criteria, although they *were* perceived to differ sharply in these qualities within their *own* speech communities. It seems therefore that evaluations of language varieties do not reflect intrinsic linguistic or aesthetic qualities so much as the levels of status and prestige that they are *conventionally* associated with in particular speech communities.

Standard versus non-standard speech evaluations

Empirical studies spanning a range of speaking situations and communities around the world have produced a generally consistent pattern of results relating to the social evaluation of standard and non-standard speakers. A standard variety is the one that is most often associated with high socioeconomic status, power and media usage in a particular community. Its particular form is due to historical influence rather than intrinsic value (as above), yet because of its extrinsic associations it is typically evaluated more favourably on traits relating to competence (such as intelligence, confidence and ambition) in comparison with other (regionally marked, non-standard urban, and minority ethnic) varieties. Even speakers of such non-standard 'subordinate' varieties will themselves tend to downgrade them. We should note here that although the studies we shall be reviewing typically take the notion of 'standardness' to be unproblematic, there have been several recent discussions of the heterogeneity and evolution of 'standard' varieties (see, for example, Edwards and Jacobsen, 1987). Ultimately, it is in the very attitudes and evaluations that the MGT researched that the most secure definition of 'standard' will doubtless lie. That said, Received Pronunciation (RP accent) and Southern British Standard (lexis and grammar) can reasonably be taken to identify standard English, as it is most commonly designated. Certainly this is the variety that has attracted the most uniformly favourable evaluations in the Anglophone world, not only in Britain but also in Australia, New Zealand and the United States. Similarly in France, Paltridge and Giles (1984) found that a Parisian guise was rated more favourably along competence traits than a Provençal guise, which was afforded more prestige than a Breton guise, which in turn was more highly evaluated than an Alsatian guise.

Other dependent measures used to examine the effects of speech style are those of recall and co-operation. With respect to memory, Cairns and Dubiez (1976) found in a Northern Ireland study that children subsequently recalled more material when it was presented in RP than in other more local guises. At the level of *behavioural* differences, Giles *et al.* (1975) showed that high-school students provided more written information to (24%), and about (48%), an RP accented speaker than they did to and about a regionally accented (Birmingham) one. Similarly, Giles and Farrar (1979) demonstrated that matched samples of housewives wrote more (as well as provided more ideas) on a three-item open-ended questionnaire when it was delivered by an RP speaker than by the same bidialectal researcher using her Cockney dialect (when the respondents' local dialect was also Cockney). This difference in co-operative behaviour in fact widened as respondents progressed from answering their first to the second and third answers (33%, 45% and 72% more, respectively). In the naturally occurring setting of a theatre foyer, Bourhis and Giles (1976) found that more people complied with a request made over the public address system when the announcer's speech style was RP than when other local, non-standard varieties were used. And in an intriguing and recent elaboration of this study in a Danish setting, Kristiansen (1989) again found the same overall pattern in favour of standard Danish in the Næstved area. However, this effect was significantly influenced by the type of audience which attended particular kinds of films (such as *Three Men and a Baby* and *Dirty Dancing*). So, for example, older (and it was argued 'more intellectual') adults of higher socioeconomic class who were watching *Cry Freedom* were equally co-operative with any request, whether in standard or non-standard language. On the other hand, adults watching *The Last Emperor*, who were relatively high in socioeconomic status but varied in age, were far more co-operative with the local non-standard (Sjællander dialect, in mild and broad forms) requests than with the standard.

While non-standard accents *per se* attract less prestige than standard accents, research in a number of cultures shows that a status hierarchy exists differentiating *among* non-standard varieties. Also, Ryan *et al.* (1977) showed that the degree of accentedness (mild to broad) *within* any one non-standard variety may also affect status evaluations. They found that students' ratings of Spanish-accented American English became less favourable the more heavily accented the speaker sounded. Such fine sociolinguistic discriminations are not made everywhere, however. Berk-Seligson (1984) found little evaluative distinction between mildly and broadly non-standard Spanish in Costa Rica, but a considerable evaluative divide between these two and the high-prestige variety.

Not surprisingly, then, listener variables can interact with speaker characteristics, and the most obvious of these is, of course, listeners' social group membership. Ethnocentrism has been shown to be positively related to downgrading of non-standard speakers while high levels of intergroup contact has been related to less downgrading. No doubt the effects of contact may become more complex when its *nature* and *quality* are thoroughly explored. Interestingly, McKirnan and Hamayan (1984) found that the narrower and more restrictive the speech norms of Americans concerning what was thought to be appropriate standard English, the more downgrading (of Hispanic speakers) occurred. Age is a receiver variable not often investigated in speaker-evaluation studies, although Rosenthal (1974) showed that three to five-year-olds held quite sophisticated views about the relationship between ethnic voices and the probable socioeconomic class of their speakers. Research has also shown different evaluative profiles at different periods in the lifespan. For instance, cross-sectional studies have shown children becoming gradually more socialized into accepting the evaluative norms of standardized speech, adolescents identifying more with local sociolinguistic ideals during their teens, and the elderly becoming seemingly more tolerant of non-standard variants in the speech of others.

In many contexts it has been shown that standard speakers are *downgraded* on traits relating to solidarity, integrity, benevolence, social attractiveness and persuasive quality, relative to non-standard speakers. In Switzerland, for example, Hogg *et al.* (1984) found that judges rated High German and Swiss German speakers equivalently on status dimensions, but Swiss Germans more favourably on solidarity traits. In Ireland, a Donegal speaker was rated the most competent of five Irish guises, but a Dublin speaker, who was regarded the lowest in this regard, was considered the highest in social attractiveness (Edwards 1977). This evaluative pattern can be qualified on some occasions by speakers' gender, as we have noted already. For instance, while white Australians and Aborigines upgraded male Aboriginal speakers as more friendly, trustworthy and gentle than white males, Aboriginal female speakers were, in complete contrast, rated less favourably on solidarity traits (Gallois *et al.* 1984).

A recent study by Luhman (1990) demonstrates the complex relationship between listener-judges' sociolinguistic identification with guises and the independence of status and solidarity traits. Luhman had Kentucky students evaluate the personalities of various speakers on tape. These were standard American and Kentucky-

Figure 2.1   Status and solidarity factor scores for Kentucky and standard
US English speakers

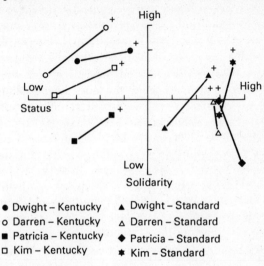

● Dwight – Kentucky	▲ Dwight – Standard
○ Darren – Kentucky	△ Darren – Standard
■ Patricia – Kentucky	◆ Patricia – Standard
□ Kim – Kentucky	✳ Kim – Standard

Source: Luhman (in press)

accented varieties produced, using the MGT, by two male and two
female speakers. The listeners were divided per stimulus condition
into those who perceived their own speech to be similar to the target
speaker in question and those who perceived dissimilarity. Figure 2.1
elegantly represents the main findings with respect to status and
solidarity rating factors. Each speaker in each guise is located in the
Figure by two connecting points; the point marked with a '+' is the
rating of the subgroup who perceived similarity with the particular
speaker, the other point represents perceived dissimilarity. First,
though admittedly as a general observation, standard speakers are
found in the high status/low solidarity quadrant, while Kentucky-
accented speakers are found in the low status/high solidarity quadrant. Second, those who identified themselves with Kentucky-
accented speech were more reluctant to accept the low status
stereotype; still, all sub-groups conceded that the non-standard
dialect – whoever spoke it – was of relatively low status. Therefore,
we find there to be an inherent variability in evaluating different
speakers from the same sociolinguistic community, an observation
that is rarely made within this literature.

The roles of context

The sociopolitical backdrop and the immediate situation

It is clear from the studies we have been reviewing that language attitudes are sensitive to local conditions and changes in the social milieu. Bourhis (1983) has also shown that the changing political climate in Quebec has been associated with modifications in attitudes towards the use of Canadian French and English. In South Wales, at a time when Welsh identity appeared to be particularly strongly sensed in the community, Bourhis *et al.* (1973) found that bilingual speakers were perceived more favourably than RP-accented ones, and in ways that were not evident some years earlier. An even more vivid illustration of language attitudes comes from Woolard and Gahng (1990) who collected MGT data in Barcelona in 1980 and then again, with a matched sample, in 1987. They found at the first time of testing that Catalan speakers were accorded more status than Castilian speakers, regardless of whether the listener-judges were Catalan or Castilian speakers themselves. The ethno-linguistic background of the judges was, however, very potent when the solidarity dimension was examined. Castilian judges gave high ratings to fellow Castilians who spoke the ingroup language, but severely downgraded them when they were heard to be speaking Catalan (notwithstanding its status in this area of Spain). Catalan listener-judges rated their ingroup variety higher on solidarity traits than the outgroup language, but were quite indifferent as to whether Castilians accommodated their language or maintained their Castilian. As Woolard and Gahng stated,

> according to the test, Castilian speakers were likely to lose the approval of their fellow Castilians if they ventured to speak Catalan, but not benefit from a compensating increase of solidarity feeling from Catalan speakers. Immediate considerations of social solidarity worked strongly against the status motivation for acquiring Catalan.

This is a cogent example of how language attitudes, interpersonal accommodation, ethnic identity and second language learning (the topics of subsequent chapters) are intimately interrelated as sociolinguistic processes in particular communities.

Since Woolard and Gahng's first testing, widespread changes appear to have affected institutional support for the Catalan language. For instance, in 1983 a law was passed giving the language co-official status alongside Castilian in government, legal affairs, education and so forth. Instruction in the language took dramatic strides forward during the decade in schools, and a Catalan-medium TV channel was also established. When replicating the study seven years later in the wake of these language planning policies, Woolard and Gahng found an even stronger status superiority for Catalan yet 'a loosening of the bond between the Catalan language and native Catalan ethnolinguistic identity. It no longer matters so much *who* speaks Catalan, but rather simply that it is spoken'. In other words, Castilian judges no longer downgraded their ingroup on solidarity scales for speaking Catalan and Catalan listeners were now more favourably disposed towards Castilians who accommodated them.

Thus, it seems reasonable to propose that when a non-standard speech style is, or becomes, a valued symbol of ingroup pride (be it working-class, ethnic, or occupational), individuals who are strongly committed to their social group membership display evaluative preferences for their own variety. In just this way, Flores and Hopper (1975) found some preference for Mexican American speech styles among people who identified themselves as *chicanos*, a term often associated with cultural and linguistic pride. In general, however, non-standard speakers adopt the stereotyped views of the majority groups in society, although ratings may also reflect the functional distribution of the varieties in some cases (cf. Fishman 1971). Thus, Adorno (1973) found that Mexican American parents considered English to be important for practical purposes, but Spanish was valued for idealistic and personal reasons. In view of the way in which different varieties may be seen as situationally appropriate, as we saw in the preceding chapter, Carranza and Ryan (1975) emphasized the need to examine reactions to speech varieties across different contexts. In their study, standard American English and Mexican American speakers were heard reading two different texts, one at home and the other in a formal school context. Bilingual Anglo-American and Mexican American students all preferred English in the school context, but showed a slight preference for Spanish in the home setting, especially on solidarity traits.

Other, more recent studies have examined and or manipulated aspects of the context of the language attitude investigations themselves. For instance, Bourhis and Sachdev (1984) found that Anglo-Canadian secondary school students had less favourable attitudes towards Italian language usage when the demographic proportions of Anglos and Italians in their immediate school environment were equal, as opposed to when Anglos were the clear majority. Creber and Giles (1983) found that the typical status-upgrading of RP was attenuated significantly when the testing situation was an evening youth club, compared with the (usual) classroom setting. On the other hand, Giles *et al.* (1983) found that the status connotations of RP were accentuated when informants were asked to discuss their speaker evaluations with each other for 90 seconds before making their ratings. The language of testing in MGT studies has also been shown to be important, as for example when Welsh bilinguals in a study by Price, Fluck and Giles (1983) made evaluative distinctions between RP and a non-standard Welsh accent on status traits when the experimental procedure was conducted in English, but *not* when it was the Welsh language. When the rating task was in Welsh, however, listeners would make social attractiveness distinctions between the varieties, a tendency which was not apparent in the other setting. So, not only can the status connotations of a standard variety be diminished or exaggerated depending on the nature of the context, but the evaluative criteria brought to bear in them can also vary.

Another important parameter of the context here is the sociolinguistic comparisons that are being made. For instance, when Abrams and Hogg (1987), using a social identity framework (see Chapter 4), asked Scottish listener-judges from Dundee to evaluate speakers from their own city alongside those from another Scottish city (Glasgow), they upgraded their ingroup representatives relative to the outgroup on both status and solidarity scales (2.94 versus 2.60 and 2.70 versus 2.44, respectively). However, when Dundee raters in another condition of the study were asked to rate these same Glasgow speakers, but this time alongside standard English speakers, these previously construed 'outgroup' (Glaswegian) speakers were rated very much higher on both dimensions (3.40 versus 2.19 and 3.10 versus 2.50 for status and solidarity, respectively). But also, as the mean values show, the evaluations made of the Glaswegian speakers were far higher than those made of their own ingroup Dundee speakers in the earlier comparison. The methodological (and theoretical) implications of this study are immense, and underscore the importance of controlling for or manipulating more sociolinguistic comparisons in matched-guise studies.

Applied contexts

Speech style is clearly an important social cue in many applied social contexts. Educational settings in general tend to encourage and reflect standard varieties of a language, the form used in writing and that associated with social advancement. Although teachers presumably have some responsibility to be alert to the prejudicial potential of language attitudes, it would be unreasonable to expect teachers, as members of society, to be totally immune to stereotyped evaluations of the sort we have been considering. Seligman *et al.* (1972) in fact found that speech style was an important cue in teachers' evaluations of pupils, even when combined with other information, such as photographs of the children and examples of their schoolwork. Choy and Dodd (1976) reported that teachers evaluating standard English and Hawaiian speakers consistently favoured the former. Overall, research indicates that the perception of children's so-called 'poor' speech characteristic leads teachers to make negative inferences about their personalities, social background and academic abilities. Clearly, these may lead to self-fulfilling prophecies to the disadvantage of non-standard-speaking children. Teachers may themselves induce behaviours from children which *confirm* their stereotyped expectations.

Language attitude studies in the medical arena are extremely rare. Fielding and Evered (1980) demonstrated that RP speakers are more likely to be perceived as having psychosomatic symptoms than patients with non-standard accents, even when they are voicing exactly the same complaints. Moreover, medical student listener-judges in this study perceived lexical and syntactic differences between two supposed patients they heard on audiotape, despite the fact that these features were in fact held constant. Patients' social class has been shown to affect the frequency of communication difficulties experienced by doctors, with working-class patients being disadvantaged as a consequence. Less information is provided to working-class patients than to middle-class patients (Pendleton and Bochner 1980) and speech style is very likely to be a potent mediating cue for physicians and patients alike.

Legal and judicial settings also offer much scope for language attitudes to intervene in crucial social episodes, although sociolinguistic research here has concentrated on so-called 'powerless' language (see Chapter 1) and its unfavourable effects on the perceptions of witnesses. However, Seggie (1983) presented voices of speakers (in RP, broad Australian and Asian-accented English) appearing in the role of defendants. RP speakers were adjudged more guilty when the crime was embezzlement, whereas Australian-accented speakers were more severely judged when the crime was physical assault. In other words, 'white-collar' crimes tend to be associated with prestige speakers whereas crimes of violence are cognitively aligned more with non-standard speakers.

Most research in occupational settings has related to employment interviews. Street, Brady and Lee (1983) found that males and females speaking the same message were more positively evaluated in informal and conversational settings than in a supposed (formal) interview. Hopper and Williams (1973) showed that speech characteristics (for standard American, black, Mexican American and Southern white speakers) were relevant to employment decisions, but decreased in importance when the interviews were for lower-status jobs. Similarly, Kalin and Rayko (1980) found discrimination against foreign-accented applicants for high-status Canadian jobs, while at the same time these speakers were judged more suitable for lower-status positions. This double discrimination would seem to inhibit the upward mobility of ethnic speakers. In Table 2.2, we see from a British study how job suitability can directly parallel accent prestige.

Seggie *et al.* (1986) also elicited evaluations of employment suitability based on ethnic accent in Australia. Two groups of subjects of European descent – owners of small businesses and female shoppers – were asked to decide whether a speaker they heard on tape was

Table 2.2   Perceived job suitability and accent usage (from Wiemann and Giles, 1988, p. 206)

Job	Perceived job status*	Prestige accent**	Non-standard accent**
Industrial plant cleaner	1.44	–	+
Production assembler	3.00	–	+
Industrial mechanic	3.55	–	+
Foreman	4.36	=	=
Personnel manager	5.79	+	–
Accounts manager	6.07	+	–
Production control manager	6.31	+	–

Source: Wiemann and Giles (1988: 206)
* As rated by an independent sample of subjects (1 = low status; 7 = high status).
** + indicates prestige-accented speaker significantly more suitable than non-standard; – indicates the opposite; and = indicates no perceived difference.

suitable to be trained for a low- or high-status job; all the speakers were presented as having identical backgrounds and qualifications. The owners of small businesses heard Asian Australian, German Australian and two (standard and broad) Anglo-Australian voices; the female shoppers heard Asian Australian and two Anglo-Australian voices. It is interesting that the businessmen did not differentiate between the two Anglo voices, whereas the shoppers regarded the standard speakers as being unsuitable for low-status job training. The businessmen rated the Asian voice equally with the standard Anglo voice, while the shoppers rated it equivalent to the broad Anglo voice. The authors offer an explanation of these findings in terms of the different cognitive schemata of the two groups. The businessmen have knowledge of the success of Asian business in Australia, whereas the female shoppers are more likely to think of Asians as restaurant workers; different evaluative profiles, it is suggested, emerge as a consequence.

Other intervening and mediating variables

It is often the case, but not always (as in the case of German-accented speech), that non-standard speakers are concentrated in the lower socioeconomic strata and are accorded lower prestige as a consequence. Thus, Ryan and Sebastian (1980) suggested that assumptions about social class may lead to the downgrading of ethnically accented speakers. They were able to demonstrate these interaction effects by presenting social class background information to judges along with the vocal guises of standard and non-standard speakers (in an orthogonal factorial design). The evaluative differences between standard American and Mexican American speakers were drastically reduced when they were both known to derive from middle-class backgrounds. Yet, this interdependence of accent and social class information has not shown up in more recent studies in other speech communities. For example, Giles and Sassoon (1983) found that whether a speaker was known to be middle-class or working-class, his non-standard speech style still evoked a lower rating on status traits in comparison with RP speakers.

The meshing of non-verbal, visual cues with vocal and verbal ones is, perhaps surprisingly, an understudied domain and one that holds out much potential for future work. The evaluative potency of accent effects was not diminished when visual cues were added to the presentation of vocal styles (Elwell *et al.* 1984). But interestingly, Aboud *et al.* (1974) demonstrated in Quebec that socioeconomically 'incongruous' presentations of photographs of people at work and their voice samples (for instance, a speaker with a middle-class appearance and a Joual accent) were reported as being a more pleasing combination for potential workmates than 'congruous' stimuli (for instance, individuals who both looked and sounded middle-class). The opposite was the case for potential superiors or subordinates. Friedman *et al.* (1988) showed that non-verbal indications of stimulus persons' emotional expressiveness were just as important as the ubiquitously important variable of physical attractiveness in viewers' ratings of targets' likeability, a finding which suggests that this facet of an individual's self-presentation is likely to be at least as important in some contexts as the ones discussed above.

In fact, relatively few studies have manipulated accent, dialect or language along with other language factors. Giles *et al.* (1981) showed that accent had as significant an effect on listeners' social evaluations as did lexical diversity in Britain, while Bradac and Wisegarver (1984), in a most ambitious design in the United States varying lexical diversity, accent, and social class background information, demonstrated that these factors were additive on status-related dimensions. This 'combinatorial model' suggests that the least favourable status judgements will be made for non-standard speakers, low in lexical diversity, with a known working-class background, and vice versa. Interestingly, accent was a less salient variable than lexical diversity on status traits in this study. Message content has rarely been examined alongside speech-style effects, although it has been shown to bear significant consequences. For instance, Powesland and Giles (1975) showed an 'incongruity' effect, again, where speakers who argued in ways not expected from their voice patterns (for example, an RP speaker advocating greater powers to trade unions) were upgraded as a consequence of their presumed integrity. More recently, Giles and Johnson (1986) showed that Welsh bilinguals rate RP speakers more positively than Welsh speakers irrespective of whether they supported or mildly threatened their ethnolinguistic identities. However, this effect was completely eradicated in a follow-up study when more culturally committed Welsh people listened to supportive and extremely threatening speakers. This time, message content almost completely determined reactions, and the threatening speakers were severely denigrated regardless of their ingroup or outgroup accent. Otherwise, the role of message content, and its underlying dimensions, have been sadly neglected in the study of language attitudes. Researchers have preferred to gain experimental control by the use of supposedly 'neutral' topics, a contentious issue that we shall address shortly.

Gallois *et al.* (1984) have also discussed the mediating influence of perceived threat in determining social evaluations, while attaching even greater weight to the role of social distance. Many recent studies have shown that standard listeners infer from a non-standard speech style that such speakers would be not only unsuitable as partners in close personal relationships but also likely to hold many dissimilar beliefs (see, for example Stewart *et al.* 1985). Also, they are perceived as being less in *control* communicatively (Bradac and Wisegarver, 1984). Future research needs to explore whether, and the precise ways in which, belief dissimilarity, direct threat, large social distance, low control (and doubtless other factors) mediate the perception of non-standard speech and low status ratings.

Theoretical developments

Essential as this descriptive groundwork is, the area of language attitudes research has, we would argue, been overrepresented by one-off studies in widely varying cultures, sociolinguistic conditions, situational and procedural domains. This has made it impossible to infer anything other than very general principles. In large part as a reaction to this atheoretical trend, the 1980s saw an array of diverse models which either focused on language attitude issues *per se* or incorporated their complexity into frameworks addressing larger communication concerns. To date, these models have not been overviewed *critically*. Space does not allow us to attempt this fully here, but we can highlight the most essential aspects of these models through five overarching questions relating to issues they (explicitly or implicitly) address:

Are there generative mechanisms operating beyond the original theoretical conception of language leading to social categorization leading to trait inferences?

Berger and Bradac (1982) contended that there were indeed four other sets of processes operating, each dedicated to the pursuit of 'uncertainty reduction' (UCR in Figure 2.2). These scholars argue, as we mentioned in the previous chapter, that an important social objective in initial interactions is to reduce uncertainty about what the other is like psychologically, and how to respond appropriately. Language cues are used therefore as a means of increasing predictability (for instance, 'she sounds rather informal and hence I can act more casually here') with perceived similarity being an important mediator in all cases. Gudykunst and Ting-Toomey (1990) have suggested that these processes are operative in different social contexts (see Figure 2.2) and can be located in two-dimensional space along 'interindividual' (high versus low) and 'intergroup' (high versus low) dimensions of social interactions.

Are language cues hierarchically perceived and evaluated?

Gallois *et al.* (1984) argue that different situations induce us to give different vocal cues salience over others. Their model suggests that in intercultural situations, ethnolinguistic cues usually assume primacy over others, especially when social distance between the groups is perceived to be high. When social distance, however, is medium or low, attributes such as gender and contextual considerations assume greater importance, and especially when expectations and appropriacy are violated. In other words, this model attends to the question of which cues assume importance, when and how.

Can language attitude situations be organized
meaningfully in terms of large-scale social forces?

Ryan *et al.* (1982) speculated that language attitude 'situations' could be placed in a dynamic and interrelated two-dimensional space of standard–non-standardness and vitality (increasing versus decreasing). The vitality dimension, which we introduce more fully in Chapter 5, refers to sociostructural factors (status, demography and institutional support) which can be to a group's advantage or not. So, for example, language attitude situations currently 'located' in the 'decreasing vitality and non-standard' quadrant might include Welsh, Breton and many ethnolinguistic minorities in the United States.

Figure 2.2   Impression formation process models.

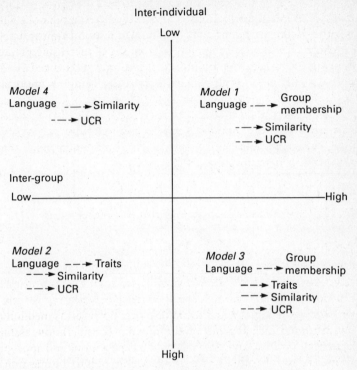

Source: schematized after Gudykunst and Ting-Toomey (1990: 317–18)

*Are there different language attitude profiles, and if so, are
they a function of perceptions of the intergroup forces
prevailing, and the nature of immediate situations?*

From the literature, these same authors identified four different
patterns of the social evaluation of contrasting speech styles in
majority and minority settings, in terms of the dependent variables of
status and solidarity. Pattern A is where there is a preference by both
groups for the dominant group's speech patterns; pattern B is where
there is a status preference for the dominant group and a solidarity
preference for the ingroup. Pattern C is characterized by ingroup
preferences by both parties; and D is where there is a consensually
agreed status preference for the dominant group and a solidarity

preference for the subordinate group. Subsequently, Ryan *et al.* (1984) associated these patterns (and other finer distinctions within them) with different historical phases of the relationships between groups in contact. An important point emerging from this rather complex analysis was that the same profile may function socio-psychologically quite differently for the groups involved, and that different members of the same social group could express the patterns variously. In our discussion of situational specificity, we argued above that such patterns depend on messages' relationships to listeners' social identities (central versus peripheral), as well as on the extent to which the evaluative contexts in which they occur stress group factors (Giles and Ryan 1982).

Are language attitudes meaningfully related to other levels of analysis and/or forms of communicative behaviour?

Bradac (1990) has also related specific language attitudes to different forms of language behaviour (see Figure 2.3). He hypothesizes that speakers' convergences towards listeners on normatively valued dimensions will be favourably perceived on dimensions of status and solidarity, whereas the converse will be the case when there is divergence on non-normatively valued dimensions. Street and Hopper (1982) have also offered a conceptual model in which such acts of

Figure 2.3   Language attitudes and accommodation.

| | SPEAKER'S LINGUISTIC | |
	CONVERGENCE	DIVERGENCE
NORMATIVE ADHERENCE	+ve status and +ve solidarity	+ve status but −ve solidarity
NON-ADHERENCE	−ve status but +ve solidarity	−ve status and −ve solidarity

Source: schematized after Bradac (1990: 406)

accommodation not only affect reception and social judgements but also influence the kinds of accommodative tactic the recipients will use in return. Finally, Giles and Street (1985) have argued that language attitudes are often crucial mediators of communicative acts, involved in presenting the individual self positively, making valued ingroup presentations, and even healthy 'couple presentations'. Hewstone and Giles (1986) develop this theorizing more in the direction of 'communication breakdown' in intergroup settings, where sociolinguistic stereotypes (that is, language attitudes) mediate (see Chapter 4). In this way, language attitudes can be thought of as a crucial point of contact between many other communicative phenomena we discuss in this volume. This will be increasingly the case as efforts at theoretical integration continue. In Chapter 5, we relate language attitude models to other intercultural phenomena and processes, in an attempt to provide a cohesive and predictive theoretical framework of our own.

Future developments

The matched-guise technique has not been without its critics over the years. Questions have legitimately been raised (some by us) about the technique's sterility in terms of its task and relational requirements the lack of programmatic, longitudinal work and linguistic sophistication, the tendency to ignore message content, and so forth. In the remainder of this chapter, we introduce two exciting prospects for further developments in the study of language attitudes – as discursive events and as linguistic action.

The MGT paradigm from a more discursive perspective

Several innovative developments are possible if, at least as an alternative design, language attitudes are approached from a *discursive* perspective (Giles and Coupland 1991). By this is meant a perspective where social meanings (and, in this case, language attitudes) are assumed to be inferred by means of *constructive*, *interpretive* processes drawing upon social actors' reservoirs of contextual and textual knowledge; such a perspective, of course, has much in common with constructivist and pragmatic orientations. Indeed, the matched-guise paradigm is one which seems to have been reluctant to move beyond a static, input–output mechanism. This is perhaps because scholars have been blinkered to some extent by the design characteristics of the traditional methods, such as the recurrent tendency for listener-judges to commence their evaluations a matter of seconds after hearing a stimulus voice. The discursive approach would attend to *processes* of meaning generation and to the way we come to construct our language attitudes, inside and beyond established MGT practices. It would explore alternative (undoubtedly less elegant) methods, through which these processes are amenable to analysis.

It is an established tenet of discourse analysis that meanings arise from the interplay of communicative acts and the full range of factors in their contextualization. Another is that texts are never 'neutral', though we noted in the introduction to this chapter that this is an avowed and valued control feature of the MGT! Texts inevitably seek to establish or subvert, through complex and often inconsistent means, rhetorical, political and ideological positions. This may seem an exaggerated claim in the case of texts we researchers may have composed *explicitly* to be uncontroversial or even trivial, and to be politically and socially inert. But to take a case in point, how is it possible to generate a text that is 'age-neutral'?

Recently, we tried to do precisely this in a matched-guise study which required listeners to evaluate a speaker varying in terms of speech rate (fast, medium or slow), accent (standard or non-standard), and age (young adult versus elderly). The passage spoken was supposedly an extract from an interview where the speaker was talking at length about his car. Adopting the traditional rating measures, we found that few effects emerged for speaker's age (Giles, Coupland, Henwood, Harriman, and Coupland 1990). However, in addition, we asked textually interpretive, qualitative attributional questions. When provided with extracts from the text – such as the speaker saying, 'I didn't know what to think' – listeners interpreted this variously depending on the speaker's age. Hence, his 'not knowing' was more likely to be attributed to his being 'confused' if elderly (the speaker was in fact perceived to be in his early sixties), but if young (early thirties), it was much more likely to be attributed to his wishing to withhold judgement given the complexity of issues at hand. In other words, listeners were interpreting the same utterances in schema-consistent ways, and ageistly so. When asked why they rated the speaker as they had done, despite the fact that he said exactly the same thing in each condition, he was described as 'arrogant and pompous' when in the guise of a young, standard speaker; 'trying to impress' or 'using the words of others' when non-standard and young; 'egocentric, living in the past, and talking of trivia' when standard and elderly; and even 'stupid, and losing his grip' when non-standard and elderly. Even more interestingly, when invited to substantiate these accounts by pinpointing textual information, respondents would very often highlight exactly the *same* utterances to justify their (very disparate) claims!

Texts themselves, therefore, no less than the vocal styles that may realize them, can never be neutral; they are interpreted and subsequent actions accounted for on the basis of pre-existing social schemata. It seems clear that whatever 'social evaluations' are produced in relation to 'stimuli' may be better conceived of as responses to textual and contextual interconnections, as indeed would be the case in any face-to-face encounter. It is also significant that attempts to minimize or deny the contextualization of stimuli are likely to fail given the natural propensity of communicators to generate contextual dimensions, 'implicatures', or propositional bridges as an inevitable component of the interpretation of texts. Therefore, language attitudes are not simply passive reactions to blocks of vocal sounds, as listener-judges are cognitively active, processing messages according to activated social representations. It follows that the more denuded a stimulus text is of contextual specificity, the more assiduous, variable and creative will be the contextual inventiveness of listener-judges. Obviously a task for the future will be to explore the kinds of cognitive responding that ensue when listeners process others' language performances.

The evaluative process needs to be separated conceptually from its reporting, since language attitudes are, after all, appraisals conveyed in a particular context. Indeed, the reporting can come about in many different forms, and may in reality never been transmitted or even mindfully appraised. Recent work in Britain has begun to challenge – if not deconstruct – the very notion of 'attitude' as currently measured and conceptualized in social psychology. And this is the very bedrock upon which language attitude studies are based. Potter and Wetherell (1987) not only point to the variability inherent in people's social attitudes when they are expressed in talk (even within the same conversation) but also question whether attitudes *can* be rarefied in the minds of individuals away from the assumed objects to which they are targeted in the 'outside world'. As we know from a myriad of studies in the social psychology of language (see, for example, Street and Hopper 1982), our judgements about how people actually sound and speak – the object of language attitudes – can themselves be a constantly redefining, social construction process and dependent on social cognitive biases. So, in a way that parallels the interdependence between language and situation that we argued for in the previous chapter, 'language varieties' on the one hand, and 'attitudes' on the other, are symbiotically related in a subjective sense, rather than the dichotomous entities they are assumed to be in the MGT paradigm. Billig (1987) also considers attitudes in a wider historical context as positions in an argument and embedded in particular social controversies. Attitudes in this sense are not only explicit appraisals pro or contra a position, but also include an implicit stance against counter-positions. Moreover, justifications and criticism are viewed as part and parcel of attitudes – not epiphenomena derived from them – and should become sharpened and modified as the argumentative context changes. Developing these two approaches to characterize the 'reporting' phase of the MGT should allow us to understand how we negotiate our language attitudes rhetorically and interactively.

In sum, then, we have arguably paid too little attention to the cognitive activities involved in recipiency, and to the complex inter-relationships between language and attitudes and the functions of these in discourse. Similarly, we have inadequately considered the role of emotional construals and expressions in MGT research. The affective connotations associated with linguistically triggered self- and other-categorizations (cf. Garza and Herringer 1987; and Dijker 1987, respectively) and the emotionally linked attributions we make about speakers who are stigmatized (cf. Weiner *et al.* 1988) may have considerable mediating significance in formulating language attitude patterns. Given that identities emerge from discourse, it seems equally apposite to determine how different speakers influence listener-judges' own conceptions of *themselves*. Along these lines, we can expect some radical shifts in the study of language attitudes in the direction of discourse and studies aimed at elucidating ongoing interpretive processes.

Language attitudes and linguistic action

It is appropriate to conclude this chapter by asking to what extent people's language attitudes predict their sociolinguistic behaviour.

Although early social psychological research on attitudes implicitly assumed that by understanding a person's attitudes one could predict behaviour, contemporary research is far more critical. Fishbein and Ajzen (1975) proposed that the predictability of a behaviour is increased by working with attitudes and behaviours defined at an equivalent level of specificity; general attitude measures (for example, English Canadians' language attitudes in response to a French Canadian guise) can only be expected to predict broad behavioural patterns (for example, amount of French spoken in a week), but not specific behavioural acts (for example, whether English or French is spoken to one's neighbour).

In order to predict specific behaviour, Ajzen and Fishbein put forward their 'theory of reasoned action'. Here, the immediate determinant of an action is viewed quite simply as a person's *intention to perform* (or not perform) a behaviour (such as speaking French to a customer in Quebec). The basic determinants of a person's intention are also specified. The person's attitude towards the behaviour is a function of *beliefs* about the consequences of performing a particular behaviour and the person's *evaluation* of these consequences. The second determinant of intention, *subjective* norms, are themselves determined by the person's normative beliefs regarding the expectations of others, and the person's *motivation to comply* with these expectations. The proposed mathematical combination of these determinants of behaviour can be represented symbolically in the following equation:

$$B = BI \left(\sum_{i=1}^{n} b_i e_i \right) w_1 + \left(\sum_{j=1}^{m} nb_j mc_j \right) w_2$$

where B is overt behaviour; BI is intention to perform the behaviour; b is the belief (subjective probability) that performing the behaviour will lead to consequences i; e is the evaluation of consequence i; nb is the perceived expectation of referent group j; mc is the motivation to comply with referent group j; n is the number of salient consequences; m is the number of salient normative beliefs; and w_1 and w_2 are empirically determined regression weights.

The adoption of such an approach to the study of language attitudes would have obvious implications for the methodology used, because rather different questions would be asked. What, for example, are the person's beliefs about the consequences of adopting a specific speech style ('I would appear less intelligent') and their

evaluations of these consequences ('very bad')? In turn, what normative beliefs are relevant ('Would one's friends laugh?') and how great
is the motivation to comply with their expectations ('Do I want to do
what my parents/friends/teachers think I should do?')? Such questions may seem to take us far away from the evaluation of speech
styles but they might help to indicate the importance of such ratings
relative to other factors. This approach should make us more
thoughtful about what language attitudes *do*, as well as what they
are.

Another approach which emphasizes the idea of attitude towards
behaviour is Jaccard's (1981) 'behavioural alternative' model which
considers situations in which an individual can perform one of a
number of alternative and mutually exclusive behaviours (for example, one must choose to speak at standard or non-standard
dialect, assuming, for simplicity, that code-shifting is not possible).
According to Jaccard, the individual may be said to possess an
attitude towards performing each of the behavioural alternatives
available. The individual will decide to perform that alternative for
which the most positive attitude is held. Thus, the prediction of
behaviour is based on an intraindividual comparison of behavioural
alternatives, and each person's attitude towards speaking a variety of
language might have to be measured (for a variety of situations) in
order to predict accurately.

Summary

We have seen how the MGT has blossomed since its inception and
language attitude studies are now at the core of SPL. Listeners can
very quickly stereotype others' personal and social attributes on the
basis of language cues and in ways that appear to have crucial affects
on important social decisions made about them, as we saw in the
medical, occupational and legal spheres. There are different kinds of
evaluative profile attending individuals who use language in different
ways in different contexts, and a wide range of contextual, speaker
and listener variables have been shown to interact in this process. We
noted that a plethora of theoretical models are beginning to emerge
at different levels of analysis, which is timely given the accumulation
of findings world-wide. Moreover, we argued that the evaluation
phase of the MGT was indeed a process – a discursive event – and
that much active interpretive work is done during these studies.

Therefore, much remains to be achieved, not least regarding the relationships between language attitudes and linguistic action. Since attitudes are created and modified as an intrinsic part of social interaction, the conceptual separation of 'language' from 'attitudes' glosses over an intriguing dynamic in SPL yet to be explored empirically.

Suggestions for further reading

Edwards, J. R. (1989). *Language and disadvantage*. London: Cole and Whurr. The second edition of an earlier classic on language and socio-economic status, an important section of which overviews educationally orientated research in language attitudes world-wide.

Ryan, E. B., and Giles, H. (eds) (1982). *Attitudes towards language variation: Social and applied contexts*. London: Edward Arnold. Still the most recent collection of critical review essays and theoretical chapters looking at language attitudes in the Anglophone, Hispanic and Francophone worlds.

Williams, F. (1976). *Explorations into the linguistic attitudes of teachers*. Rowley, MA: Newbury House. Overview of one of the first programmatic sets of empirical studies concerning evaluations towards black, Hispanic and white speakers in the United States.

3 / ACCOMMODATING LANGUAGE

Having established that language behaviours have diverse and complex meanings, we now come on to explore how such meanings are manipulated and accessed by communicators in order to fashion their self- (and also group) presentations through dynamic language use in social contexts. Each one of us will have experienced 'accommodating' verbally and non-verbally to others, in the general sense of adjusting our communication actions relative to those of our conversation partners, and been aware of others accommodating (or failing to accommodate) to us. The phenomena we describe and model as accommodation in this chapter have been recognized under a variety of labels; for example, scholars have considered 'interactional synchrony' to be a universal characteristic of talk, stemming from the very earliest months and years of life. But through the accommodation framework, we hope to impose some order on this literature and find generalizations about the origins, processes and effects of manipulating sociolinguistic 'distance'. Accommodative processes can, for example, facilitate or impede language learners' proficiency in a second language (Chapter 5), as well as immigrants' acceptance into certain host communities (see Chapter 4). In media settings, they can affect audience ratings; elsewhere, they can influence job-satisfaction, affect reactions to defendants in court (and therefore the nature of the judicial outcome), or influence satisfaction with medical encounters (and thereafter whether we comply with medical regimens); they can constitute an enabling or detrimental force in handicapped people's quest to fulfil their communicative and life potentials (see Giles *et al.*, in press).

At one level, accommodation is to be seen as a multiply-organized and contextually complex set of alternatives, regularly available to communicators in face-to-face talk. It can function to index and achieve solidarity with or dissociation from a conversational partner, reciprocally and dynamically. At another level, accommodation strategies can characterize wholesale realignments of patterns of code- or language selection, though again related to constellations of underlying beliefs, attitudes and sociostructural conditions. A noteworthy, and perhaps unique, characteristic of 'communication accommodation theory' – the model we progressively develop in this chapter – is precisely this openness to micro- and macro-contextual communicative concerns within a single theoretical and interpretive framework.

But there is necessarily some slippage between everyday and academic uses of terminology in this area, and indeed variation across academic treatments of 'accommodation' and related concepts. Many different approaches have made inroads into what 'being accommodative' may constitute linguistically and interactionally, and the model we develop in this chapter is an attempt to integrate them. In the primarily historical overview that follows, it will be apparent that accommodation research has spanned several radically different methodological designs. Consistent with its sociopsychological origins and interests in motivational and evaluative trends, much of the earliest work was laboratory-based and relatively insensitive to the descriptive linguistic dimensions of the varieties and speech styles it researched. In fact (see below) it was precisely to counteract an insensitivity to social contextual variables in early (linguistically sophisticated) sociolinguistic research that basic tenets of accommodation theory were developed. Today, however, we can point to a good deal of sociolinguistic and discourse analytic research explicitly within the terms of the accommodation model. There is a most valuable balance of experimentally controlled *and* naturalistic studies to report. This chapter presents accommodation theory as a robust paradigm for communication research, in the particular sense that it is, perhaps uniquely, able to uttend to (a) social consequences of interaction (attitudinal, attributional, behavioural and communicative); (b) ideological and macro-societal factors; (c) intergroup variables and processes; (d) discursive practices in naturalistic settings; and (e) individual, lifespan and other language shifts, and group-language shifts (see Chapters 5 and 6). The origins of communication accommodation theory, the basic accommodation strategies and important conceptual distinctions will be introduced first. Then we examine the motives underlying the much researched strategies of convergence and divergence as well as their social consequences, introducing complexities and caveats that arise when they are analysed in particular contexts. Finally, we introduce a recent elaboration of the theory and discuss it in relation to other contemporary approaches to interpersonal influence in language and communication research.

Basic concepts and strategies

Convergence and divergence

The first publications on the subject of 'speech accommodation theory' (SAT) emerged in 1973. Giles (1973) demonstrated the phenomenon of interpersonal accent convergence in an interview situation, and introduced his 'accent mobility' model as a result of critiquing some aspects of Labov's (1966) very influential paradigm of sociolinguistic research (see also Bell 1984; Coupland 1988). It was argued that the formality or informality of context and the criterion of 'attention to speech' which was what Labov took to explain situational variation in his interview data, could be reinterpreted, at least in part, as interpersonal accommodation processes. For example, casual speech may have been produced not only because of the informality of the context (and we have already discussed the problems inherent with such a deterministic approach – see Chapter 1), but perhaps because the interviewer (who would be equally prone to sociolinguistic forces) had shifted to less standard speech forms. The ending of the interview (when the tape-recorder was supposedly turned off) or the introduction of certain emotive topics (for example, being near to death, nursery rhymes), when the least formal pronunciation styles were elicited in Labov's data, might not have been as significant as the cues the interviewer was providing. An interpretation in terms of interpersonal influence – interviewee convergence to the interviewer – at least needed serious consideration. As Krauss (1987: 96) argued:

> the addressee is a full participant in the formulation of the message – that is, the vehicle by which meaning is conveyed – and, indeed, may be regarded in a very real sense as the cause of the message. Without the addressee that particular message

would not exist. But the message, in the concrete and particular form it takes, is as much attributable to the existence of the addressee as it is to the existence of the speaker.

The original insight that styles might be determined interpersonally opened the door for studies which manipulated a wide variety of speech variables (Giles and Powesland 1975). Giles *et al.* (1973) empirically confirmed some fundamental 'speech accommodation' ideas in the bilingual context of Montreal. They found that the more effort in convergence a speaker was perceived to have made (for example, the more French English Canadians used when sending a message to French Canadians), the more favourably the speaker was evaluated, and the more listener would converge in return. After that study, a plethora of convergent strategies were discovered in what for some would be described as a socially sterile laboratory setting. Theoretical refinements have come in profusion, particularly in the 1980s, and have intermeshed with significant empirical developments as well (see Coupland and Giles 1988, for an overview of some of these).

In its earliest years, SAT focused on the social cognitive processes mediating individuals' perceptions of the environment and their speech styles. Its theoretical framework developed out of a wish, in those days, to demonstrate the value and potential of social psychological concepts and processes for understanding the dynamics of speech diversity in social settings. Specifically, it originated in order to elucidate the cognitive and affective processes underlying speech convergence and divergence, although other speech and interaction strategies (complementarity, over- and underaccommodation – see below) have more recently been recognized theoretically. As we shall see later in this chapter, SAT has been moving in a more interdisciplinary direction and the focus has broadened from exploring specific linguistic variables to encompass non-verbal and discursive dimensions of social interaction; hence, the wider notion of *communication* accommodation theory (CAT) (see Giles *et al.* 1987).

Convergence has been defined as a strategy whereby individuals adapt to each other's communicative behaviours in terms of a wide range of linguistic/prosodic/non-vocal features including speech rate, pausal phenomena and utterance length, phonological variants, smiling, gaze and so on. Most studies of this genre were laboratory-controlled investigations, but many studies have also emerged showing convergence in naturally occurring contexts, such as the demonstration of John Dean's convergence of median word frequencies (a measure of formality) to his different Senate interrogators in the Watergate trials (Levin and Lin 1988) and Coupland's (1984) phonological analysis of a travel agent's convergence to her many individual clients, varying in socioeconomic status and education. Although most studies have been conducted in the West and in English-language settings, convergence on temporal, phonological or language-switching dimensions has been noted in many different languages including Hungarian, Frisian and Dutch, Hebrew, Taiwanese, Mandarin, Japanese, Cantonese and Thai (see sources in Giles *et al.*, in press). Pertinently, Yum (1988a) argues that East Asian communication is far more receiver-centred than the more sender-orientated West. Gudykunst *et al.* (1987) also observe that members of collectivistic cultures (such as Japan and Korea) perceive their ingroup relationships to be more synchronized than individualistic societies (such as Australia and the United States).

While convergent communicative acts reduce interpersonal differences, variability in the extent and frequency of convergence is also apparent, corresponding to sociodemographic variables such as age (see, for example, Welkowitz *et al.* 1976). Bilingual convergence in interethnic settings has been shown to exist at six years of age (Aboud 1976) although a fuller knowledge of sociostructural norms relating to language use is usually acquired slowly throughout childhood and adolescence, at least in the West (Genesee 1984). Many interindividual differences have also been detected. It has been founded that 'field dependents' (individuals who find it difficult to disembed core perceptual features from their field – see Welkowitz *et al.* 1972) and those with strong interpersonal orientation (see Murphy and Street 1987) converge heavily on non-content features of speech. High self-monitors match the emotionality, intimacy and content of their interactant's initial self-disclosure more than low self-monitors (Schaffer *et al.* 1982). Extroverts, as well as cognitively more complex communicators who are high on construct differentiation, are more listener-adaptive than introvert and low differentiators (Hecht, Boster and LaMer 1989). Obviously, other measures of cognitive and perceptual functioning, as well as those of social sensitivity (see, for example, the functional flexibility construct of Paulhus and Martin 1988) should provide positive relationships with convergence.

Divergence was the term conceived to refer to the way in which speakers accentuate speech and non-verbal differences between themselves and others. Bourhis and Giles (1977) designed an experiment to demonstrate the use of accent divergence by Welsh people in an interethnic context. The study was conducted in a language laboratory where people who strongly valued their national group membership and its language were learning Welsh (only about 26% of Welsh people at that time, as now, could speak the language). During one of their weekly sessions, Welsh people were asked to help in a survey concerned with second language learning techniques. The questions in the survey were presented to them verbally in English in their individual booths by a very English-sounding speaker, who at one point arrogantly challenged their reasons for learning what he called a . . . 'dying language with a dismal future'. Such a question was assumed to threaten their feelings of ethnic identity, and the informants broadened their Welsh accents in their replies, compared with their answers to a previously asked, emotionally neutral question. In addition, some informants introduced Welsh words and phrases into their answers, while one Welsh woman did not reply for a while and then was heard to conjugate a less than socially acceptable verb gently into the microphone. Interestingly, even when asked a neutral question beforehand, the informants emphasized their Welsh group membership to the speaker in the content of their replies (so-called 'content differentiation'). Indeed, it may well be that there is a hierarchy of divergent strategies available to speakers, from indexical and symbolic dissociation (for example using in-group-stereotyped pronunciation), through explicit propositional non-alignment (expressing disagreement or hostility) to physical distancing (ending or avoiding interaction).

Language divergence was investigated in a follow-up study by Bourhis *et al.* (1979). The study involved different groups of trilingual Flemish (Flemish–English–French) students being recorded in 'neutral' and 'ethnically threatening' encounters with a Francophone (Walloon) outgroup speaker. As in the previous study, the context of the interaction was a language laboratory where participants were attending classes to improve their language skills (this time English). Many Flemish and Francophone students converse together in English, as an emotionally neutral compromise between maintaining rigid differentiation and acquiescing to pressures to converse by using the other's language. In this experiment, the speaker spoke to students in English, although revealing himself as a

Walloon by means of distinctive Francophone pronunciation. It was found that when the speaker demeaned Flemish people in an ethni-cally threatening question, listeners rated him as sounding more Francophone (a process termed 'perceptual divergence') and themselves as feeling more Flemish. This cognitive dissociation was manifested behaviourally at a covert level by means of muttered or whispered disapproval (which was being taperecorded, unknown to the informants), while the Walloon was speaking, and at an overt level through divergent shifts to own-group language. However, this divergence only occurred under certain specific experimental conditions, and then for only 50% of the sample. It was found that these listeners only diverged when their own group membership and that of the speaker was emphasized by the investigator, and when the speaker had been known from the outset to be hostile to Flemish ethnolinguistic goals. But in a follow-up study, language divergence into Flemish did occur for nearly 100% of the informants under these same conditions, but only when the Walloon speaker himself diverged into French in his threatening question. Interestingly, the form of the language divergence in the first of these Belgian studies differed from that in the second. It was found that, in the first, the ingroup initially replied to the outgroup threat in English – and then switched into Flemish. In the second (more threatening) setting, listeners replied in a directly divergent manner by an immediate shift into Flemish.

Like convergence, divergence can take on many forms, verbal and non-verbal (LaFrance 1985). Scotton (1985) introduced the term 'dis-accommodation' to refer to those occasions when people switch registers in repeating something uttered by their partners, as a tactic to maintain integrity, distance or identity. For example, a young speaker might say, 'OK, mate, let's get it together at my place around 3.30 tomorrow', and receive the reply from a disdainful elder, 'Fine, young man, we'll meet again, 15.30, at your house tomorrow'. Although keeping one's speech style and non-verbal behaviours congruent across situations may be construed as a communicative *non*-event, Bourhis (1979) has pointed out how, in many interethnic contexts, 'speech maintenance' is a valued (and possibly conscious and even effortful) act of maintaining one's group identity. Similarly, at the level of personal identity, those individuals Hart *et al.* (1980) take to embody 'Noble Selves' would be predicted to maintain their idiosyncratic speech and non-verbal characteristics across many situations. Noble Selves are those straightforward, spontaneous persons who see deviation from their assumed 'real' selves as being against their principles and thus intolerable.

Some important distinctions

These basic convergent/divergent shifts are, of course, not as descriptively simple as they might at first appear. Table 3.1 outlines several of the principal distinctions that have been made at varying times in the accommodation literature; others will emerge later in the chapter. Both convergence and divergence may be either 'upward' or 'downward' (see Giles and Powesland 1975), where the former refers to a shift towards a consensually prestigious variety (for example, accent), and the latter a shift away from it. Adopting the high-prestige dialect of an interviewer would be an example of upward convergence, and shifting to street language in certain minority communities would be downward convergence.

Convergence on some features of language does not mean speakers will converge all available variables and levels (Giles *et al.*, 1987); hence, the distinction between uni- and multimodal convergent/divergent shifts. Beyond this, we should not conceive of convergence and divergence as necessarily mutually exclusive phenomena. Bilous and Krauss (1988), in their study of same- and mixed-sex interactions, showed that females converged to males on some dimensions (including total words uttered and interruptions) but simultaneously diverged on others such as laughter. Similarly, informal observations of bilingual switching in Montreal in the 1970s sometimes showed mixed accommodation strategies, apparently motivated, such that French Canadian shoppers addressed Anglophone store assistants in fluent English while requesting the

Table 3.1 Distinctions in the characterizing of convergence
and divergence

Upward versus downward
Full versus partial versus hyper-/cross-over
Large versus moderate
Uni- versus multi-modal
Symmetrical versus asymmetrical
Subjective versus objective

services of a Francophone assistant instead: convergence in code but propositionally the message is one of dissociation.

The distinction between partial and full convergence has proved valuable for some methodological designs, too (Street 1982). For example, a speaker initially exhibiting a rate of 50 words per minute can move to match another speaker's rate of 100 words per minute (total) or can move to a rate of 75 words per minute (partial; and cf. the notion of 'underaccommodation' that we introduce later). Similarly, Bradac *et al.* (1988) distinguish between extents of shifts of lexical diversity. Also, in any interaction, convergence and divergence can be 'symmetrical' or 'asymmetrical'. An example of mutual convergence can be found in an investigation by Mulac *et al.* (1988: 331), who reported that 'in mixed-sex dyads, it appears that both genders adopted a linguistic style more like that of their out-group partner than they would have maintained with an in-group partner'. Similarly, in Booth-Butterfield and Jordan's (1989) study of intra- and intercultural encounters between female students, blacks were rated as far more expressive in within-group encounters than whites when talking with their peers. However, blacks were rated to be less expressive when conversing with whites than they were when talking with other black women, and whites became more communicatively expressive in the mixed-racial than in the same-racial encounters – both thereby converging, presumably, to outgroup norms.

An example of *a*symmetrical convergence can be found in White's (1989) study of American–Japanese interactions where convergence by one party was not reciprocated by the other. When speaking with other members of their culture, Japanese informants in this study produced far more backchannels of certain kinds (for example, 'mmhm', 'uh-huh') than their American counterparts in within-culture situations. When it came to cross-cultural encounters, however, Americans used significantly more backchannels when speaking with Japanese (that is, they converged), though Japanese speakers maintained their high levels of backchannelling. Speakers can 'overshoot' full convergence and 'hyperconverge' (see Bradac *et al* 1988, for social evaluations of hyperconvergence in lexical diversity). Again, this can be accomplished asymmetrically or symmetrically where both parties overshoot (see Bilous and Krauss 1988). Relatedly, divergence of a sort may occur not only by simple dissociation away from the interlocutor towards an opposing reference group, but by sociolinguistically expressing greater identification with that other's reference group than that other is able to display. For example, when talking to an old school friend who is using a lower-prestige code than you and perhaps disdainful of your 'superior' manner, you might adopt an even more basilectal code to show your greater identification with local values. These strategies can be termed upward and downward *cross-over* divergence respectively, though they are, of course, achieved by initial (and often substantial) convergence.

The final distinction in Table 3.1 arises from the work of Thakerar *et al.* (1982) and emphasizes SAT's truly sociopsychological core. Because our perceptions of speech styles are dependent on various social and cognitive biases, speakers believed to be relatively competent may be heard to be more standard-accented than they actually are. Hence, Thakerar *et al.* invoked the conceptual distinction between 'subjective' and 'objective' accommodation. The objective dimension refers to speakers' shifts in speech *independently measured* as moving towards (convergence) or away from (divergence) others, whereas the subjective dimension refers to speakers' *beliefs* regarding whether they or others are converging or diverging. Thakerar *et al.* found that interlocutors would shift their speech styles (speech rate and segmental phonology – for example, glottal stop in place of word-final /t/) towards what they believed their partners sounded like, irrespective of the descriptive realities. For instance, initially similar-sounding low- and high-status interactants were measured objectively as diverging from each other, though the low-status one was subjectively converging (towards the interlocutor's faster speech and more standard accent, stereotypically associated with a higher-status speaker); and the higher-status speaker was accomplishing precisely the converse.

These kinds of process may be partly responsible for the kinds of 'behavioural confirmation' demonstrated by Snyder (1981). For instance, Snyder showed that if males believed they were interacting with attractive (rather than unattractive) females over an intercom link, the females would sound lively and outgoing (the known social stereotype of physically attractive women). Although no data on the sociolinguistics of behavioural confirmation as yet exist, it could well be that the males in this condition facilitated and even constructed these women's styles by themselves converging to the stereotype; put another way, the women may have converged on objectively linguistic criteria to the males' stereotype-based convergence. Interestingly, Cohen and Cooper (1986) describe situations where visitors to foreign countries actively converge over time towards the (often

Table 3.2   Subjective and objective dimensions of speech accommodation

| | | SUBJECTIVE ACCOMMODATION | |
		Convergence	Divergence
OBJECTIVE ACCOMMODATION	Convergence	A	B
	Divergence	C	D

Source: Thakerar *et al.* (1982: 238)

ill-conceived) convergent attempts of individuals from the host community towards them! Relatedly, it may be argued that not only do speakers converge to where they believe others to be, but in some (as yet unspecified) conditions to where they believe others *expect* them to be. The notion of prototypicality (see below) is relevant here, and in some role-relevant situations people may gain kudos for 'acting their age', taking a professional line, and so forth.

As Table 3.2 indicates in cells A and D, speakers' beliefs about their own shifts are often reasonably in accord with objective sociolinguistic realities; in other words, they 'get it right'. Mis-attributions are potentially rife when motives, beliefs and behaviours fail to coincide, as in cell C of the table. Giles and Bourhis (1976) found evidence that black West Indian immigrants in a British city thought they were converging towards local white speech norms – actually the working-class variety of the neighbourhood – and they did in fact (as an evaluative phase of the study showed) sound indistinguishable from local whites. Yet, whites did not interpret blacks as behaving convergently, but heard them to be moving towards a speech style – the same non-standard urban dialect – that they themselves were striving to abandon. In a very different cultural setting, Beebe (1981) found that Chinese–Thai bilingual children would use Chinese phonological features when being interviewed by an (objectively) standard Thai speaker who looked ethnically Chinese. Similarly, some Singaporeans' and Australian immigrants' attempts – lexically, grammatically and prosodically – to match 'upwardly' the speech of native English speakers may miscarry; and in other cases, native English speakers mismanage their downward attempts to converge towards what they believe Singaporeans and Aborigines sound like (Platt and Weber 1984). From these examples (and we have no empirical illustrations as yet of the kind of feasible mismatches implied in cell B), we can conclude that accommodation is often cognitively mediated by our stereotypes of how socially categorized others will speak.

Gallois and Callan (1988) have developed the notion of stereotypically driven accommodation further by invoking Turner's (1987) notion of prototypicality. They developed an index for measuring the extent to which Australians (including recent immigrants) accommodated the non-verbal prototype of 'what it was to be an Anglo-Australian'. They found that prototypicality indices were in fact much better predictors of raters' social evaluations of these individuals than their actual or even perceived behaviours. Those who accommodated the prototype effectively received moderately favourable ratings on a solidarity factor (not aggressive, good, kind and friendly), while those further from the prototype were downgraded. That said, those who deviated from the prototype, but in a socially desirable manner (that is, who smiled and gazed more and had softer voices), were judged most positively. It is as if new members to a community get first-base support for moving towards the group prototype as an indication of being willing to adopt group attributes, but there is still further room for positive evaluation if the person can assume other societally valued speech habits. In sum then, people use whatever resources are available to them in terms of accommodating to others and the actual focus of such movements may not be the addressees' communicative style themselves. Prototypicality is likely to be just as important an issue in the process of (linguistic) self-stereotyping in the context of divergent as it is in convergent acts.

Accommodative motives and consequences

In this section, we discuss the basic motives that have been demonstrated or inferred to hold for convergence and (though less studied) divergence, and the complex ways they function psychologically.

Convergence and integration

CAT proposes that speech convergence reflects, in the unmarked case, a speaker's or a group's need (often non-conscious) for social integration or identification with another. In the early days of its development, the theory relied heavily on notions of similarity attraction (Byrne 1971) which, in its simplest form, suggests that as one person becomes 'more similar to' another, this increases the likelihood that the second will like the first. Convergence through speech and non-verbal behaviours is, of course, a central instance. Thus, for example, Welkowitz and Feldstein (1970) reported that dyadic participants who perceived themselves to be similar in terms of attitudes and personality converged pause-duration patterns more than those who perceived dissimilarities. Also, Welkowitz *et al.* (1972) found that participants in a dyad who perceived themselves to be similar converged vocal intensity more than informants randomly paired, presumably because perceived similarity induces a more positive orientation and a relatively high level of interpersonal certainty.

Through convergence, a speaker's attractiveness, perceived supportiveness, intelligibility, and interpersonal involvement (see Giles *et al.* 1987) in the eyes of the recipient are also liable to be increased. Moreover, Buller and Aune (1988) found that slow- and fast-speaking informants who were addressed at their own rates of talking by a target male rated him as more 'immediate' (that is, as having verbal and non-verbal patterns indicative of closeness) and as more intimate; they were also more likely to comply with his request for volunteered assistance than when appealed to by speakers with non-accommodated rates. From the above data, then, although largely by inference from studies of adjudged effects, convergence may plausibly be considered a reflection of an individual's desire for social approval: if people recognize positive cognitive, affective and behavioural outcomes to follow from convergence, this is sufficient for us to consider that an approval motive may often trigger it. In this way, Purcell (1984) observed that Hawaiian children's convergent shifts in prosodic and lexicogrammatical features depended on the likeability of the particular peers present when talking together in small groups; and Putman and Street (1984) reported shifts in interviewees' speech rates and turn duration when intending to sound likeable to an interviewer.

As we noted earlier in the bilingual setting of Montreal, several studies of impression formation have shown speech convergence (over speech maintenance) to have been positively evaluated. Putman and Street (1984) found that interviewees who converge toward their interviewers in terms of speech rate and response latency are reacted to favourably in terms of perceived social attractiveness. Other research, too, indicates that relative similarity in speech rates, response latencies, language and accent is viewed more positively, on dimensions of social attractiveness, communicative effectiveness, perceived warmth, and co-operativeness (see Giles *et al.* 1987). Furthermore, professional interviewers' perceptions of student interviewees' competence also has been shown to be positively related to the latter's convergence on speech rate and response latency (Street 1984), while Bradac *et al.* (1988) showed *downward* convergence in lexical diversity to be very favourably perceived.

It seems to follow from this that the greater the speaker's need to gain another's social approval, the greater the degree of convergence there will be. Factors which influence the intensity of this particular need would include the probability of future interactions with an unfamiliar other, an addressee's high social status, and interpersonal variability in need for social approval itself. In the last respect, Natalé (1975a; 1975b) found that speakers scoring higher on a trait measure of need for social approval converged more to their partner's vocal intensity and pause length than speakers who scored lower. Furthermore, Larsen *et al.* (1977) showed that the greater one's desire for specified others' approval, the more similar overall these others' voices will sound subjectively to one's own (even if they contain stigmatized speech features such as lisping). This sense of a reduced linguistic barrier between oneself and another, termed 'perceptual convergence', no doubt facilitates the convergence process itself.

The power variable is one that emerges a number of times in the accommodation literatures and in ways that support the model's central predictions. Hamers (pers. comm.), using role-taking procedures in a bilingual industrial setting in Quebec, has shown greater convergence to the language of another who was an occupational superior than to one who was a subordinate; foremen converged more to managers than workers, and managers converged more to higher managers than to foremen (see also Bourhis 1989). Van den Berg (1985), studying code switching in commercial settings in Taiwan, found that salespersons converged more to customers than vice versa, presumably because the customers in these settings hold more of the economic reins. Interestingly, Cohen and Cooper (1986), drawing upon data in Thailand, show how many tourists to the Third World do not expend effort acquiring much, if any, competence in the language of the country visited, whereas locals in the service industries whose economic destiny is in many ways tied to tourism often become proficient in the foreigners' languages.

It is evident just from the above studies that the mechanics of everyday interpersonal convergence in important social networks provides a breeding ground for longer-term shifts in individual as well as group-level language usage, as argued by Trudgill (1986) (and in Chapter 5, below). The potentially different trajectories of long-term accommodation effects in different situations are certainly worthy of longitudinal study, as are the different clusters of motives driving diverse accommodative acts. Accommodation theory has had much recourse to *approval* motives as being the main trigger of convergence. However, it is clear that from the last study cited that *instrumental* goals more adequately represent the conditions for convergence under some conditions. Moreover, integration and approval are not necessarily coterminous, and future analyses need to reflect on the nesting of perceived task, identity, and relational goals, global and local.

Much of the literature on long- and medium-term language and dialect acculturation can also be interpreted in convergence terms (see Trudgill 1986), where immigrants may seek the economic advantages and social rewards (though there are clearly also costs) that linguistic assimilation sometimes brings. In other words, group-level accommodation here may often be unilateral towards the power source. Hence, Wolfram (1973) reported that in New York City, where both Puerto Ricans and blacks agreed that blacks held more power and prestige, Puerto Ricans adopted the dialect of blacks far more than vice versa. Moving to the gender context, Mulac *et al.* (1987) found that women, but not men, converged toward their partners' gaze in mixed-sex dyadic settings. Still, Genesee and Bourhis (1988) make a telling point about the role of sociostructural conditions mediating accommodative evaluations. In their study contrasting bilingual shifts in Montreal with Quebec City, they show that convergent shifts towards a less prestigious minority can sometimes bring considerable social accolades.

At least four sets of interrelated caveats can be suggested to the overriding social benefits which are claimed to accrue from convergence (and what will later be extended into 'attuning' strategies). These relate to: multiple meanings and social costs; social and societal norms; causal attributions and intentions; and optimal levels.

Caveats

Multiple meanings and social costs

In the same way that interactions usually have multiple goals, language behaviours often have multiple social meanings for hearers (see Chapter 2). Convergence may, therefore, entail some rewards as well as some costs. As we have seen, rewards could include gains in listeners' approval and perceived co-operativeness, with the specific rewards depending on the particular sociolinguistic dimensions converged (see, for example, Giles and Smith 1979). Potential costs, on the other hand, could include possible loss of personal and social identity, and expended effort, especially if accommodation is widespread, not reciprocated and long-term.

An illustration of the multiple meanings of convergence was provided by Bourhis *et al.* (1975). Six groups of Welsh respondents were told that a Welsh athlete had recently been placed seventh in a Commonwealth Games diving competition, and that they were to hear him in two consecutive radio interviews, purportedly taped after the competition. In one of these, the athlete's interviewer was a standard English speaker, while in the other the interviewer possessed a mild Welsh accent. With the mild-accented interviewer, the athlete also consistently employed a mild Welsh accent, but with the standard interviewer, his speech style varied from condition to condition. In one condition he maintained his Welsh accent, in another he modified it towards that of the interviewer (so that it was more standard and less Welsh-like), and in yet another condition he diverged his accent away from the interviewer towards broad Welsh. The order of the interviews was counterbalanced and the different texts were matched for duration, information content, vocabulary and grammar. It was found that the athlete was perceived as more intelligent when he shifted into standard forms than when he did not shift at all, and more intelligent in the latter case than when he broadened his Welsh accent. But convergence also involved a decrease in perceived trustworthiness and kindheartedness relative to the no-shift condition. The divergent shift to broad Welsh (although associated with diminished intelligence) resulted in the athlete's being rated as more trustworthy and kindhearted than in the other conditions.

Social norms

Genesee and Bourhis (1988, for example) have shown how

situational norms may well override accommodative tendencies at certain sequential junctures during an interaction. For instance, they found that the act of salesmen converging to customers does not necessarily result in positive evaluations, because of the established situational norm that 'the customer is always right'. Even so, we should acknowledge the additional or confounding attributed motive of ingratiation in the context of this particular norm, which makes us somewhat wary of its (as well as perhaps other norms') autonomy and purity.

Further complexities abound, and they underscore the need for research into the relationships between the management of social identities and the sequential dilemmas of 'appropriate' interpersonal accommodation in context. Having converged towards each other, interlocutors may feel less socially constrained and thereby feel released to adopt preferred speech patterns. Alternatively, some may feel the need to establish their own identities through talk at the outset, and then may feel more comfortable about accommodative behaviour. Also, what can parsimoniously be interpreted as accommodation can sometimes be an artefact. For instance, an interviewee who sounds more like her/his prestigious interviewer may not have shifted strategically in the latter's direction. The interviewee may simply have been attempting a so-called 'assertive self-presentation' to portray a competent persona. Put another way, whatever speech patterns the interviewer may have encoded at the time would have had little impact on the interviewer's face intents; any 'addressee focus' here would have been very limited.

Causal attributions, awareness and intentions

Attributional principles suggest that very often we evaluate behaviour directed towards us in the light of the motives we assume gave rise to it (Hewstone 1989), and this analysis has been applied to linguistic and communicative behaviours, paradigmatically so in the work of Grice (1971) and Brown and Levinson (1987). It has been proposed that a perceiver takes into account at least three factors when attributing motives to others' actions: their ability, effort and external pressures impelling them to act in a particular way. Simard et al. (1976) examined the implications of attribution principles for the evaluation of convergence and non-convergence. They found that listeners in an interethnic laboratory task who attributed another's convergence toward them as a desire to break down cultural barriers perceived this act very favourably. When this same shift was attributed externally to situational pressures forcing the speaker to converge, then the act was perceived less favourably. Similarly, when a non-convergent act was attributed externally to situational pressures, the negative reactions were not so pronounced as when the maintenance of speech was attributed internally to the speaker's lack of effort.

The discussion thus far has linked accommodative acts implicitly to strategic communication and intentions. In this respect, Giles *et al.* (1973) suggested that different forms of convergence (for example, complete language shifts, slowing speech rate) may be placed along a continuum of perceived effort where both speaker and listener might construe a given linguistic strategy as involving high, medium or low social concessions. Indeed, it was suggested that apologizing for a lack of ability to converge towards another language may be emotionally more 'giving' than simply switching into the other's language. Needless to say, the relationship between perceptions of accommodation and social consequences is one when misattribution is again common. For instance, Canadian patients report converging to medical language when interacting with their physicians who in turn report moving more into everyday language with them (Bourhis *et al.* 1988). Unfortunately, neither side acknowledges perceiving such moves by the other; here, nurses act as 'linguistic brokers', taking on the role of intermediaries and claiming to converge to both parties.

Adopting a self-regulation perspective (Gilbert *et al.* 1988) would lead us to predict that when convergence is deliberate and mindful, encoders will be less able to process accurately the intentions of their accommodating or non-accommodating partners. This would be so because regulating certain kinds of own-behaviour (for example, bilingual convergence when non-fluent in a second language, feigning involvement, deceiving another, creative accounting) can be so cognitively involving that insufficient resources are left for detailed decoding processing, to the extent that the listeners' responses are more likely to be taken at face value. It should be noted however that seemingly purposive designs are not necessarily either enacted or evaluated with full awareness; indeed, even accommodative bilingual and dialectal code switching can occur without the sender's knowledge or memory of it. Berger and Roloff (1980) suggest that much communication is produced and received at low levels of awareness, and that in many instances speech accommodation may be *scripted* behaviour. Factors such as a discrepancy between expectations and what is encountered may, however, intervene and bring speech and non-verbal behaviours to a state of greater awareness. Certainly, evidence attests to the fact that some accommodated features are more consciously self-perceived under some conditions than others. In Street's (1982) study, subjects were unaware of response-latency and speech-rate convergence, but were highly aware of divergence of these behaviours, while in Bradac *et al.*'s (1988) study, decoders were more accurate in perceiving downward (than upward) accommodative movements in lexical diversity. In complete contrast, Bourhis *et al.* (1975) found a distinct tendency for listeners to claim they perceived upward shifts in interviewees' accents with high-prestige-sounding interviewers even though maintenance was actually in evidence – an effect due perhaps to the social expectation that convergence would be normative here. In other words, awareness is not commensurate with perceptual accuracy.

It seems, then, that a speaker's goals may be more or less overtly represented, and that speech adjustments cannot uniformly be taken as indicative of wholly intentional orientations. An interesting instance relating to both scripted and overtly intentionalized behaviour is Bourhis's (1983) study in Quebec. The results of this sociolinguistic survey showed that speakers can occasionally be consciously aware of convergence and divergence in language switches, as well as of the probable reasons for them. For example, English Canadians reported being more likely to converge to French in Montreal today than in the past; they also reported that French Canadians were less likely to converge to them in English today than in the past. The converse was true for the French Canadians' reports. However, in a follow-up set of field studies designed to test how these reports matched actual accommodative behaviour, Bourhis (1984a) found little overlap. French Canadians were more likely than English Canadians to reciprocate convergence in intergroup encounters, and English Canadians were more likely than French Canadians to maintain their own language. Bourhis suggested that in spite of sociopolitical changes favouring the ethnolinguistic ideals of French Canadians in Montreal, English Canadians are still in the habit of maintaining English when interacting with French Canadians, and French Canadians are still in the habit of converging to English with English Canadians. That is, it may be that, contrary to their avowed intentions, old habits of intergroup communication 'die hard'.

Optimal levels

As discussed thus far, CAT would suggest that full convergences would be more positively evaluated than partial convergences, and this was the empirical concern of a study by Giles and Smith (1979) who intuited that such a linear relationship would not hold. They presented eight versions of a taped message to an English audience. The taped voice was that of a Canadian, showing various combinations of convergence/non-convergence on three linguistic dimensions (pronunciation, speech rate, and message content), in a factorial design. Listeners appreciated convergence on each level separately but found that convergence on all three levels was perceived negatively as patronizing; content plus speech-rate convergence was the interpersonally effective optimum. By the same token that recipients may find non-convergence a blow to their esteem, as it implicitly indicates the speaker finds them unworthy of seeking their approval, it could well be that recipients of multimodal accommodation will feel extremely uncomfortable with those who can demonstrate that their own idiolectal features are so easily matched. Hence, and in the same way that listeners have ranges of acceptable or preferred linguistic and non-verbal behaviours (see, for example, Cappella and Greene 1982), listeners may have a *tolerance* for certain amounts of convergence. In this way, a move beyond a certain threshold (which may vary situationally) may be negatively perceived by them.

Besides optimal 'magnitudes' of convergence, Giles and Smith (1979) speculated that there might also be optimal *rates* of convergence (and divergence). Aronson and Linder's (1965) gain–loss theory of attraction proposed that we feel stronger liking for those people whose respect we are acquiring than for those whose admiration we already possess. It could be that convergence is more effective when it takes place by perceptible degrees than all at once. Interestingly, there are data showing that non-familiars converge towards each other gradually across subsequent occasions (see, for example, Ferrara, in press), thereby appearing to conserve some convergent acts as bargaining tools. In this way, the structure and process of mutual convergences can be quite negotiative and precursors to communicative innovations at the lexical, grammatical, prosodic and non-verbal levels. Gain–loss theory also claims that individuals will most dislike someone else not when they have never been shown respect by her/him but when it appears that respect is gradually being eroded. In accommodation terms, then, disapproval would be levied against those who diverge sequentially away more than against those who diverge fully on one occasion.

Divergence and intergroup processes

Giles and Powesland (1975) argued that both speech convergence and divergence may be seen as representing strategies of conformity and identification. Convergence is a strategy of identification with the communication patterns of an individual internal to the interaction, whereas divergence may be regarded as a strategy of identification with regard to the linguistic and communicative norms of some reference group external to the immediate situation. If, as seems probable, divergent strategies are adopted more often in dyads where the participants hold different social identities, the incorporation of ideas from Tajfel's (1978) theory of intergroup relations and social change is directly appropriate (see Chapter 4 for a detailed discussion). Divergence can therefore be a tactic of intergroup distinctiveness employed by people in search of a positive *social* identity, as has been well exemplified in the studies by Bourhis and others reported above. By diverging and emphasizing one's own social (and sometimes idiosyncratic) communicative style, members of an ingroup may accentuate differences between themselves and outgroup members along a salient and valued dimension of their group identity.

Taylor and Royer (1980) found, in Quebec, that French Canadian students who expected to meet in person an Anglophone speaker they heard on audiotape anticipated speaking more French with someone who completely agreed with (rather than disagreed with) their ethnolinguistic ideals. Furthermore, their anticipated divergence was accentuated after they had together discussed the language strategies they would probably use. In post-experiment questionnaires, the French Canadians attributed this 'linguistic polarization' directly to their feelings of ingroup belongingness and to the need to assert their positive ethnic identity.

A number of other studies of impression formation have shown that maintenance and divergence is often seen by recipients as insulting, impolite or downright hostile – that is, unless it is attributed situationally to extenuating circumstances (Simard *et al.* 1976) and/or to the adherence to valued norms (see, for example Bradac 1990). Such negative reactions would make perfect evaluative and attributional sense in the light of what the absence of convergence implies, as discussed above. While some social situations would value divergent over convergent speech patterns in certain competitive contexts, as shown in Switzerland by Doise *et al.* (1976), social norms in many other kinds of situation would make divergent patterns costly. As an example, Gorter (1987) discusses the general norm of convergence in Dutch society where two bilingual Frisian speakers may converse together in Dutch. Similarly, in the context of Wales, it was found that situations had to be very 'intergroup' in nature (see Chapter 1) for bilingual Welsh people even to anticipate diverging into Welsh with an English person (Giles and Johnson 1986). For this to occur, an English speaker had to threaten core elements of the Welsh subjects' committed ethnic identity very overtly. Hence, the dimensions of intergroup salience, the nature of communicative norms, and the degree of commitment to social identification are all crucial interacting variables, in determining not only whether or not divergence occurs but also the form it takes.

It is certainly not being claimed that all divergences are intergroup in nature. Divergence to another communicative form may signal *personal* disdain regarding another's dress, mannerisms, habits, language style, and so forth. For example, when Putman and Street (1984) required interviewees to act out being 'dislikeable' in an interview setting, they were found, predictably, to diverge away from their interviewers on non-content speech features. Indeed, sometimes it is virtually impossible to disentangle the intergroup from the interindividual dimension (see Seltig 1985). To add one further complexity here, we would like to attend to Giles and Wiemann's (1987) notion that people not only construe encounters in terms of their individual and group identities, as discussed in Chapter 1, but also their *relational* and/or *couple* identities. Indeed, it is possible to conceive of a romantic, heterosexual relationship, for instance, as on some occasions being simultaneously high on all three dimensions: that is, 'I'm me, but I'm a feminist, although I am us'. Hence, when it suits desired needs, an individual could diverge from another by adopting couple-talk (Giles and Fitzpatrick 1984), even with their partner not present, perhaps through proliferating couple disclosures and airing an obviously privately constructed code.

Further distinctions

Studies that have probed even deeper into contextual particularities have been able to reveal some further complexities of motive and effect – for example, that some divergent acts can in fact be enacted for seemingly convergent motives, and even some convergent acts accomplished towards 'divergent' ends. For these purposes, we need to introduce the further distinction between psychological and communicative accommodation, as well as a more differentiated account of the *functions* of accommodative strategies.

Psychological versus linguistic accommodation

Thakerar *et al.* (1982) defined psychological convergence and divergence, respectively, as individuals' integrative and differentiative orientations to others; linguistic convergence and divergence are, of course, the speech strategies (objectively or subjectively viewed) that may realize these orientations. Very often, psychological and communicative accommodations will be perfectly isomorphic. But psychological convergence attending communicative divergence may be vividly evident in role-discrepant situations where dissimilarities are not just acceptable but even expected. For instance, a sociolinguistically sensitive interviewee is hardly likely to be evaluated favourably if s/he assumes communicatively the directive, interrogative language and non-verbally controlling styles of her/his interviewers; complementarity on certain levels, then, is expected by both parties.

A complementary relationship obtains when participants are mutually acknowledged to hold subordinate and superordinate positions (Watzlawick *et al.* 1967). Many examples can be given where a status or power discrepancy exists in a dyad, including employer–employee, teacher–pupil, veteran–novice and other relationships. However, not all relationships can be classified in such power terms, and talk in many stable, intimate relationships veers in a status-equivalent and then in a status-unequal direction, depending on the nature of the topic discussed or on some other situational dimension. It is important to emphasize that complementary relationships require a measure of consensus from the participants involved. Indeed, complementarity would appear to increase mutual predictability (Berger and Bradac 1982) as proposed with respect to convergence earlier in this chapter. Miller and Steinberg (1975: 235) commented that:

> Many people do indeed seem to choose to be one-down in their relationships with others; they consistently adopted sub-

servient, deferential or even totally dependent positions. In doing so, they are able to achieve some measure of certainty in their communication transactions. Their consistently one-down behaviour tends to elicit predictably one-up kinds of responses from their companions. In this sense, any role is preferable to a variable one, or to no role at all.

Classic examples of speech complementarity might include when two young people are out on a date. Even though laboratory problem-related tasks have shown mutual convergences by males and females in situations where gender identity was probably low in salience (Mulac *et al.* 1987; 1988), males and females with initial romantic inclinations are likely to diverge towards prototypically strong and soft communicative patterns, respectively, at least in the many communities where traditional sex-role ideologies abound. Montepare and Vega (1988) found that women sounded more 'feminine' (for instance, used higher and more variable pitch) when talking to an intimate, as opposed to an unknown, male other over a telephone link. We would take this to be an instance of complementarity rather than as descriptive divergence (as the authors themselves described it). This does not, however, preclude the possibility of convergence simultaneously occurring on other linguistic dimensions. For instance, a woman may adopt a soft voice and certain paralinguistic and prosodic features with an eligible male, yet may wish to gain his attraction, approval and respect by not only fulfilling her feminine role requirements but also converging to his higher-prestige dialect. As we noted earlier, Bilous and Krauss (1988) showed that women converged towards men's utterance length, interruptions and pausing, but diverged on backchannels and laughter. These last two behaviours could again be taken as instances of speech complementarity, signalling traditionally sexist, role-related female involvement with and endorsement of male discourse.

Speech convergence, then, is often accompanied by speech complementarity of other linguistic features. Naturally, the optimal degree and rate of convergence, together with the optimal balance of complementarity, is difficult to encode from situation to situation. As Goffman (1967) stated, 'the image that emerges of the individual is that of juggler and synthesizer, an accommodator and appeaser, who fulfils one function while he is apparently engaged in another'. Seen in this light, it is no wonder that interpersonal communication is often fraught with difficulties and misunderstandings. Street (in press) provides a compelling analysis of doctor–patient relationships in which he argues that a fine meshing of physician convergence and complementarity is essential for patient satisfaction and compliance to health regimens.

The other 'incongruent' combination remaining to be discussed is psychological divergence allied to linguistic convergence, as for instance in the reciprocation of both verbal abuse and interruptive behaviour – referred to by Giles and Powesland (1975) as 'negative response matching'. Drawing once again on observational experience from Montreal in the 1970s, many English Canadian students reported effortful instances of accommodating to presumed French Canadians in non-fluent French, and then being replied to, and often interrupted, in fast fluent English by those French Canadians. Woolard (1989) has reported similar patterns in Catalonia (in the early 1980s, see Chapter 2) where the linguistic etiquette of an 'accommodation norm' was that 'Catalan should be spoken only between Catalans' (1989: 69). Hence, Castillian people who accommodated Catalan speakers by shifting into that language would more than likely have been responded to in Castillian. Similarly, Miller (1982) has claimed that a common strategy adopted by Japanese to show displeasure at a Caucasian who is speaking Japanese is to adopt a 'foreigner talk' register, or to refuse to carry on a conversation in Japanese, and instead to 'diverge' in the direction of English. Such patterns of response have been shown experimentally to be highly favoured by the Japanese (especially women), even in response to highly proficient Japanese-speaking Westerners; but the reasons for it are self-presentationally complex and perhaps not as divergent as Miller has assumed (Ross and Shortreed 1990).

CAT has tended to focus on acts of accommodation in which speakers have specific and clearly-defined *repertoires* enabling them to switch codes or styles. However, this restriction may have turned out to be theoretically limiting given the relationship between accent mimicry, everyday humour and media portrayals. Coupland (1985) has shown in a case study how a Cardiff DJ frequently shifted pronunciations in a consciously mimicked yet comfortable 'convergent' manner across a whole range of British and American dialects, in seeming solidarity with particular listeners, singers and figureheads. Nevertheless, mimicking can often be accomplished with divergent aims, as in Basso's (1979) data where Native American Indians mocked whites by mimicking their communicative behaviour. Such negative mocking, but with more critical intent, has been observed by Shields (pers. comm.) among Jamaican school-teachers (who usually adopt standard forms in the classroom) converging towards or mimicking their pupils' creolized styles when they are deemed disruptive, inattentive or lazy. Indeed, the sender motives and recipient attributions of mimicking and mocking are an intriguing dynamic deserving further research.

Cognitive organization versus identity-maintenance functions

Thus far, convergence and divergence have been treated essentially as affective phenomena. Thakerar *et al.* (1982), however, suggested that such shifts may function psychologically for two main reasons – cognitive organization and identity maintenance (see Giles *et al.* 1979). The cognitive organization function involves communicative features being used by communicators to organize events into meaningful social categories, thereby allowing the complex social situation to be reduced to manageable proportions. In this way, speakers may organize their outputs to take into account the requirements of their listeners; listeners may select from this discourse and organize it according to the cognitive structures most easily available for comprehension (Brown and Dell 1987). As mentioned earlier, increased intelligibility is a valuable byproduct of convergent acts and may on occasion be the principal motive for accommodating. Indeed, 'babytalk' – which undoubtedly fulfils a cognitive organiza-tion function in providing simplified input – could very usefully be considered in CAT terms. Similarly, Pierson and Bond (1982: 136), investigating American–Cantonese bilingual interviews, reported that:

> During the interview itself, Cantonese bilinguals broke up their speech units with filled pauses more when working in Can-tonese with Americans. They also slowed down their speed of speaking Cantonese by 8.4%, even though this reduction was not statistically significant. Both changes functioned to assist the interviewer in decoding their meaning by giving him more time.

On other occasions, interlocutors may wish to communicate in a manner that will allow them to present themselves most favourably and listeners may, in turn, wish to select creatively from the multiple

Figure 3.1   Accommodative functions arranged in two-dimensional space

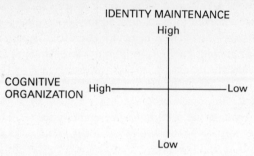

Source: Thakerar *et al*. (1982: 240)

messages they hear in ways that maintain or even enhance their own self- or group esteem. So, the identity-maintenance function of communication fulfils the emotional needs of participants, as they attend to speech markers and non-verbal features that positively reinforce their egos, and fail to process any information that may have a negative effect on their images. As Figure 3.1 suggests, these two dimensions may be considered orthogonal, allowing for the likelihood that virtually every social episode has a modicum of both functions operating and often several other goals to achieve. In other words, those whose approval we desire may come to be those with whom we wish to, or want to be thought to wish to, establish clarity. Relatedly, and some British migrants to areas of the USA may identify with this example, speakers may want speedy and effective service interactions and so converge – not in any sense to glean approval but as a tactic to reduce their perceived cultural distinctiveness. In doing this, they might intend to avoid the routinized (but often well-disposed) metalinguistic commenting ('Such a cute accent!') which non-convergence would predictably elicit. Also, convergence would avoid the predictable repeat requests that might allow interested recipients to inspect these 'cute' accent performances!

In the Thakerar *et al*. studies outlined earlier, it was suggested that the low-status speakers were converging towards where they *believed* the standard speakers to be as an act of identity maintenance; that is, they wished to be seen as more competent than they had been credited with being up to then. The high-status speakers converged, it was argued, towards where they believed the low-status speakers were as an act of cognitive organization, in order to promote comprehension. In this way, the same accommodative acts may fulfil different and complex functions. A further salutory consideration, however, is that locating goals exclusively in the heads of speakers (as Figure 3.1 unfortunately implies) is a conceptual convenience that ignores the many occasions when convergences or divergences are *collaborative* acts reflecting *emergent* goals.

Divergence, too, may function not only as an expression of attitudes but also to put order and meaning into the interaction, and to provide a mutually understood basis for communication; in other words, to fulfil a cognitive organization function. For example, the broadening of an accent, as well as content differentiation or other forms of divergence, may serve to indicate that interlocutors are not members of the host community or familiar with the current situation in which they find themselves. This kind of self-handicapping tactic (Weary and Arkin 1981) increases the probability that norms inadvertently broken can be attributed externally, and that a greater latitude of acceptance will be made available for the speaker; divergence here has some real social utility (Ryan, pers. comm.), perhaps particularly in intercultural environments. This divergence, moreover, acts as a form of self-disclosure to indicate that certain spheres of knowledge and behaviour may not be shared, and that intersubjectivity is, in consequence, at a premium.

In other situations, speech divergence may be a strategy employed to bring another's behaviour to an acceptable level or to facilitate the co-ordination of speech patterns. Studies have indicated that inter-actants (for example, therapists and more generally adults) may sometimes diverge in the amount they talk in order to encourage their listeners (clients and children) to talk more (Street, Street and Van Kleeck 1983). Anecdotally, it is not uncommon for people to slow down their speech rate with extremely fast-talking and or excited others in order to 'cool them down' to a more comfortable communicative and cognitive level. Although in a different theoretical context, Ickes *et al.* (1982) showed that when males were expecting to talk via an intercom system to a 'cold' rather than a 'warm' interlocutor, they sounded far warmer in the former than the latter conditions, presumably to enhance the projected warmth of their partners.

Discourse attuning

We should note that the *addressee focus* in the above discussion has centred around the other's communicative *performance*, or at least perceptions or expectations of this performance. From this perspective, convergence, divergence and complementarity as we have discussed them may be labelled *approximation strategies*. Coupland, Coupland, Giles and Henwood (1988) elaborated CAT so as to include a broader range of addressee foci, and hence *attuning* strategies, than the approximation ones, and so open the door to the reconceptualizing of accommodation in terms of discursive and sequential acts. One alternative addressee focus involves attending to the other's interpretive competence, which we often assess through their social category memberships (by such cues as accent, lexical diversity, skin colour and so forth) and the inferences we derive on the basis of these. Sometimes, as we shall see with the case of the supposedly generic 'elderly' in Chapter 6, such competences are stereotyped rather negatively – for example, as an impaired ability to understand. This then leads to a set of *interpretability* strategies which can be used to modify the complexity of speech (for example, by decreasing diversity of vocabulary, or simplifying syntax), increase clarity (by changing pitch, loudness, tempo by incorporating repetition, clarification checks, explicit boundarying devices and so on), and/or by influencing the selection of conversational topics (by staying in familiar and unthreatening areas for the other).

Two other addressee foci involve attending to the addressee's conversational needs and role relationships which lead to sets of *discourse management* and *control* strategies, respectively. The first of these is to be seen as a highly diverse set of discursive options whereby a speaker may facilitate a partner's own contribution to ongoing talk – for example, in offering turns, eliciting disclosable information, repairing problematical sequences and generally working to redress positive or negative face-threats to a recipient (Penman 1991). Alternatively, attuned discourse management will involve supportive recipiency strategies whereby a speaker's contribution can be endorsed and accredited through backchannelling or more explicit approbatory moves. Control strategies likewise embody degrees of attuning, reflecting the disposition of role options in talk, as, for example, when a young speaker may suppress her own disclosure and offer 'the floor' to an elderly partner.

The explanatory value of this more propositionally and functionally based specification of CAT is only now beginning to be demonstrated (see Giles *et al.*, in press). The *theoretical* necessity for this expanded perspective is, however, already clear. Accommodative or attuned talk is very frequently achieved strategically when behaviour matching, participant to participant, is either not the evaluatively salient criterion or is even highly inappropriate. One interesting case emerges from the conversation-analysis literature on troubles-telling. Although 'laughing together is a valued occurrence which can be the product of methodic, coordinated activities' (Jefferson 1984: 348), the established pattern in troubles-telling is that 'the troubles-teller laughs, and the troubles-recipient declines to laugh by talking to the prior utterance and thus by talking to the trouble' (1984: 350). So, laughter by teller and recipient enter quite polarized strategies and evaluative frames during troubles-talk, *vis-à-vis* the 'laughability' of circumstances from one or other perspective. An objective similarity between teller's and recipient's behaviour—laughter—is in this case not in itself the interpersonally meaningful concern; rather, it is the contextual and sequential organization of laughter, and its highly attuned *absence*, that signifies.

More generally, a high level of psychological and subjective attuning along these dimensions (approximation, interpretability, discourse-management and control strategies) can attenuate sociolinguistic distance, bring the other person psychologically closer, and also enhance conversational effectiveness and smoothness; in other words, fulfil both cognitive organization and identity-maintenance functions as discussed above. Of course, the converse can occur by means of *contra*-attuning. The Coupland, Coupland, Giles and Henwood (1988) exposition outlines further possibilities of *under-* and *over*attuning when interactional strategies deemed appropriate by one or other party (for example, an elderly recipient, as in Chapter 6) are perceived to have been under- or overplayed. Thus, for example, 'overattuning' (or overaccommodation) can be specified to characterize demeaning or patronising talk – often well intentioned in its own terms – when excessive concern is paid to vocal clarity or amplitude, message simplification or repetition, as well as 'overaccounting' when excuses, justifications, and apologies are proliferated but unwarranted. Similarly, Fanon (1961) has discussed the patronizing speech whites sometimes adopt with blacks, making them feel that they have been considered childlike or even sub-human. Alternatively, excessively authoritarian and dismissive styles may, for example, be characterized as underattuned (or underaccommodative) along dimensions of control and discourse management.

Future rapprochements

Interpretive competences are, of course, more dynamic than we have suggested this far, and can, for example, change as topics do. In other words, and particularly with unfamiliar others, we are constantly needing to assess and reassess the amount of shared knowledge we have on particular issues, events, and people as these are sequentially focused upon during a conversation. Sometimes this will be not simply to accommodate others' lack of expertise, but, more strategically, to ensure that our own discourse does not appear naive or ill-fated given our addressees' competences, dispositions, and evaluative tendencies. Commenting on research on (mainly referential) perspective-taking, Krauss and Fussell (1988) have outlined the kinds of appraisal (and social comparison) individuals need to make if they are, in our terms, to estimate their partner's interpretive competences. These are the extent to which interlocutors share the same: (a) background knowledge in topic-relevant areas, and affective orientations to these; (b) situational definition, goals, plans and task orientations; (c) definition of the relationship (for example, intimacy); and (d) definition of the speaking situation (for instance, norms of appropriate behaviour). Processing such social data is often achieved swiftly and implicitly, as reported by Anderson and Garrod (1987). They observed misunderstanding occurring between pairs of speakers co-operating to solve a problem involving the movement of pieces in a maze. As the dialogue continued, the speakers gradually began to adopt the same terms to describe and refer to items in the maze without any discussion of this strategy or apparently the need for it. Similarly, Isaacs and Clark (1987) found that subjects in their experiment swiftly appraised whether or not their interlocutors had expert knowledge about New York City, without any explicit indication and often within their first exchange of utterances. This *collaborative* and dynamic venture requires that individuals negotiate what is conversationally necessary, by way of attuning, to ensure that ongoing interpretive competences are optimal. Indeed, Clark and Wilkes-Gibbs (1986: 33) claim that conversationalists take this process for granted, and operate their so-called 'principle of mutual responsibility':

The participants in a conversation try to establish, roughly by the initiation of each new contribution, the mutual belief that the listeners have understood what the speaker meant in the last utterance to a criterion sufficient for current purposes.

Schober and Clark (1989) argue that a significant portion of this collaborative process is rather *opportunistic* – what they term 'grounding' – to the extent that participants in novel communicative contexts try out various referential (and presumably also affective) 'short-cuts', which are either accepted by the others and acted upon, or else rejected and alternatives negotiated.

Attuning to others' interpretive competences would seem essential under conditions where we wish to persuade them, attempt to regulate their behaviour, or induce them to comply with a request. The extensive work of Delia and his associates (see, for example, O'Keefe and Delia 1985) has examined the kinds of listener-adapted message respondents claim they would use to persuade another in an imaginary situation. The strategies reported as indicative of cognitively complex individuals give us guidelines as to the kind of interpretability strategies accommodating persuaders might adopt in regulative disputes. Based on this research tradition and specifically the work of Clark (1984) and Kline (in press), sophisticated social influencers would attempt to use language so as to co-ordinate their recipients' beliefs and actions with those of their own. More specifically, this attuning process should include the following strategies: (a) expressing mutually held values; (b) outlining problems and inducing reflection and changed perspectives; and (c) creating a resolution that is appealing to the other and does not damage (and even promotes) her/his positive identity and face-needs. It is interesting that this constructivist school of listener-adaptive communication and the cognitivist, referential school of perspective-taking rarely cross-cite each other, though they would doubtless profit from each other's insights. Obviously, the time is ripe for theoretical as well as empirical rapprochements; the elaborated format of CAT we present here allows these cross-fertilizations to occur, in understanding the negotiative character of interpersonal, small-group and intergroup relations and communication.

Another task for the future is certainly to impose further conceptual and taxonomic order on the range of sociolinguistic processes that may be implicated in interpersonal attuning. One intriguing area of overlap will be with Brown and Levinson's (1987) specification of 'positive politeness' strategies, which they characterize as highly diverse discourse moves to claim common ground with an inter-locutor, convey interactants as co-operators, and generally fulfil interlocutors' wants. Though Brown and Levinson discuss such strategies exclusively in terms of moves made to redress face-threat, their currency is presumably broader, fulfilling face-*promotion* and face-*maintenance* goals, too (Penman 1991). They would appear to fall well within the remit of traditionally invoked accommodative motives (to gain approval and increase communication efficiency). Correspondingly, CAT seems well suited to supply the contextual elaboration Brown and Levinson themselves suggest (in the Intro-duction to the 1987 volume) their framework requires, and which has apparently limited its predictive power to date.

Theoretical models, perhaps particularly those seeking to capture generalizations about communication and relational processes, are unlikely to achieve stasis. As this chapter has amply demonstrated, CAT has attracted scholars from a range of disciplines and in so doing has seen major shifts of emphasis and incorporated their new insights into its explanatory compass. This productive interchange will doubtless continue.

Summary

Accommodation theory has developed a long way since its inception. We now consider that accommodative processes can, in the long-term, affect even issues of life and death across the lifespan, as we shall see in Chapter 6. This chapter has located accommodation theory among other traditions of research concerned with adaptive interpersonal processes in language and communication. We saw how converging towards and diverging away from another could be indexed along multiple structural dimensions, and then considered some of their motivational determinants, social consequences and interactional and identity functions. The important distinction of psychological versus linguistic accommodation was introduced, leading to a complex web of language strategies that could be seen as both divergent and convergent from different perspectives. Recent discursive developments were then elaborated, showing that a wider range of discourse acts are inherent in attuning, for example, to the interpretive competences of others. This opened up new vistas of interpersonal language alignments which were more contextually grounded and context-shaping than in earlier forms of the accommodation model. Finally, we suggested exciting prospects for meshing accommodation research and theory with other research areas, with particular respect to the constructivist tradition and work on collaboration in referential communication. The chapter has therefore built on the previous two to the extent that accommodative behaviours are both dependent variables reflecting and independent variables determining the meaning of social contexts for interactants. Much of this strategic interactional 'work' – interindividual and intergroup – is culled from the idiosyncratic and shared language attitudes we hold as social schematas. In the next chapter, we explore further the intergroup dynamics of language forms which attenuate and accentuate social identity, but we do so in the framework of language and ethnicity. There, we focus on the ways in which these processes contribute to interethnic communicative success and failure.

Suggestions for further reading

Brown, P. and Levinson, S. (1987). *Politeness: Some universals in language usage*. Cambridge: Cambridge University Press. An increasingly influential theoretical position relying on notions of face; the volume should be mandatory reading for all interested in language and society.

Cody, M. and McLaughlin, M. (eds) (1989). *The psychology of practical communication*. Clevedon: Multilingual Matters. A collection of diverse, mostly data-orientated papers dealing with the language of strategic interpersonal communication.

Clark, H. H. and Brennan, S. E. (in press). Grounding in communication. In L. B. Resnick, J. Levine and S. D. Behreno (eds), *Socially shared cognition*. A chapter concerned with important facets of interpersonal collaboration in language use in different media.

Graumann, C. F. and Herman, T. (eds) (1988). *Other-relatedness in language processing*. Special double issue of *Journal of Language and Social Psychology*, 6 (3/4). Reprinted as a (1989) monograph titled *Speakers: The role of the listener*. Clevedon: Multilingual Matters. An important collection of data-driven papers from the Mannheim–Heidelberg school on reference with a cognitive-referential bias deriving from a different theoretical base than accommodation theory.

4 / LANGUAGE, ETHNICITY, AND INTERGROUP COMMUNICATION

Language and ethnicity are, as we shall see, very widely recognized to be closely intertwined, though social psychological accounts of intergroup relations more generally have afforded language behaviours and processes little attention. Despite this, no one can doubt the prominence of language issues in cultural conflict worldwide. Throughout history there have been countless instances where efforts at linguistic and political change have coincided. For example, the official language of the Ottoman Empire for the previous 400 years was repressed by the leaders of post-1922 Turkey in favour of a new form of the language (modern Turkish) to emphasize linguistic identification with central Asia. In India, Sikh writers promoted a standard variety of their language in order to differentiate it from Hindu since the two languages were originally very similar in spoken form. Macedonian writers in Yugoslavia sought words and grammatical structures from remote rural areas in order to establish a standard which would distinguish their language from Serbo-Croatian, and the struggle for a separate Macedonian republic in Yugoslavia coincided with these efforts at linguistic differentiation.

More recently, one recalls the Soweto riots in South African in the summer of 1976 when large numbers of blacks and whites were killed. The catalyst of this situation was a language issue. When the confrontation with the police occurred, black students and other groups were protesting against the white government's insistence that their educational curricula be presented in the Afrikaans language. In commenting on this situation to the press, black leaders made the following statement, reported in a London newspaper, *The Times* (23 June 1979):

> the situation has unearthed the innermost frustrations of Black people which were hidden from the outside world. Although there is a prevalent belief in some quarters that Afrikaans as a medium of instruction was not a direct positive factor in these riots, this is not so. Afrikaans was forced down Black students just as much as the Trust Land Act, pass laws, and migratory labour . . .

For black people in South Africa, Afrikaans is undoubtedly seen as a very potent symbol of white domination and oppression. It can be argued that their being forced to 'taste it in their mouths' (if you like) was perceived by blacks as an intolerant, abhorrent attack on their social identity. In the same summer of 1976, commercial air services at Montreal's airports were halted for a week when Quebecois air traffic controllers engaged in industrial action for not being allowed to use French as a work medium. Indeed, this (essentially sociolinguistic) dispute was described by the Canadian Prime Minister at the time as potentially the most divisive the country had faced for 30 years.

More recently, media attention has been focused on the numerous ethnic groups in the Soviet Union airing nationalist sentiments and pleas for political independence. Language has again been a critical concern here – for example with appeals for a local parliament to be conducted in the Estonian language; a Bill to this effect passed in January 1989, was in fact the Soviet Union's first language law. This new concern for minority language rights (see Chapter 5) has had its effects on Soviets in other Baltic republics, too. The *Los Angeles Times* (2 September 1989) reported an interview with a Russian resident in Moldavia:

> 'Everyone is becoming so strident,' he complained. 'One man, a Moldavian writer who has been my friend for 12 years, knows that my ability to speak Moldavian is not up to the mark. We always spoke in Russian. But suddenly he has begun speaking to me only in Moldavian, and elaborate, literary Moldavian at that'.

In this chapter, we examine *why* language is important to ethnic relations and, to do this, we develop a social psychological perspective by drawing on theory and research in the social psychology of intergroup relations. Then we shall examine the role of social stereotypes in 'breaking down' communication between groups in contact.

The salience of language

There are at least four reasons for the salience of language in ethnic relations: language is often a criterial attribute of group membership, an important cue for ethnic categorization, an emotional dimension of identity, and a means of facilitating ingroup cohesion (see also Maas *et al.* 1989).

There are different criteria for membership of an ethnic group, involving ancestry, religion, physiognomy and other dimensions of ethnicity (Fishman 1977). Most ethnic groups also have a distinct language or dialect, and these can often be considered necessary attributes for full and 'legitimate' membership of the group. This links up with notions of paternity/maternity, through concepts such as 'mother tongue', where language is seen as an aspect of ancestry. For example, one definition of an Arab (from Article 10 of the Constitution of the Socialist Arab Resurrection Party) is: 'A person whose mother tongue is Arabic, who has lived or who looks forward to living on Arab soil, and who believes in being a member of the Arab nation' (cited in Fishman 1972: 44). Similarly, it was not uncommon in Hispanic communities in the southwestern United States in the 1970s to hear that: 'A Mexican American who can't speak Spanish should choke on his chilli beans!'; such individuals may not be afforded full membership by other group members, and may themelves feel that their identity is incomplete. Even when there are strong and clear criteria for ethnic group membership such as skin colour, an ethnic language variety often remains a criterial attribute. One Afro-American member of the Peace Corps Volunteers was surprised and upset to find that when he met his African 'brothers' in Sierra Leone they called him *oyimbo* ('white man'), because of his standard American English and behaviour (Hancock 1974).

Giles (1979) introduced a model of ethnic boundaries which bears upon this very issue. He presented a 2 × 2 model in which perceived linguistic boundaries ('hard' versus 'soft' – for example, distinctive language and mild accent, respectively) intersected with hard–soft *non*-linguistic ethnic boundaries (for example distinctive religion and some dissimilar values, respectively). It was argued that ethnic minorities would accentuate their ingroup communicative markers in an interethnic encounter where they felt their linguistic boundaries were soft (or being made increasingly soft by the outgroup) rather than hard, and also when they felt their non-linguistic boundaries were soft rather than hard; both undertaken as a means of strengthening overall boundary 'hardness'. This is a desirable process for most ethnic groups as it enables them to differentiate more clearly, on valued dimensions, between own-group and outgroup. By these means, they can achieve a positive social identity and allow ingroup norms to be established more effectively. Using an analysis of variance model, it is possible to predict that the manipulation of the independent variables linguistic–non-linguistic and hard–soft boundaries will have main effects on the dependent measure–use of ethnic language markers. Figure 4.1 schematizes degrees of ethnic language accentuation accordingly. The model suggests that the most linguistic differentiation occurs, paradoxically enough, with the very groups (in the lower right-hand quadrant) which have the softest perceived overall ethnic boundaries and hence the greatest similarity with the ethnic outgroup.

Support for this notion comes from the work of Turner *et al.* (1984). They suggested, on the basis of cognitive dissonance and commitment principles, that when individuals voluntarily choose to take up membership of a social category, group cohesion will be

Figure 4.1   Perceived linguistic and non-linguistic boundary continua.

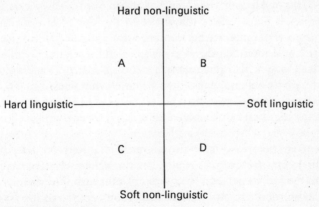

Source: Giles (1979: 279)

greatest when the group *fails* on a task, but that for involuntary category members the reverse is true; that is, group cohesion will be greatest when the group succeeds. Therefore, *defeat* in conditions of voluntary commitment to membership actually facilitates ingroup cohesion and outgroup differentiation. In the quadrant where both boundaries are perceived as soft, the individual has the choice of self-identifying with his/her ethnic ingroup or moving out of it, to perhaps a greater extent than in any of the other quadrants. When individuals do commit themselves to ethnic identification under these conditions, the 'failure' of the group in terms of the softness of its boundaries will mobilize the person to a greater sense of ingroup cohesion and collective action on behalf of the group – more so than if the boundaries were perceived to be more secure. Because ethnic verbal markers are usually a very direct and overt expression of social differentiation in interethnic interaction (that is, individuals can easily hear and monitor their distinctiveness tactics), it is the linguistic boundary that tends to become hardened. Indeed, such reasoning might help to explain the rebirth of ethnicity in the last generation or so.

For orientation in a complex and rapidly changing environment, individuals need to organize their world cognitively, and this includes the social categorization of its inhabitants. Language is central to these categorizations, because it has the flexibility and overt, physical presence to reference a range of social categories. Language characteristics are often necessary to distinguish group memberships – for example, an American from a Canadian, perhaps Catholics from Protestants in Northern Ireland (see the discussion of linguistic shibboleths by Hopper 1986), an Australian from a New Zealander, and between many ethnic minorities in the United States. Again, many aspects of language performance (for instance, accent) can be acquired and modified developmentally and situationally. Therefore, language is also potentially a stronger cue to an individual's sense of ethnic belongingness than inherited characteristics (such as skin colour). Others may certainly take this to be so, since acquired characteristics may be attributed 'internally' (as conscious decisions about how to self-project) rather than 'externally' (as historical accident). In other words, while paternity (inherited characteristics) may be the key to ethnicity for the individuals themselves, patrimony may be the key to perceptions of others' ethnicity (Fishman 1977). Even when there are clear and unambiguous non-linguistic cues to people's ethnic group membership (such as skin colour and dress),

speech style and linguistic self-labelling can still be used interpretively by others to make inferences about their *strength* of ethnic
identification, and so about personality traits, job suitability, and so
on, as we saw in Chapter 2.

It is certainly the case that the ethnic salience of language is a
fluctuating one. For instance, Smolicz (1984) argued that language
was not a core value of Dutch people in Australia whereas it was far
more so for Polish and Greek communities there. Contrastingly, in a
series of multidimensional scaling studies, it was shown that some
French Canadians felt closer to an English Canadian who spoke
French than to a French-Canadian who did not (Taylor *et al.* 1973).
In a case study, Banks (1987) has shown the ways in which some
Hispanic managers can face pressures to de-ethnicize their discourse
before higher-power positions in an Anglo-American organization
are available to them, and how this can have an adverse affect on
their feelings of Mexican identity. Among Lithuanians in the United
States, language is the variable on which the group shows least
assimilation. Although they have become fully integrated into American life, they have nevertheless maintained their language for use
among themselves (Baskauskas 1977). The Catalonian Cultural
Committee sees language as the cultural linchpin: 'Our language, the
expression of our people, which can never be given up, is the spiritual
foundation of our existence . . . a people without a language of its
own is only half a nation' (cited in Fishman 1972: 46). Not surprisingly, then, ethnic group members in some communities who do not
endorse their ethnic affiliation linguistically may be labelled cultural
traitors and their language regarded as improper, insulting and
disloyal. An example is the following extract from an interview with
a Puerto Rican boy in New York:

> I have to answer in Spanish. My father asks me a question in
> Spanish. He won't take it in English. I have to answer in
> Spanish 'cause he says I'm not Italian and I'm not a Negro but
> I'm a Puerto Rican and have to speak to him in my language.
> He says I was born in Puerto Rico and . . . I'm gonna raise you
> like Puerto Ricans. So if we speak in English in front of him . . .
> it's like cursing right in front of him (Wolfram, 1973: 171).

Sometimes, it has been argued, it is not necessary for members of
an ethnic group to speak the language so long as they have it
available. As De Vos (1975, p. 15) says: 'ethnicity is frequently
related more to the symbol of a separate language than to its actual

use by all members of a group'. Examples might include Gaelic, Welsh and Breton, which are not spoken by the majority of those who identify with their respective groups, but which nevertheless are highly valued as aspects of ethnic identity. De Vos (1975: 16) goes on to suggest that 'group identity can even be maintained by minor differences in linguistic patterns and by style of gesture'. For example, many people of Jewish origin (not unlike the majority of Scots, Irish and Welsh) speak their host language (usually English) with a distinctive accent, and with words and phrases borrowed from their own ethnic tradition, culture and religion. In a similar way, Australians have begun to reappraise their own distinctive cultural identity and the way in which they had assimilated to American and European traditions. In an article about the Australian Renaissance ('Ockerism') in the (London) *Observer Review* (27 June 1976), attention was drawn to language as a core issue:

> Americanization of the language is much more significantly pervasive than the high incidence of skate-boards and roadside fast food parlours . . . The American invasion of the Australian stomach was always on the cards. But the invasion of the language is less easy to laugh off . . .

Approaches and problems

Given the cultural significance of language, it is not surprising to find language issues at the heart of interethnic conflict. Studies of language and ethnicity across the disciplines have in fact been caricatured as falling into three overlapping categories: the sociolinguistic, sociological, and communication breakdown approaches (Giles and Johnson 1981). The *sociolinguistic* approach examines the different kinds of speech markers used by different ethnic groups in contact when they are using supposedly the same language. This approach implicitly counters stereotypes of ethnic dialect speakers in an appreciation of the richness of, say, black verbal genres such as signifying, marking, sounding and rapping (see, for example, Kochman 1986). As Taylor *et al.* (1985: 161) argued: 'if teachers could find a way to capitalize on these verbal skills, they might find a gold mine for enhancing academic achievement'. The *sociological* approach (briefly considered in Chapter 5) examines the kinds of factors which affect the maintenance or death of a minority language. The *communication breakdown* approach looks at the ways in which the differential use of verbal, vocal and non-verbal features can lead to misunderstanding and misattribution.

While these approaches have provided us with fruitful data, they do not provide a fully adequate basis for comparative and integrated theorizing. In other words, while a group in one place is using and thinking about its language varieties in one way, a group elsewhere appears to be doing and believing quite the opposite. The heterogeneity of interethnic situations, language strategies, and language attitudes is, of course, a problem in this regard. But this multidisciplinary area is limited, we suggest, by failing to recognize socio-psychological dimensions and distinctions, which we can usefully review at this point.

First, as we showed in Chapter 1, different ethnic groups vary on many macro-contextual dimensions, including history, geography, territory, as well as in their economic and political relations with other groups. Berry, Kim and Boski (1987), in a 2 × 2 model, distinguished between groups who valued their ingroup identity and those who did not, as well as between those with valued links with the broader society and those without, producing the four quadrants of Figure 4.2. Relating to our concerns in Chapter 5, Angie Williams (pers. comm.) has suggested that moving from the 'separation' to the 'integration' quadrant and then on to 'assimilation' may be the psychological route to a group losing its language. An important source of *linguistic* variation between ethnic groups is the degree of overlap of the speech repertoires of the ingroups and outgroups concerned. In order to illustrate the complexity of the possibilities existing in this respect, Giles (1978) proposed a 4 × 4 matrix of 16 interethnic situations. In this model, the possibilities for both in- and outgroup were: (a) monolingual in the ingroup language; (b) monolingual in the outgroup language; (c) bilingual in the in- and outgroup languages; and (d) bilingual in the ingroup language and lingua franca. Perhaps a more parsimonious way of conceptualizing this would be to locate relevant in- and outgroups on the two-dimensional space displayed in Figure 4.3.

Subsequently, three of these cells were highlighted by Giles (1979) as comprising the most typical situations, and these are represented in Figure 4.4. The *language choice* paradigm exists in many multilingual communities where a large number of ethnic groups coexist in the same social space, having their own (often mutually unintelligible) language codes but with one or more languages in common. A prime concern with such contact situations has been which

Figure 4.2   Adapted from Berry *et al.*'s (1987) model.

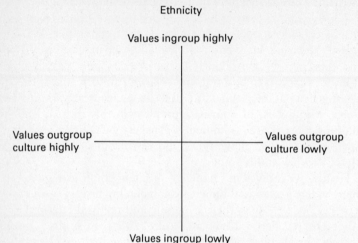

language each group chooses, and whether speakers maintain it or switch during social encounters. The accommodation and assimilation models side-step this problem to the extent that one ethnic group (usually the economic, social and political subordinate, group B in Figure 4.4) has opted either from choice or necessity to use the language of the other in interethnic contacts. This group has often chosen to become bilingual so as to function more effectively in a group A-dominated society, but maintained its own ethnic language

Figure 4.3   A model of intergroup bilingualism

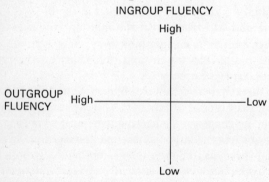

Source: Giles (1978: 363–78)

Figure 4.4   Typical language use in interethnic contact situations
(lower-case letters refer to the language(s) in which the speaker is fluent).

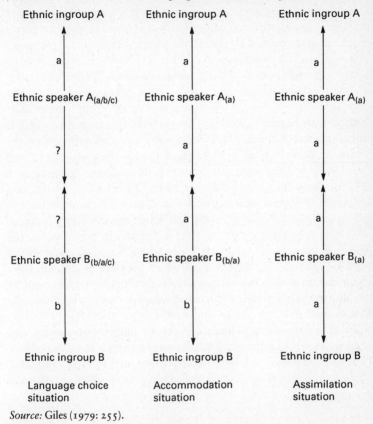

Source: Giles (1979: 255).

(b in Figure 4.4) diglossically for within-group interactions (as with Hispanic groups in the United States).

In the assimilation paradigm, group B could have been, to varying degrees, deliberately *de*-ethnicized (cf. Giles 1978: 366) by the policies of group A (Hellinization, Arabacization, Russification, for instance). De-ethnicization is evidently a modern as well as a historical phenomenon, as for example documented by Hurtado and Rodriguez's (1989) study of Hispanic students' recollections of the recent repression of Spanish in their south Texan schools. Alternatively, group B could have voluntarily assimilated into the dominant society (see the notion of 'individual mobility' below). As with all such models, we should, of course, be cautious of caricaturing particular objective situations in terms of one paradigm, because of interindividual differences (see below). The point is nevertheless that interethnic settings do fall into gross but important sub-categories which are underpinned by distinctive sociopsychological processes.

Second, and relatedly, types of ethnic groups do show characteristically different patterns of language use. While some groups attenuate their ethnolinguistic varieties — even to the extent of their languages disappearing without trace — other groups *accentuate* these features, create new forms, or even take direct action on behalf of their neglected languages. To take some contrasting instances, the speech of West Indians in Cardiff, Wales, in the early 1970s was found to be indistinguishable from that of working-class whites in 80% of cases (Giles and Bourhis 1975). In the USA, blacks and whites have been distinguished with an accuracy of 80% on the basis of speech samples (Shuy *et al.* 1969), reflecting the retention, accentuation and even creation of ethnic speech style. In recent years, the Welsh, Bretons and particularly Catalans, far from assimilating into dominant ethnic groups with which they are in contact, have attempted to foster the economic viability of their languages by pressing forcibly for their wider use in such domains as the media and education.

Third, there is often heterogeneity in language attitudes and behaviours across different factions and members of the same group. This is exemplified among Indians living in Leicester, England, whose ethnic language is Gujarati. One person interviewed commented:

> If I didn't speak Gujarati, I would feel drowned . . . I would suffocate if I didn't speak Gujarati. If an Indian tries to speak to me in English I always ask 'can't you speak Gujarati?'. If he can't I feel distant from him.

Another member of the (supposedly) same group is quoted as saying:

> I was at a polytechnic in London and a year passed before I spoke any Gujarati. Even when I met a Gujarati from Leicester, we got to know each other in English and wouldn't dream of speaking anything else (Mercer *et al.* 1979: 23).

In short, an approach is required which will take into account between-group and within-group diversity in language and ethnic attitudes, speech repertoires and strategies, as well as structural features of, and influences on, groups in contact. The next section provides such a sociopsychological perspective and enables us better to specify who uses which language strategy, when, and for what purposes.

Ethnolinguistic identity

'Ethnolinguistic identity theory' was introduced by Giles and Johnson (1987), but has its roots in a good deal of earlier research. One foundation is social identity theory, a robust approach vital to understanding ethnolinguistic issues, despite several existing critiques (see, for example, Rabbie *et al.* 1989). Social identity is built around a sequence of processes which can be expressed as follows (deriving from Tajfel 1978; Tajfel and Turner 1979). Social categorization of the world involves knowledge of our membership in certain social categories. This knowledge of our category memberships, together with the values (positive or negative) attached to them, is defined as our social identity and has meaning only in social comparison with other relevant groups. Social identity forms an important part of the self-concept and it is assumed that we try to achieve a positive sense of social identity in such a way as to make our own social group favourably distinct from other collectivities on valued dimensions (such as power, economic and political resources). This process of achieving positive distinctiveness enables individuals to achieve a satisfactory social identity and thereby enhances their own positive self-esteem. Thus, when ethnic group identity becomes important for individuals, they may attempt to make themselves favourably distinct on dimensions such as *language*. The accentuation of a whole panoply of ethnic speech and non-verbal markers (such as vocabulary, slang, posture, gesture, discourse styles, accent) can therefore realize a process termed 'psycholinguistic distinctiveness' (Giles *et al.* 1977). In line with the previous discussion, the encoding of linguistic distinctiveness is not an all-or-nothing process. Indeed, Brennan *et al.* (1975) found nine identifiable degrees of Spanish influence in the English accents of Mexican Americans; all of these small increments were identified by linguistically naive listeners as having distinct social meanings.

The essence of social identity for us here is again *cognitive*. Debate about the adequacy of different criteria for defining a collectivity as an 'ethnic group' has continued for decades. Ross (1979: 3) sums up some of the problems here as follows:

> Ethnicity has proven to be a very difficult concept to define with much precision. Indeed those who have approached the task has not been able to achieve a consensus. Most usages are both vague and ambiguous in their application to empirical research. What some scholars consider to be exemplars of ethnicity, others would consider to be cases of such variables as regionalism, religious sectarianism, class conflict and even sheer opportunism. When ethnicity is at best a fuzzy concept, it becomes rather difficult to convincingly establish its relationship to language.

The definition of an ethnic group we adopt is an amalgam of subjectivist definitions (see, for example, Barth 1969). We take an ethnic unit to be: those individuals who say they belong to ethnic group A rather than ethnic group B, are willing to be treated as A rather than B, allow their behaviour to be interpreted and judged as A's and not B's, and have shared systems of symbols and meanings, as well as norms and rules for conduct, normatively associated with community A.

This social psychological and interpretivist definition has three main features. First, in line with Chapter 1, it avoids categorization of individuals on the basis of supposedly 'objective' ethnic criteria. Most research studies use such external criteria, and many of their confusing and sometimes apparently contradictory results may be attributable to inadequate initial assumptions. For instance, presumably our first Gujarati above would identify himself as a 'Gujarati', while the second would probably self-identify as 'British'. (For an exploration of how language habits can themselves influence ethnic labelling, see Hurtado and Arce 1987.) Interestingly, Ros *et al.* (1987) found that their measure of 'subtractive identity' (that is, the difference between identifications with specific groupings – for example, Catalan, Basque, Valencian, Galician) was a better predictor of attitudes towards Spanish languages than was the identification with the ingroup alone.

Second, the definition does not rely on notions of physical proximity or even liking between members. In other words, Welsh people could be far more sociolinguistically Welsh in the United States than ever they were when resident in Wales. Third, it implies a notion of ethnicity which is contextually based, so that one can feel a group member in certain situations but not others, recognizing that we have multiple identities open to negotiation. In this way, the discursive tradition is most important (Collier and Thomas 1988) to the extent that feelings of ethnicity surface, are revealed and negotiated in social interaction and are not necessarily a priori categories merely waiting to be accessed trans-situationally. Moreover, social interaction allows for the symbolic meanings associated with ethnicity to be constantly redefined, for as Ross (1979: 8) argued,

> in the process of self-definition, the group myths and cultural values, including language, ... may be substantially revised, altered, and reinterpreted so as to fit with changing conditions. Clearly, ethnic identity is a distinctly modern phenomenon rather than a mere reiteration of primitive or traditional images.

This issue is important to stress as so many studies to date in the social psychology of ethnolinguistics and elsewhere have 'frozen' ethnicity at a particular historical moment, manipulating it as an independent variable. Rather, we need to recognize its function as a determining force in emergent discourse and as a socially constructive resource for negotiating complex and ambiguous affiliations. From this perspective, social categories themselves are socially constituted, emerging from social interaction and conflict (Potter and Reicher 1987), and mediated by contextual considerations. The labels for own- and outgroups are a clear instance. Husband (1977) noted that terms for Romani travellers in Britain changed from 'nomads' to 'itinerants' to 'gypsies' to 'tinkers'; that is increasingly more derogatory labels or so-called ethnophaulisms. Our tendency to refer to the ethnicity–language 'relationship' – and the experimentalist tradition itself through which we have researched it – has probably blinded us to the ways in which sometimes ethnicity itself *is* what is going on discursively. As Cronen *et al.* (1988) suggest, culture and communication are not mere interacting orthogonal concepts; rather, culture can be viewed as derived from, if not constituted in, communication and language practices.

No single perspective can, of course, accommodate all facets of ethnicity. The one that stems from our initial definition above, for example, fails to explain instances where a particular ethnic status is attributed to an individual and s/he is dealt with accordingly, without her/his own ethnic affiliations coming into question. In this instance, Louw-Potgieter and Giles's (1987) model of language and

Table 4.1   The dominated as defined by self and the dominant

Self-definition (provided by the dominated)	Other-definition (provided by the dominant)	
	Defined in	Defined out
Defined in	A	B
Defined out	C	D

Source: Louw-Potgieter and Giles (1987: 263)

social categorization might be useful. They explored the congruous and non-congruous relationships operating in terms of (a) being defined in and out of a group and (b) who is doing the defining, as shown in Table 4.1. The model suggests how group members will attempt to escape the identity imposed from without by using language strategies to change the criteria for group membership, and by differentiating themselves from the group with which they are being associated. McNamara (1987) provides a cogent example of an outgroup inducing individuals to redefine their social identity with Israeli *émigrés* in Melbourne, Australia. Upon arrival they construed themselves as 'Israelis', but very quickly found that the identity being foisted upon them was actually a 'Jewish' one.

Returning to social identity theory, it now becomes clear why the goal of imposing a stable world language such as Esperanto is unlikely to be realized, at least until a time when linguo-national identities are less socially salient. Linguistic similarities between ethnic groups act as cues for comparison, giving rise to competition between the groups for positive differentiation. Collaborative goals (like those of achieving a universal, or even in some cases a national language) are likely to heighten assessments of similarities between the groups in values or attributes. This in turn may lead to further comparisons, competition and linguistic *differentiation* between groups. This can be illustrated in studies of English and French Canadians in Quebec learning French and English, respectively. Reportedly, they start introducing ingroup phonological markers into the second language they are learning (Lambert and Tucker 1972), restoring psycholinguistic distinctiveness.

Strategies of language change

Social identity theory is a dynamic perspective which also has the potential for considering ethnolinguistic change. In particular, a negative social identity would be expected to act as a pro-change motivating factor; on the other hand, a dominant group, satisfied with its ethnolinguistic identity, would presumably desire to maintain the status quo. But there are many examples of ethnic groups in low-status positions for whom a subordinate power position does not seem sufficient motivation to initiate sociostructural changes: blacks in South Africa, minority groups in the United States, *Gastarbeiter* in Germany, isolated German and Italian groups in Brazil might constitute examples. The emphasis here is on perceived rather than actual conditions and conflicts which exist psychologically for groups involved. As Gurr (1970: 24) puts it, we need to access 'the perception of deprivation . . . People may be subjectively deprived with respect to their expectations even though an observer might not judge them to be in want'. From this viewpoint, a positive ethnic identity is achieved to the extent that group members can make social comparisons with relevant ethnic outgroups in their favour. Should social comparisons with an ethnic group on valued dimensions result in a negative ethnic identity for ingroup members, in Tajfel and Turner's (1979) view they will adopt strategies to achieve a more positive self-concept. Of these, we suggest that upward mobility is to be seen as an 'individualistic' strategy aimed at a dis-identification with a former ethnic category, whereas strategies such as social creativity and social competition are considered more 'group-orientated', because they imply individuals are attempting to achieve a positive ethnic distinctiveness. These strategies and their tactics can be seen to have important *language* correlates, and these will be introduced below together with some of the conditions considered most likely to bring about their occurrence.

Individual mobility and group assimilation

This general strategy is one where individuals wish to pass out of a group in which they experience comparative discomfort into a more positively valued one, usually the dominant ethnic collectivity. They will attempt to acquire, or at least aspire towards, the characteristics (physical, linguistic and/or psychological) of this other group. This strategy is most likely to be used when objections raised by either ingroup or outgroup for the shift are not considered strong. An important tactic for individual upward mobility in such a situation is, of course, *convergence* towards the linguistic characteristics believed prototypical of the ethnic outgroup (as discussed in Chapter 3), and attenuating the ingroup's own distinctive speech and non-linguistic markers. Banks's (1987) study is again relevant here. He argues that ethnolinguistic minorities in some organizational settings, such as Hispanics in Anglo-American settings, must cross the boundary from 'marked' usage (that is, interactionally salient, non-normative speech) to 'unmarked' usage (normative, taken-for-granted, probably standard speech) if they are going to bridge the great divide between low and high managerial positions.

Large numbers of the ingroup acting in this assimilationist manner can have serious collective consequences, including the 'erosion' or even 'death' of the ingroup language, as represented in Figure 4.4. Such a process might be more appropriately termed 'language suicide' (Denison 1977) according to the social identity explanation we have given. Albo (1979) has studied the effects of group assimilation on two subordinate collectivities in the Andes. As the subordinate ethnic groups there attempt to assimilate into the dominant Spanish-speaking group, their ethnic languages become restricted to certain domains of usage. This results in the languages lacking neologisms for technical advances and so forth, with Spanish words used instead to denote high-prestige items. For example, a modern kitchen would be referred to through the Spanish vocabulary item, whereas the ingroup word is used for a traditional kitchen; Spanish words are preferred for telling the date or time while native numerals are allowed for counting sheep. The frequency of borrowing of Spanish words varies with topic; for example only 11% of words are borrowed for a theme such as 'fears of spirits', but over 40% are borrowed in discussions of politics or modern medicine.

Ultimately, the strategy of upward mobility is not always a successful means of attaining a more satisfactory social identity, as we shall argue in the next chapter. It may instead lead to anomie and a loss of cultural distinctiveness for those individuals who still in some respects value their ethnic group membership. Acquiring another ethnic group's speech style (as in the Soweto instance we mentioned earlier) can sometimes lead to 'subtractive bilingualism' for an ethnic group with an inadequate social identity (Lambert 1974). Further, and despite the rewards for increased social stability and control, the dominant group frequently does not fully accept the subordinate group even after it has attempted to assimilate, as this in turn diminishes its own psycholinguistic distinctiveness. First the dominant group could refuse to acknowledge linguistically assimilated individuals as sounding fully 'correct'. In other words, however much the individual objectively has acquired competence in the dominant group's variety or code, the latter may still perceive the former to sound 'ethnic' if they can predicate this from other cues, such as name or skin colour (see Williams 1976). Second, if linguistic assimilation by ethnic minorities occurs with such levels of proficiency and in such numbers as to dilute the dominant group's cultural distinctiveness, powerful members of the latter may respond by 'upwardly' diverging away from them (again, see Chapter 3), and thereby create a new standard for comparison. In such circumstances, subordinate groups may find the high-prestige language or dialect of the dominant group an ever-shifting target to pursue (see Ullrich 1971).

In any case, individuals who attempt to pass into the dominant group are often, as we noted above, stigmatized as 'cultural traitors' by other members of their own group who value their ingroup identification very highly. Kochman (1976: 19) notes that in America:

> Blacks speak of toms and oreos, Chicanos about coconuts, Native Americans about apples, and Orientals about bananas. Those denoted by such labels have been judged by their respective communities to have let the mask become the man, i.e., metaphorically, to have become 'white' on the 'inside' in terms of value, attitudes and behaviour, while ostensibly remaining 'black', 'brown', 'red', and 'yellow' in their racial/ ethnic affiliations on the outside.

It is also likely that individuals will not wish to pass comprehensively into the dominant ethnic collectivity, and will not want to resign membership of some *other* social category whose associations they value. A Welsh person's accent in English, for example, might promote his/her acceptance into working-class categories; resisting passing into RP might stem from *class* rather than ethnic concerns. At the level of the (minority) group itself, large-scale defection can blur group boundaries, decrease ingroup cohesiveness, and reduce the potential for collective awareness. Assimilation may come to be deemed unworkable for attaining status parity and the minority may seek this instead through other forms of collective action, aimed at redefining the group *in and on its own terms* rather than in and on the pre-existing terms of the dominant group. This, of course, still represents a definite psychological shift for group members (Tajfel 1978).

Psycholinguistic distinctiveness

According to Tajfel and Turner's (1979) theorizing, we would expect to find that there are at least two strategies of positive and linguistic differentiation available to subordinate ethnic group members – social creativity and social competition. *Social creativity* refers to those strategies which attempt a redefinition of different elements of the comparison between subordinate and dominant ethnic groups. In contrast to the previous (mobility) strategy, which implied an abandonment of the ethnic group, the present strategies are aimed at protecting the group's identity and restoring its positive distinctiveness. In this sense, they are considered 'group-orientated' even though the solutions, as opted for by individuals, may not actually alter the objective relationship existing between ingroup and outgroup on dimensions of subordination. Social creativity strategies, of which there are at least three, are likely to be adopted when individuals find it impossible to leave their ethnic group and identification with it is unavoidable.

The first of these refers to an avoidance of 'painful' comparisons with the outgroup which is deemed responsible for their negative ingroup image. Where a lack of comparability can exist, evaluative deficiencies should be diluted and an inadequate identity less apparent. This can be achieved by individuals selecting other subordinate ethnic groups (or even particular members within them) with which they can make favourable comparisons. For instance, Asian immigrants in Britain might compare themselves with West Indians and gain more positive culture-identity from this comparison, since, among other cultural and religious traditions, they have distinct languages for differentiation and do not rely on what might be construed as 'mere substandard' dialects. But it is unlikely that groups can be successfully insulated from interethnic comparisons in the long term, especially in situations of close proximity, so the strategy seems precarious, and other creativity strategies will often need to be undertaken.

Another is an attempt to change the values attributed to ingroup characteristics in a more positive direction, so that negative ingroup comparisons are much mollified. The example *par excellence* is, of course, the 'Black is beautiful' slogan. Again, language assumes significance in that the often-termed 'inferior' or 'substandard' language or dialect of ethnic ingroups are no longer stigmatized but heralded proudly as symbols of group pride. If the value shift succeeds, we would find strategies of language retention and dialect maintenance within the minority group. An intriguing instance of alteration of existing linguistic dimensions of comparison, but this time by the dominant group, is the changes in Swahili made by the Boers in Kenya resulting in a new dialect, Kiselta (Muthiani 1979). The dominant group, by altering the subordinate group's tongue, defined the situation via language as one in which they became superior and more powerful. The indigenous population was in no position to enforce a 'standard' form of their language, but in many instances adopted the Boers' form of their own, previously ingroup, language.

The third creativity strategy is a tendency to compare the ingroup with the outgroup on some new dimensions. The resurrection of Hebrew from virtual extinction to the status of a national language in a very short time, the revival of Punjabi in Pakistan, and appeals for Romani leaders to devise a linguistic system to increase intra-group communication, and the deanglicizing of English in Third World countries can sometimes be considered instances of such a strategy. Again, Ukranian nationalists replaced letters of the Russian alphabet with new Ukranian ones to emphasize the distinctiveness of Ukranian, and Bones (1986) refers to lexical and semantic aspects of Rastafarian language, called Afro-Lingua, as instances of linguistic creativity. However, having these new forms recognized and legitimized by the dominant outgroup could well prove difficult.

Social competition refers to the strategy adopted by certain indi-viduals who wish to reverse the perceived status of ingroup and outgroup on valued dimensions. Direct competition is viewed as taking place when (a) group members identify strongly with their group, and (b) intergroup comparisons are still active (perhaps despite previous attempts at social creativity) or have become so. One set of determinants besides proximity and perceived similarity that Tajfel and Turner (1979) considered crucial in fostering 'in-secure social comparisons' is the awareness of cognitive alternatives to a group's status. This is conceived of in terms of two dimensions:

perceived legitimacy–illegitimacy, and stability–instability. Thus, when subordinate group members come to attribute their inferiority externally to historically oppressive and discriminatory measures of the outgroup – and do *not* now attribute it internally to the ingroup's inadequate own qualities – and see their subordination as illegitimate and potentially changeable or even reversible, between-group comparisons will become more active than quiescent. In Gurin *et al.*'s (1980) terms, the group will now become more politically conscious and collectively mobilized into redressing the power imbalance and their social discontent.

A large number of situational factors may induce an awareness of alternatives, among subordinate group members, to their relative inferiority. Taylor and McKirnan (1984) proposed, in their cyclic theory of intergroup relations, that it is in the interests of the dominant group to allow some subordinate members to pass into the dominant group if they have the necessary qualifications, such as education and speech patterns. The intergroup structure is thereby seen as legitimate but a little unstable. Nevertheless, some sufficiently qualified members of the subordinate group may not be admitted into the dominant group beyond a manageable number of such 'tokens', and assimilated individuals may not be *fully* accepted if their ethnic group membership is visible. It is these individuals, who may then come to see the intergroup situation as *illegitimate*, that may return to their original group to instigate group action. Individuals in these circumstances come to see that their social and economic destinies do not depend on their own personal motives and skills, but rather on the status of the *group* from which they derive; changing the group is then seen as more urgent than individual change.

Examples of linguistic competition abound cross-nationally (for instance, in Spain, France, India, Sri Lanka) where individuals take part in civil disobedience on behalf of their beleaguered languages. Another instance is the Welsh Language Society's fight for the language to be represented in the media and in education. Not only do group members wish to revitalize their traditional languages, but they move to have these recognized in formal public contexts. In this sense, people will wish to accentuate their ingroup language markers and actively diverge away from what they perceive as focally outgroup styles. Testing ethnolinguistic identity propositions, Giles and Johnson (1987) found that Welsh people who valued their cultural identity strongly and who believed the intergroup hierarchy was illegitimately biased against them, claimed that they would use more divergent language strategies in their discussion of such matters with an English person. They would, for example, use more Welsh vocabulary, phrases, and accent than those who identified less with their Welshness and saw prevailing intergroup relations as more legitimate.

Here we have the seeds of potential ethnic conflict since dominant groups are unlikely to ignore actions which not only increase the status of the subordinate group but also, by implication, threaten their own valued distinctiveness. Indeed, it would appear that dominant group members being aware of cognitive alternatives (recognizing, for example, that their superiority is illegitimate and unstable) makes them prime candidates for adopting reciprocal strategies of social creativity and competition in order to restore *their* positive ethnic identity. Interestingly, Brown (1978) suggested an extension to the notion of illegitimacy to include cases where the dominant group saw its superiority – through comparisons with other dominant groups (for example, colonial powers) – as illegitimately small. In such circumstances, we would witness derogatory language, abrasive verbal humour and oppressive language policies – such as, with patriotic rhetoric, elevating the dominant group's language to the only one with official status and currency. In this vein, recent work on the discourse of intergroup relations is showing that the rhetoric of equal opportunities and liberal intergroup stances can often conceal acts of ingroup legitimation and racism (see, for example, van Dijk 1987).

We have seen that the awareness of cognitive alternatives by subordinate group members will determine whether or not they will wish to use ethnic language markers to differentiate themselves from the outgroup. And in the next chapter, more specific elements of this process will be elaborated in propositional terms. To the outside observer, the different self- and group-orientated strategies adopted in a wide range of structurally different ethnic contexts may seem confusing, diffuse and even perhaps irrational. Some members of dominant collectivities who enjoy the privilege of speaking world languages, and not least English, will doubtless scorn the 'deviance' of those who emphasize and fight for what they take to be linguistic 'trivia'. But we hope to have shown already how language and identity impinge on some of the most fundamental human and relational issues. Fishman's (1968: 40–1) observation that 'language becomes not merely the means of communication but a priceless heritage of group culture' is inescapable, and in the next section we see the enormous range of everyday social situations to which this general principle, and its consequences apply.

Intergroup communication 'breakdown'

As we mentioned earlier, there is a growing interdisciplinary literature documenting miscommunication between social (including ethnic) groups (see, for example, Gumperz 1982). In the remainder of this chapter, we shall examine models of intergroup communication 'breakdown', which for us constitutes mutual psycholinguistic distinctiveness, generated through *stereotyping* processes. Similar culturally based analyses have considered communication 'problems' between, for example, able-bodied people and the physically handicapped (Emry and Wiseman 1987), and the sexes (Maltz and Borker 1982). Broadly 'cultural' and other components of miscommunication have recently been identified and interrelated in handbook-length treatment by Coupland, Giles and Wiemann (1991). Key contributing processes are lack of shared sociolinguistic backgrounds and knowledge, different beliefs about talk and silence, cultural values in terms of individualism or collectivism, dimensions of ingroup communicative satisfaction, and rule systems.

In this paradigm, McNabb (1986) established that Eskimo verbal and non-verbal communicative patterns can lead to attributions of inconsistency and unpredictability by non-Eskimos. Eskimo 'taciturn reserve', remaining quietly non-committal while awaiting further information, may be interpreted by non-Eskimos as apathy or animosity. Albert (1986), investigating differences in the importance of 'shame' between Hispanics and Anglo-Americans, required informants to consider various vignettes and attribute causes for behaviour depicted in them. One vignette was: 'Maria didn't speak up in front of her classmates because . . .'. Respondents were asked to choose between the following attributions: because she (a) was ashamed; (b) was shy; (c) was afraid her classmates would make fun of her; and (d) had been taught that girls do not speak in front of a group. Hispanics tended to choose the 'shame' attributions more often than Anglo-Americans did, and as Albert argues (as does Kochman 1986, with respect to black–white differences in verbal insults), this can have important implications in intercultural communication and especially so in educational settings.

Relatedly, Rubin (1986) has shown the likelihood of ambiguities in classroom questioning. Typically, white teachers use quasi-questions which hint at the information required and the white child knows that it is a test of his/her knowledge and understanding. This kind of questioning is quite unfamiliar to black group members for whom a direct request may be needed to elicit information. Rubin describes how ethnic minority children come to be seen as unresponsive and lacking in understanding and, as a result, tend to underachieve. Pedersen (1983: 405) discusses the problems faced by Americans in counselling Chinese students, in that

> even when the words in Chinese and English were the same, the contexts in which the words were interpreted were completely different. Some of the more common counselling words such as concern (e.g., *I am concerned about you*) simply do not exist in Chinese.

Pedersen then provides an insightful analysis of how Chinese pictographs can allow one access into the semantic and cultural differences inherent in Chinese words *vis-à-vis* English. For example, 'good' is represented as the combination of the figures of a woman and children, indicating that familial issues constitute much of what is cared for and good. Cheung and New (1984) give a fascinating historical account of miscommunication apparent when Canadian Protestant missionaries attempted to provide Western medical services to Chinese people in the early part of this century. Based on analyses of correspondence and reports mailed from China to the home church, these authors were able to pinpoint how the Chinese medico-culture and its practices on the one hand, and Western medicine on the other, were mutually misunderstood by both parties, leading to a lack of the communicative empathy necessary for truly effective treatment to be accepted.

In another absorbing study, Cohen (1987) has proposed, on the basis of an analysis of politicians' autobiographical accounts, that the crises (including that of Suez) that arose in American–Egyptian relations in the 1950s are in part attributable to the communicative misunderstandings of diplomats on both sides. Cohen relates these problems to the fact that the United States and Egypt represent respectively 'low-context' and 'high-context' cultures. Essentially, in low-context cultures, meanings are conveyed explicitly in messages with relatively little need for contextual specification; high-context cultures tolerate or require more implicit expression, requiring greater contextual support. Cohen argues that many communicator characteristics will differ radically between the two culture types (including, of course, directness–indirectness and exaggeration–understatement) and it is in these terms that diplomatic statements were open to misinterpretation.

An interesting series of studies by Taylor and Simard (1975) in Canada and the Philippines showed that objective similarities in intercultural communication can still lead to psychological discomfort and misattribution. For instance, they showed that in structured and unstructured tasks, dyadic communication within ethnic groups was just as 'efficient' (along a host of dependent measures) as between ethnic groups. Nevertheless, after the event, subjects reported much less satisfaction and efficiency with inter- than intra-ethnic communication. It is clearly the case that knowledge of communicators' different characteristics, interpersonal accommodation, and contact are not sufficient for promoting intercultural harmony and particularly so when social prejudice abounds.

Models of 'breakdown'

Models of communicative 'non-success' or 'breakdown' have traditionally been interindividual, highly cognitive and/or rule-governed (see, for example, Patterson 1983). The first truly intergroup model that emerged was that of Dubé-Simard (1983), who claimed that intergroup communication breakdown occurs when the three conditions (schematized in Figure 4.5) coexist. While the psychological climate characterized in the model certainly suggests a breeding ground for breakdown, there are several areas where elaborations and extensions can usefully be made.

First, stereotyping processes play a less than central role in this theoretical framework. This is surprising, given the range of belief-based instances of miscommunication we have just considered and the extent to which it is acknowledged that stereotypes mediate language production and reception. Second, the three conditions Dubé-Simard specifies for determining intergroup communication breakdown are, we would suggest, neither necessary nor sufficient. For instance, according to social identity theory, mere categorization of individuals into distinct (even equal-power) groups can be suf-

Figure 4.5   Schematic representation of group processes to be considered in the breakdown of intergroup communication

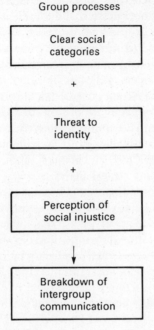

Source: Dubé-Simard (1983: 188)

ficient to cause intergroup discrimination in the search for a positive group identity and self-evaluation. If language is a valued dimension of group identity, then the desire for positive differentiation is likely to show up sociolinguistically, increasing communicative distance and the potential for breakdown to occur. In other words, although the perception of social injustice can historically be an important determinant of the breakdown in relations between many groups, it *need not* be a precondition. The mere existence of two comparative groups is likely to foster ingroup forms (for example, jargon, mutually unintelligible technical terms, abbreviations and so on) as a means of preserving or achieving preferred identities for their members. Also, even when social injustice *is* in question, situational constraints and/or societal or contextual norms of politeness and co-operation (Genesee and Bourhis 1988), might override any identity-prescribed linguistic differentiation or breakdown from occurring.

Third, the notion of 'breakdown' itself is, of course, highly amorphous. The construct is implicitly static, overinclusive, and glosses over a heterogeneous range of objective and subjective ineffectualities of communication. It is for this reason that Coupland, Wiemann and Giles (1991) have proposed a multilayered model of 'miscommunication'. At one extreme, miscommunication may be taken to designate local, routinely effortful characteristics of inter-action, where 'problems' may not be orientated to as such. The intergroup processes we are considering in this chapter occupy the middle levels of Coupland, Wiemann and Giles's model, where beliefs, construals and attributions intervene to influence strategies of talk. At the most global level, 'miscommunication' refers to ingrained sociostructural imbalances and inequalities, often accessible only through critical analysis.

Beyond this, we should also recognize that miscommunication can be experienced unilaterally as well as bilaterally (cf. Baxter 1984). Also, the concept of 'breakdown' risks understating the *process* nature of communication difficulties and dissatisfactions. It may be that work at the interpersonal level on relational dissolution can inform future theory-building at the intergroup level (see below). For present purposes, given that stereotypes may be both antecedents to and consequences of intergroup communication breakdown, we turn to a brief consideration of Hewstone and Giles's (1986) more contextual model, which aims specifically to take into account the content and functions of stereotypes in breakdown processes. While its implied focus is on interethnic communication, we suggest that the model is relevant to most, if not all, intercategory settings.

The stereotype process framework

Hewstone and Giles work with a relatively conservative and inclus-ive definition of 'intergroup communication breakdown', as a feeling of dissatisfaction resulting from the perception, by one or more of the participants in an interaction or a relationship, that its full potential is not being realized, in ways that are attributable to memberships of contrasting social groups. Let us overview the core constructs in the model – schematically presented in Figure 4.6 – and their major relationships with each other.

Context
As in our discussion in Chapter 1, context refers to both macro-

Figure 4.6   A stereotype model of intergroup communication breakdown.
(1 = consequences of the breakdown of intergroup communication.)

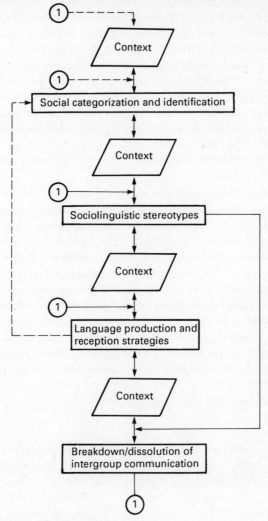

structural and micro-interactional concerns, and to both objective and perceptual dimensions. Aspects of the historical and changing relationships between groups are seen as crucial components here, including their (a) relative efforts at mutual social and linguistic accommodation, and (b) fluctuating sociostructural positions in society, including their perceived group 'vitalities' (see Chapter 5), a notion which subsumes Dubé-Simard's 'perceived social injustice'. More immediate situational features such as the perceived probability of evaluative comparisons being made between ingroup and outgroup communicators are also relevant here. Finally, the perceived dimensions of the situation, and their appropriate norms and goals, will influence language-encoding and decoding processes operative, as the figure suggests.

Social categorization and identification

It is the social meanings of the features mentioned above, together with the perceived characteristics of the participants in the situation (for example, the prototypicality of outgroup speakers, relative numbers of ingroup and outgroup members) that will determine the perceived salience of intercategory memberships, their clarity, and the strength and dimensions of social identification involved. Gudykunst and Ting-Toomey (1990) suggest that strong ingroup identification in an interethnic context would invoke social identity processes, which could be the breeding ground for breakdown. In contrast, possessing a weak ingroup identity would predictably lead to seeing an interethnic encounter in interpersonal terms (Chapter 1) and would reduce intergroup misunderstandings and misattributions.

Sociolinguistic stereotypes

Under conditions where individuals subjectively define the situation as an intergroup one, there is a tendency to depersonalize outgroup speakers, and ingroup speakers are likely to self-stereotype, in a similarly deindividuating manner; social stereotyping thereby assumes considerable cognitive significance. Because of this, less emphasis is given to individual differences in personality and communicative style. At the same time, individuals' degrees of cultural flexibility in terms of their social cognitions and communicative habits are important in determining which dimensions of stereotypes (for example, status or solidarity) are considered relevant. As Figure 4.6 also indicates (and cf. Tajfel 1981), the content of these stereotypes is also *functionally* dependent on what aspects of people's social identities are salient at any one moment. For instance, we could hypothesize that if young people failed at some cognitive task in competition with elderly people, they would invoke stereotyped elderly traits such as 'wise', 'mature' and 'experienced' as a means of repairing their threatened esteem, and more so than in less age-salient, comparative situations.

Language production and reception strategies
Given the lack of (much needed) research into how stereotypes relate in detail to actual intergroup communicative behaviour (see, however, Maas *et al.* 1989), comments here are speculative. Following from Gudykunst and Kim's (1984) development of Lukens's (1979) work on communicative distance, we can suggest the following. When relations between social categories are co-operatively stable and intergroup stereotypes are complementarily positive, we might expect to find a 'distance of sensitivity', with speakers attempting to converge towards each other (as discussed in Chapter 3). But as conflict develops, sociolinguistic stereotypes will increasingly impinge. And here, what Lukens terms communicative distances of 'indifference', 'avoidance', and 'disparagement' would predictably be reflected in denigrating acts of 'underaccommodation', 'over-accommodation', behavioural confirmation and verbal derogation (or ethnophaulisms). We could add that a 'distance of aggression' might also be established, where verbally hostile acts are superseded by physical aggression.

As we argued in Chapter 2, stereotypes exert considerable influence over reception processes, too. Figure 4.6 shows that outgroup stereotypes are likely to be used attributionally and functionally to explain away communicative difficulties, thereby confirming suspicions about outgroup competence and integrity. For instance, some doctors may attribute the difficulty they experience in dealing with working-class and immigrant patients to the patients' incompetence or unco-operativity or some other stereotyped trait, rather than to different dialect or discourse norms, perhaps low proficiency in a second language or stress in an unfamiliar environment. Indeed, when communications difficulties arise between groups, the degree of personal endorsement of social stereotypes (Henwood, pers. comm.), as well as the perceived history of strained relations between the groups, are likely to be related to cognitive biases.

The dichotomized encoder/decoder perspective we are adopting here should not be overemphasized. As speaker-hearers, we reflexively monitor our own utterances, perhaps especially when we are open to criticism as being naive or ethnocentric, even racist, sexist or ageist, and so on. Again, we know that our recall of events is determined at least in part by our expressed descriptions of them to others (Higgins and McCann 1984). In other words, the language patterns of speakers-hearers feed back, as indicated in Figure 4.6, to solidify social stereotypes.

Breakdown/dissolution of intergroup communication

The contextual dimensions we have considered may then translate into 'dissatisfaction', in the terms of our initial definition of 'breakdown'. A *process* perspective on 'dissolution' would be valuable for future research, allowing us to trace multiple trajectories and implications. It is also likely that while many similarities exist between processes of dissolution at the interpersonal (cf. Duck 1984) and intergroup levels, important differences may, none the less, be evident. To consider just a few possibilities, participants anticipating intergroup breakdown may seek the advice and consolation of ingroup members (the 'intragroup' phase). During what we might term the 'encounter phase', attempts at repair might be made or participants might engage in direct confrontation about group alignment. If disengagement results, there may be a 'social' phase when group members generate accounts for the breakdown and creatively attribute its origins to the outgroup. Any subsequent repair and rapprochement similarly has to be socially engineered at the intergroup level.

Finally, as Figure 4.6 indicates, the various phases of breakdown are likely to feed back to other components of the model, including obviously the nature of the context in which it has occurred. Outgroup stereotyping is likely to be reinforced and new stereotypical inferences drawn – for example, perceived outgroup coldness/remoteness on the one hand, or emotion/intrusiveness on the other. Identification is also likely to be strengthened as perceived failures in intergroup encounters tend to strengthen ingroup solidarity and cohesion when individuals are known to have committed themselves to their category memberships.

In these ways, the model recognizes many of the complexities of intergroup communication breakdown with particular reference to the mediating roles of stereotyping processes. Many further processes could elaborate the model, such as the (presumed) debilitating roles of heightened cognitive uncertainty (Gudykunst and Ting-Toomey 1990). Likewise, considerations of arousal and anxiety (as emphasized in Chapter 1). It is more than three decades since Allport (1954) acknowledged the major role played by language in the development and maintenance of ethnic prejudice. Closer attention to the interplay between social identity, stereotypes and intergroup communication and miscommunication (see also Chapter 7) will allow us to document the diversity of 'breakdown', which is no doubt a broader construct than we have suggested here.

Summary

In this chapter, we examined some of the important roles language plays in establishing and challenging an individual's sense of cultural and ethnic identity. We reviewed multidisciplinary work in the area under the headings of sociolinguistic, sociological and communications breakdown approaches. A fourth approach was needed, however, to explore who uses which language forms, when, and particularly *why*. We developed a perspective based on social identity principles to account for ethnolinguistic strategies and change, which allows us to appreciate the heterogeneity of forms of 'ethnic talk'. Key concerns were individual mobility and the attenuation of distinctive group language habits, the creativity of a group in redefining old linguistic evaluations and definitions, the formation of new patterns of language usage, and the psychological climate needed to foster the accentuation of group language patterns under conditions of unrest. This psychological analysis, based as it is on individual cognitions and behaviour, nevertheless alerts us to the possibility that social psychologists, as Tajfel intended, have considerable resources for assisting in explanations of larger-scale social and language movements. We made the important point that language and ethnicity are not conceptually distinct. Again, and in the spirit of previous chapters, we argued that feelings of ethnic belonging are not static variables impinging on interethnic (or intraethnic) encounters but can emerge from and be changed during ongoing discourse. The remainder of the chapter reviewed approaches to 'communication breakdown'. We considered a schematic framework which helps us understand breakdown as a process, and one mediated by social stereotypes and diverse other contextual dimensions – the starting point of this book. In the next chapter, we show that these same processes are relevant to understanding not only who learns another language and to what level of proficiency, but also to the more societally related issue of when languages prosper, survive or die.

Suggestions for further reading

Coupland, N., Giles, H. and Wiemann, J. M. (eds) (1991). 'Miscommunication' and problematic talk. Newbury Park, CA.: Sage. A comprehensive examination of approaches to miscommunication, prefaced by a theoretical integration, across a range of intergroup settings (for example, intercultural, between-gender, intergenerational), modes of communication (for example, telephonic, human–computer, broadcast news, language learning) and in applied contexts (for example, medical, clinical, legal).
Edwards, J. R. (1985). Language, society and identity. Oxford: Blackwell. An important book looking at different disciplinary approaches to language and ethnicity with a critical appraisal of social psychological approaches. An invaluable appendix, listed by country, explores a host of language situations across the world.
Gudykunst, W. B. (ed.) (1986). Intergroup communication. London: Edward Arnold. A diverse collection of essays looking at language and communication from an intergroup perspective. The editor's attempt to integrate different approaches theoretically is especially welcome. ·
Gudykunst, W. B. and Ting-Toomey, S. (1989). Culture and interpersonal communication. Newbury Park, CA: Sage. An award-winning and very readable book exploring how cultural values affects language behaviours and communicative processes.
Gumperz, J. J. (ed.) (1982). Language and social identity. Cambridge: Cambridge University Press. An invaluable collection of essays and data looking at social identity from an interpretive and ethnographic perspective. Its attention to notions of miscommunication throughout is very useful.

5 / BILINGUALISM AND THE SURVIVAL OF LANGUAGES

Bilingualism has already featured in many areas of this book. In the first chapter we discussed bilingual code switching as a clear instance of situationally based repertoire selection. Chapter 3 showed how we form attitudes to speakers who use different languages, and in Chapter 4 we examined how interlocutors accommodate others in bilingual settings. In the last chapter we noted that language can be an important aspect of cultural identity for many ethnic groups in multilingual settings. Like many of the topics we have chosen to focus on, the study of bilingualism is multidisciplinary and vast, and we cannot claim to give an exhaustive coverage here. We intend to focus on sociopsychological concerns, and on two questions in particular: under what conditions a person becomes bilingual, and what climates render a language viable in the long term. In the course of exploring the second of these questions, we shall try to integrate some of the diverse traditions of current intercultural communication research.

The field and its importance

Although sociopsychological examinations of bilingualism have been largely confined to Canada and Scandanavia, the study of bilingualism is important for very many reasons. Most societies in the world are multicultural and most of these are multilingual, and the problem of selecting national official language and/or a mutually accessible language (a lingua franca) is one many governments have to face. For instance, 200 languages are spoken in the Soviet Union,

100 in the Philippines (which is no bigger than the state of Nevada in the USA), and 15 in Romania. Indeed, it is difficult to think of more than a handful of settings, such as Portugal, which are in reality monolingual. So the fact that many middle-class white students in areas of the UK and the USA feel that this topic is peripheral to their concerns is in itself interesting. From a global perspective anyway, the Anglophone experience is hardly representative. Most children are schooled in their second language, usually the language of a dominant colonial group or ethnic elite, and in fact most English speakers have learned that language as their *second* one. Some might suspect that with increasing centralization and modernization, not to mention the spread of economically and politically powerful languages world-wide, bilingualism would be a disappearing condition. But, as we have observed in previous chapters with the resurrection of Hebrew, the renewed growth of Catalan, the Arabicization of North Africa and the role of Tagalog in the Philippines, languages do not necessarily capitulate to their larger brothers. Bilingualism is a perennial state and is likely to become even more important with the dissolving of trade barriers in the European Community, increased economic and cultural exchanges with and within the Eastern bloc, and the explosion of commerce with technologically-advanced societies in East Asia.

Gardner (1979) suggested that second language acquisition had traditionally been thought of as an educational topic and as such the learning of a second or foreign language had been viewed as just another area of the academic curriculum. He opposed such a perspective, arguing that the general school curriculum is embedded within the students' *own* culture. In the acquisition of a second language, on the other hand, 'the student is faced with the task of not simply learning new information (vocabulary, grammar, pronunciation, etc.) ... but rather of acquiring symbolic elements of a different ethnolinguistic community' (1979: 193). The student, Gardner (1979: 193) argued, is not being asked to learn *about* the linguistic elements of the new code; rather, 'he is being asked to acquire them, to make them part of his own language reservoir. This involves imposing elements of another culture into one's own lifespace'. The consequence, Gardner (1979: 193) suggested, is that 'the student's harmony with its own cultural community and his willingness or ability to identify with other cultural communities become important considerations in the process of second language acquisition'. The school context remains a crucial one for matters multilingual, as Edwards (1985, for example) has argued. But more generally, Gardner's last-quoted sentence establishes a rich agenda for social psychological research into language acquisition.

Despite a very long tradition of interest in the cognitive correlates of language learning, it is only over the last couple of decades that data have emerged showing the cognitive benefits (rather than deficits) of bi- and multilingualism, such as increased construct differentiation and earlier cognitive development among children (Hakuta 1986). Indeed, experiments have been ambitious and programmatic in following through, under controlled conditions, children who have been 'immersed' in a second, locally prevalent language (sometimes their own heritage language for ethnic immigrants). Many bilingual immersion programmes, including the first in St Lambert, Montreal (see Lambert and Tucker 1972), have shown widespread cognitive and social advantages for such bilingually educated children (given families' support for the initiative) over matched peers schooled in their mother tongue. Interestingly, young children of around five or six, after a year's immersion in the second tongue, not only speak, read, write and understand the language well but also do at least as well in school subjects in which they had been immersed as 'control' children taught in their first language (Swain, in press).

Of the many absorbing empirical studies of bilingualism we now have, a large number have correlated particular variables such as age, personality and sex with various measures of second language proficiency (see Gardner 1985). But Tucker (pers. comm.) found in Jordan that proficiency in a second language was unrelated to time spent learning it, a finding which many of us would perhaps endorse. Similarly, German research has shown that Spanish and Turkish migrant workers' competence in German is not correlated with duration of residence in the country but with the number of contacts these *Gastarbeiter* have with other Germans. Such findings, of course, indicate social psychological processes at work. But the accumulation of empirical studies has not been matched, until rather recently, by corresponding *theoretical* developments, and it is on these that we shall mainly focus. In the first part of this chapter, we examine three social psychological models of second language acquisition that have emerged. The first is Gardner's (1985) model – a useful place to start given that it brings together under one framework factors which have been deemed as important in second language acquisition for many years. Later in the chapter we consider the sociopsychological climates which enable a language to survive, and which, of course, also predispose it to be relatively widely acquired.

Influential frameworks

Gardner's model

This model arose after Gardner's empirical and theoretical involvement with Lambert in a series of studies looking at the role of motivation, *vis-à-vis* natural language aptitude, in predicting second language outcomes. Gardner and Lambert (1972) found that learners' motivations for learning outweighed their aptitudes on many occasions. Moreover, in these studies, an integrative motive (for example, wishing to know more about the second language community or to be like its speakers) proved to be more important than an instrumental motive (for example, because knowing the language was useful for job promotion) in accounting for second language success.

The model has four phases (see Figure 5.1). The first specifies the broad social context in which both the student and the language-learning programme exist, including the social implications of learning a second language (L2) and developing bilingual skills. The second phase identifies the four individual difference variables Gardner considered most influential in L2 achievement. 'Motivation' here refers to those affective characteristics orientating the student to try to acquire elements of L2, the desire the student has for achieving such a goal, as well as the amount of effort expended in this direction. 'Situational anxiety' refers to the tension experienced in specific learning situations (including, of course, the classroom) where the student may feel embarrassed, unsure and awkward about attempting the L2 publicly. The third phase establishes a distinction between formal and informal acquisition contexts. Classroom instruction or any other teacher–pupil context is 'formal', whereas 'informal' includes situations where language skills may be improved without direct instruction (for example, casual conversations with members of the L2 community, or watching L2 television). The final phase of the model grossly distinguishes 'linguistic' and 'non-linguistic' outcomes. Linguistic outcomes are test indices such as course grades, or scores on vocabulary or general proficiency tests; non-linguistic

Figure 5.1   Schematic representation of the theoretical model

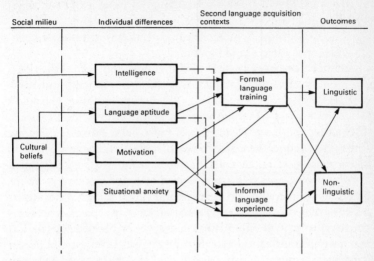

Source: Gardner (1979: 196)

outcomes of L2 acquisition include favourable or other attitudes towards the target cultural community, interest in further language study, general appreciation of other cultures, and so on.

Through this model, Gardner attempts a detailed examination of how these variables can operate together developmentally in the acquisition process. It is claimed that cultural beliefs prevalent within the social milieu (including whether the learning community is monolingual or bilingual) influence the *extent* to which achievement in L2 is mediated by different individual difference variables. For instance, Gardner (1979) found that English Canadian adolescents' achievements in learning French in Anglophone-dominant areas of Canada were correlated more highly with motivation than situational anxiety, whereas the reverse was the case in provinces where biliguality was more normative (so that motivation was already high). The individual difference factors were also argued to impinge on the two acquisition contexts to different extents. As Figure 5.1 suggests, Gardner argues that motivation and situational anxiety are influential in both formal and informal L2 learning contexts, while intelligence and language aptitude have little relevance to informal learning (as indicated by the broken arrows).

Predictably enough, it was proposed that the different acquisition contexts themselves may foster particular outcomes, in the sense that formal ones are likely to generate specifically linguistic achievements, while learning in more informal contexts might rather facilitate attitudinal and cultural outcomes.

A number of other models also highlight the importance of a positively affective motivational component to the acquisition process (see, for example, Schumann 1986). As we saw above, Gardner's model emphasizes a favourable disposition towards the L2 speech community, the integrative motive. He argues, however, that we need to distinguish explicitly between attitudes and motivation. In his empirical research, he finds that while attitudes are highly related to motivations, which in turn were correlated strongly with L2 achievements, there was no direct relationship between the attitudes and achievements themselves. Hence, attitudes were argued to function so as to provide motivational support for achievements. The same level of motivation can then be derived from quite different attitudinal profiles, which have themselves been moulded from distinct cultural beliefs inherent in different social milieux. Moreover, Gardner's perspective assumes an important dynamic element by proposing that these attitudes can also ultimately be bolstered or deflated by learners' successful or unsuccessful L2 outcomes, in an essentially cyclical manner.

Clément's model

Clément (1980) took up the challenge of explaining how aspects of the social milieu influence individuals' linguistic outcomes in the L2 acquisition process. An important dynamic feature of his analysis is that particular individual outcomes can give rise to collective consequences. One important instance is linguistic assimilation to the dominant group, which modifies the structure of the original social milieu and through this the individual mediating processes. In his framework, Clément subsumes Gardner's linguistic and non-linguistic outcomes under the term 'communicative competence' (see Figure 5.2), assuming that the same processes are responsible for the acquisition, maintenance and practice of both.

Although it is not specified in the schematic representation of Clément's model, the concept of ethnolinguistic 'vitality' is recognized theoretically as an important structural feature of the social

Figure 5.2   Schematic representation of individual mediational processes

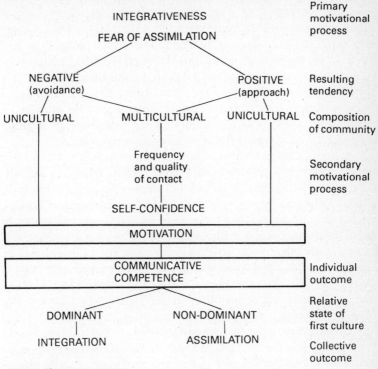

Source: Clément (1980: 150)

milieu. For the moment, we can define 'vitality' as the set of factors (such as status, demography and institutional support) which are to varying degrees in a group's favour; that is, a group can have high, medium or low vitality. In line with our previous discussions in this book, Clément argued that the language of the group with the highest vitality would predominate, and that there is a direct relationship between the ethnolinguistic vitality of a culture and its attractiveness to outgroup members. Again, the individual mediational processes operating between the conditions prevailing in the social milieu (that is, the *relative* ethnolinguistic vitalities of the ethnic ingroups and outgroups) and communicative competence in L2, comprises for some individuals what Clément terms the 'primary motivational process'. Two antagonistic forces are seen as operating here: 'integrativeness' and 'fear of assimilation'. The first of these represents the desire to become an accepted member of the L2 culture and is the positive affective basis of the primary motivational process, while fear of assimilation is the negative affective basis represented in a fear that learning will lead to a loss of first language (L1) and its culture correlates. The resulting motivational impetus released by the primary motivational process is a delicate balance of integrativeness and fear of assimilation. In unicultural settings, it is hypothesized that those for whom fear of assimilation predominates would be less motivated to acquire, and (if they do attempt L2 learning) eventually less communicatively competent, than those who have a relatively high level of integrative motivation.

In multicultural settings, Clément contends that a 'secondary motivational process' is also operative. This is related to the self-confidence (cf. Gardner's 'situational anxiety') experienced by individuals when communicating in the L2. Self-confidence, for Clément, depends on the interactive function of the frequency and quality of contact with L2 group members. So, in multicultural settings, it is hypothesized that individuals' L2 competence will be determined by both the primary and secondary motivational processes operating in sequence, such that competence will be a function of high levels of integrativeness and self-confidence (see Figure 5.2). Clément also suggests that L2 acquisition can result in various social consequences. Two of the more important ones are that individuals may completely lose their L1 and pass into the outgroup (assimilation, as seen in Figure 4.4 of Chapter 4), particularly if they are a subordinate ethnic group; or they may still retain their L1 while participating in both cultural communities (that is, integrate) particularly if they are the dominant group. Finally, it is again suggested that these kinds of social outcome fashion the very nature of the milieu in which L2 learners find themselves, thereby feeding back into the climate in which integrativeness or fear of assimilation will be constructed for or by the individual.

The intergroup model

These models have contributed significantly to our understanding of sociopsychological aspects of L2 acquisition. Gardner's model gives explicit theoretical status to specific individual difference variables and examines these in the light of different acquisition contexts and individual outcomes in a developmental sequence. Clément's approach points to the important functions of collective outcomes in L2 acquisition. Giles and Byrne (1982), in the first version of the intergroup model (IGM), acknowledged these features as well as the centrality of motivation to understanding L2 proficiency. They also agreed that there may be contradictory tendencies within the individual, in the light of instrumental purposes possibly conflicting with the desire to retain an ethnic ingroup language.

The IGM continues to attend to important facets in these previous models (individual differences, acquisition contexts, linguistic outcomes and collective outcomes) and hence owes much to them. But Giles and Byrne depart theoretically from them in recognizing that L2 learning is centrally an *intergroup* process. While both Gardner and Clément acknowledge that L2s are often learning in interethnic contexts, they do not directly address intergroup variables (see Chapter 5) such as ingroup identification, ethnic boundaries and so forth. The IGM also affords significance to factors *impeding* L2 proficiency, with the contention that different processes underlie successful and non-successful outcomes. That is, L2 failure may not be explicable simply as the converse of proficiency, though the literature to date has assumed this; and this in itself could have profound pragmatic implications. The IGM originally narrowed its focus onto minorities' learning of a dominant group language or dialect, but more recently other intergroup and *foreign* language learning possibilities have been accommodated. The IGM has undergone some revisions since 1982 and we trace these historical developments in the following account.

It may help to realize that the IGM is premised on the assumptions of ethnolinguistic identity theory, as discussed in the previous chapter, which itself emerged out of speech accommodation principles (introduced in the chapter prior to that). In its simplest terms, the IGM contends that the sociopsychological conditions stimulating the widening of communicative distance in face-to-face, interethnic encounters (that is, divergences) would resemble those leading to group members setting up barriers to learning a relevant other's L2. Laid out below, propositionally, are the five sociopsychological variables Giles and Byrne saw as *inhibiting* L2 acquisition in *subordinate* groups, where the language of acquisition is that of a possibly threatening majority group. Learning would be inhibited when potential L2 learners:

a   identify strongly with their own ethnic group, and the ingroup language (L1) is considered an important dimension of their cultural identity;

b   construe 'cognitive alternatives' to their intergroup status – for example, feeling that their own relative position was *illegitimately* created historically by outgroup oppression (rather than it being part of the accepted order of nature), and that there is some possibility now of the status hierarchy being changed;

c   perceive their ingroup, and the outgroup, boundaries to be hard and closed;

d   identify with few *other* social categories, each of which provides them with inadequate identities and low intragroup statuses relative to their ethnic identification; and

e   perceive their ingroup's ethnolinguistic vitality to be high and to compare favourably with that of the outgroup.

Let us consider (e) further, since 'vitality' will appear elsewhere in this volume and has evoked some interesting and vigorous debate in the literature (see, for example, Johnson *et al.* 1983) and allows us analytical access to the contextual conditions under which a second language is acquired or not.

Ethnolinguistic vitality

The concept of ethnolinguistic vitality originated as an attempt to incorporate individuals' construals of societal conditions as factors mediating individuals' interethnic attitudes and behaviours. In this way, interethnic dynamics are viewed against the backdrop of their sociostructural contexts (Giles *et al.* 1977). In the sense that 'perceived vitality' is a way of construing the social environment, it might well be profitable to view it as an important element of what Triandis (1972) refers to as 'subjective culture'. Vitality has three major components – status, demography and institutional support – whose sub-constituents are shown in Figure 5.3. Groups that have institutional support for their culture and language, a reasonable social standing in terms of their historical past and economic situation, and a strong demography such as large numbers and an increasing birthrate, may be considered to have 'high vitality'. Hence, subordinate ethnic minorities and many immigrant communities would clearly possess lower vitalities than their dominant counterparts.

Figure 5.3   A taxonomy of the structural variables affecting
ethnolinguistic vitality

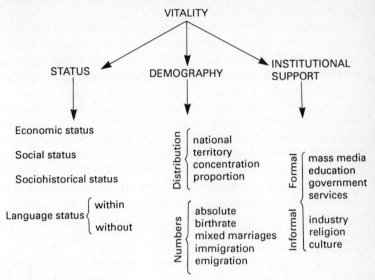

Source: Giles *et al.* (1977: 309)

This objective analysis of ethnic groups in contact has been fruitfully
applied in a number of European interethnic settings (see, for
example, Saint-Blancat 1985).

It has been argued that the more vitality a group *considers itself to
have* the more likely it is that individual members will be disposed
towards investing psychological energy in it, conceptualize relevant
situations in interethnic terms, and therein emphasize their own
ethnolinguistic identity (Giles and Johnson 1981). The current climate of Hong Kong, in the run-up to cession of British sovereignty
and the colony becoming an autonomous region of the People's
Republic of China in 1997, gives us an interesting instance. English-
language newspaper and magazine headlines over the late summer
months of 1988 included: 'Migration fever', 'New figures reveal
brain drain crisis', and 'Record exodus to continue'. The vitality
portrayals embedded in these vivid statements would hardly induce
middle-class Cantonese bilinguals in the colony to invest further in
their Hong Kong social identity (and its related economic destiny),
perhaps even in long-term residency.

Individual *perceptions* of the components of vitality have been measured by the 22-item subjective vitality question (SVQ) devised by Bourhis *et al.* (1981), which has been shown to have a reasonable internal validity (Labrie and Clément 1986), and doubtless has considerable utility in other kinds of intergroup setting (for example, between-gender, intergenerational). A study of Anglo and Greek Australians in Melbourne (Giles *et al.* 1985) showed that the three components of vitality do in some cases have psychological reality; that is, people have corresponding subjective images (or social representations) of how their group stands in relation to relevant others which do correspond with more objective measures. The same Australian study showed that vitality may be affected by intergroup dynamics and loyalties. In Melbourne, although there is a large Greek community, institutional support, status and demography are objectively in favour of Anglo-Australians. The data suggested that while both groups recognize this reality, across some (notably language) scales Anglo-Australians polarized the differences between ingroup and outgroup vitalities in their favour, whereas Greeks significantly *attenuated* such discrepancies.

Similar findings emerged in an Israeli study by Kraemer and Olshtain (1989), where Jewish majority students in a central region of the country accentuated differences in relative vitality between themselves and Arabs, whereas the Arab minority group attenuated these differences. Somewhat different findings emerged in a recent study in the Francophone-dominant canton of Neuchâtel in Switzerland (Young *et al.* 1988). Although Swiss German adolescents conceded, like the Greeks in Melbourne, much more vitality to the Swiss French than to their own group on most items, on some scales they elevated the majority outgroup to a greater extent than even the Swiss French themselves. These investigations show how psychological weightings of vitality can vary considerably.

Vitality-perception studies were also carried out in Hong Kong to tap the sociopsychological climate regarding sovereignty (see above). Pierson *et al.* (1987) found that Western and local Cantonese students differed in their relative vitality perceptions to a far greater degree than in the above-cited studies. Some items revealed strong indications of 'ingroup favouritism', where both Western and Chinese students saw their respective ingroups as having more vitality than the outgroup. However, the opposite profile emerged on other items, showing that each group felt that the other had more power and control. In a further study, it was possible to embrace the effects of sociopolitical change on perceptions of vitality that were collected prior to the Sino-British treaty of 1983 and compared with a matched group some 18 months later. Findings showed that Chinese subjective vitality increased while Western subjective vitality diminished in parallel on some measures, even though there were no real changes in objective indices (Young *et al.* 1986). Interestingly, Yaeger-Dror (1988) has data from an Israeli study showing that increasing accentuation of ethnic speech markers in the recorded Hebrew singing of certain Arab-speaking Jews maps directly the increased ingroup vitality of this group over the same period.

Through the notion of vitality, we see that social structure is best regarded as a variable and multidimensional, sociopsychological construct for the individuals involved in language learning and other language activities (cf. Allard and Landry 1986), operating through their particular social networks (Clément, pers. comm.). Vitality, then, plays a crucial role in our understanding of language in society – and the ways in which it emerges and is negotiated in intra- as well as intergroup discourse are a compelling topic for the future. Which constituents of vitality are contextually important appears to vary, as indicated in a study of the perceived vitalities of three Indian languages in South Africa (Louw *et al.*, in press). Despite the very high objective vitality of English, these authors concluded:

> the subjective vitality of Hindi, a language perceived to have high status and institutional support, seems quite robust. Even outgroup members (and those outgroup members whose home language was English) indicated that they would like to speak Hindi fluently. For Gujarati, a language spoken by an exclusive group with high economic and sociohistorical status, the picture also appears to be quite positive. It could be speculated that the economic power and, paradoxically, the exclusivity of this speech community might provide the necessary maintenance factors for this vernacular. Tamil, on the other hand, might survive because of its strong demographic support.

The intergroup model revisited

What we outlined earlier as the IGM's propositions (c) and (e) are in fact developments of original propositional summaries which referred to *ingroup* boundaries and vitality only. In line with Genesee *et al.* (1983), who pointed to the role of perceived motivational support from the L2 community in facilitating L2 acquisition, the value of acknowledging *outgroup* boundaries also needs to be recognized. As stated above, (c) posits that ingroups and outgroups have their own perceived boundaries, *both* of which will impede or promote movement between groups, as well as opportunities for L2 learning. Similarly, in (e) above, we recognized the importance of *outgroup* vitality. *Relative* vitality in favour of the L1 will predictably reduce the incentive for investing energy in acquiring the L2, and therefore seems a more potent theoretical construct (Clément 1980). These two modest revisions enhanced the 'intergroup' character of the IGM.

Of course, the group perceptions specified as conditions (a)–(e) relate only indirectly to learning propensities and outcomes, and the factors bear influence in somewhat different ways. Not only is acquisition of the dominant outgroup language ideologically dispreferred (condition (a) and especially in combination with (b)), but it is also difficult (in the sense of (c)) and possibly even unnecessary under conditions (d) and (e). Members of a minority group embracing *all* of the perceptions and identifications (a)–(e) have previously been identified as 'Subgroup A' (Giles and Byrne 1982). 'Subgroup B' consisted of those with the converse beliefs, who are more likely to approximate the language patterns and communicative styles of outgroup members. But it is important to recognize that there will be heterogeneity across and even within members of a group along the different dimensions.

Garrett *et al.* (1989) redefined the notion of 'subgroups A and B', and not solely in terms of concrete subcategory memberships; rather, as alternative 'learning orientations'. They argued for the conceptual merit in construing conditions (a)–(e) and their converses as a 'low' or 'high propensity to learn the majority L2', respectively. This conceptual refinement not only acknowledges that quite diverse and complex sociopsychological climates may underlie the *same learning orientation* (whether high or low) but also provides a more robust framework for modifying the IGM further as empirical work develops. It is in any case an empirical issue as to whether the types designated by the abbreviations A and B constitute significant proportions of a minority collectivity and are socially distinguishable and labelled as discernible sub-categories within the ethnic collectivity or by outsiders.

Returning to the IGM's central predictions, those with a *low* propensity to accommodate the majority L2 are predicted to experience a 'fear of assimilation' as a disincentive to learn the majority L2, and will see L2 acquisition, if it occurs, as 'subtractive' to their identity. Their learning orientation towards the L2 and its users will tend to be 'segregative' or even 'disintegrative'. They will steer away from informal acquisition contexts, particularly those involving personal encounters with members of the L2 community. Of course, learning contexts and pedagogic concerns will cut across these predictions (cf. below). But we might more probably expect positive outcomes in narrowly linguistic respects such as course grades and grammatical competence, but less so along the dimensions of communicative competence. Intelligence and aptitude levels will presumably mediate the extent of any of their achievements here (cf. Gardner's model, above). As an additional consideration, conditions (a)–(e) may well be those necessary for fostering a *high* propensity for acquiring the minority language amongst those of the ingroup who cannot speak it. The successful maintenance of minority languages such as Catalan, Welsh, Frisian and so forth may (other macro-contextual forces notwithstanding) in fact be explicable in these terms.

On the other hand, those with a *high* propensity to accommodate the majority L2, will see acquisition as 'additive' to their identities and will have an 'integrative' orientation towards the language and its speakers, seeking out informal learning context and opportunities. Individuals with such a learning orientation will work hard to compensate for, and transcend, the limitations of pedagogic practice by actively involving themselves in the acquisition process (Krashen 1982) and maximizing its potential. They are likely to achieve not only high oral proficiency and communicative competence in the L2 (Rivera 1984), but also additional non-linguistic outcomes, such as an increased knowledge and liking for L2 speakers and their culture. In turn, these gains will lead to greater self-confidence in using the L2 in public and their accomplishments will grow as their situational anxiety decreases. Recently, some empirical data have been provided by Hall and Gudykunst (1986) which show some support for the IGM. Their study, in Arizona, employed a LISREL model-testing procedure and involved over 200 international students from a wide range of cultural and linguistic backgrounds. The IGM was found to provide a good and significant fit to their data for English-language competency (as well as non-linguistic outcomes).

Integral to the IGM, and in line with a social attribution perspective (Hewstone 1989), are the social ramifications of L2 performance *feedback* as discerned by members of the ingroup and outgroup. The lack of proficiency evident in those with a low propensity to accommodate the L2 would be interpreted positively by those similarly inclined as the successful retention of their L1, in the face of threat imposed by the L2 and its culture. Those with a high propensity to accommodate the L2, on the other hand, would define the same group's non-acquisition as 'failure', but might explain it in terms of pedagogical limitations, poor supportive environments and so on. The dominant outgroup, however, who might not even consider the possibility that others have no desire to acquire their language or savour their culture, might well see this failure as confirmation of their preconceived ideas regarding the communicative and cognitive shortcomings of the particular ethnic group.

Those whose high propensity to accommodate the L2 is translated into actual mastery of it would be viewed very positively by others similarly inclined, and this would further strengthen their integrative orientation. Those with a low propensity, however, would regard such 'success' as cultural betrayal, and this could well aggravate their fears of assimilation as well as increase their reluctance to learn the L2. This pattern is in fact consonant with findings in Giles and Johnson (1987) in that a *decrease* in ingroup vitality can stimulate ethnic mobilization. They found that the degree to which Welsh people anticipated diverging from a culturally threatening English person (by use of Welsh words, phrases, and the use of the full language code) was an interactive function of their degrees of cultural identification and perceived ingroup vitality. More specifically, when Welsh people identified very strongly with their group, a low sense of ingroup vitality would be associated with divergent code switching. However, when individuals identified only moderately with their group, it would take them to perceive a high level of ingroup vitality for divergence to be envisaged. In the first case, it is as though decreasing vitality is perceived to be mobilizing to those already committed to the group, and communicative distinctiveness would emerge as a compensating consequence to the threatened identity; but equally those committed but feeling their group has enough 'going for it' are secure enough not to feel the need to dissociate face to face. On the other hand, those not entirely committed to the group (and who in any case have other valued social group memberships on which to call) need to feel that the group has sufficient sociostructural strength for it be worthwhile investing effort, and being seen to do so, and suffering derisory feelings from the diverged recipients.

Lastly, where sufficient numbers of those with a positive learning orientation attempt to 'cross over' and adopt the primary linguistic ethnicity of the (former) L2, this will reduce the distinctiveness of the outgroup, especially if its members value their own distinctive L1 highly. This may precipitate a qualitative shift in the L2, so as to maintain their own advantages (Ullrich 1971), establishing an ever-shifting target to pursue. Individuals whose positive learning orientation has led them to proficiency in the L2 may nevertheless have adopted a speech style which can be stigmatized. They may then find themselves 'between two stools' in terms of the outgroup and those members of their ingroup with a low propensity towards learning the dominant tongue.

Within the framework of the IGM, and specifically with reference to minority-group perceptions, bilingualism is a two-edged sword. It can bring positive cognitive gains and social benefits to those inclined to learn the L2, whereas for those with a low propensity, where *non*-competence is a goal, it may be redefined as cultural suicide. Furthermore, the IGM sees L2s as dynamic, changing entities, evolving in response to the sociohistorical fluctuations of intercultural relations and communication.

The intergroup model revised

Although the brief of the IGM can be usefully extended to encompass a wider variety of language-learning settings than was originally envisaged, data from Lambert *et al.* (1986) suggest that the propositions we have discussed this far are still overgeneralized. These researchers have found some support for a 'multiculturalism hypothesis' which contends that the more secure and positive a minority group feels about its identity, the more tolerant it will be towards the ethnic characteristics and activities of other non-majority groups in the community. By this account, strong ingroup identification and security can sometimes be an important condition for *embracing* the L2 and other (though, we assume, *non-threatening*) group attributes. Interestingly, Bond and King (1985), in relation to Hong Kong, have pointed to the fact that Chinese social identity actually incorporates the value of change, and that 'modernization' does not necessarily equate with 'Westernization'. Thus, the acquisition of English need not be regarded as 'subtractive' to their cultural identity. Indeed, they may feel that, far from L2 learning leading to cultural assimilation, it could be invaluable in maintaining or bolstering their cultural resources in the face of sociotechnological advance. This suggests that L2 learning on occasions can actually be an intergroup strategy aimed at *preserving* ingroup identity, and adds to the observation that group identity can survive the disappearance of the original language.

Relatedly, Edwards (1985) has strongly questioned the fundamental association between language and identity (that we argued for in the previous chapter), at least to the extent of claiming that language loss does not inevitably lead to a lessening of identity. San Antonio (1987), in an ethnographic study of the use of English and associated communicative norms in an American corporation in Japan, shows that acquiring English to improve one's status in the organization does not involve any loss of Japanese identity. Groups with low ethnolinguistic vitality have been shown to adopt particularly *creative* (and *non*-linguistic) strategies for maintaining their group identities. In studying the Valdotans (a French-speaking community in northern Italy), Saint-Blancat (1985: 22) found that they try to achieve socioeconomic parity with the dominant group by speaking Italian (their L2), yet still 'perpetuate traditional values by maintaining family land property and securing its survival by handing on religious beliefs and a sense of work and duty'.

In recognition of the role of *non*-linguistic factors as core values of cultural identity, as acknowledged in the ethnic boundary model (see Figure 4.1 in Chapter 4), and of the claims that L2 gains are not commensurate with identity loss in all cases, propositions (f)–(j) are set out below (after Garrett *et al.* 1989). These are revisions in so far as they modify the earlier reliance on the *converse* of propositions (a)–(e) as orientations conducive to acquisition. Hence, a *high propensity* to accommodate the dominant L2 (or dialect) may also exist when minority group members:

(f) identify weakly with their ethnic group, and their language is not a salient dimension of ethnicity; *or*, if L1 is a salient dimension, it is not perceived to be threatened by L2 acquisition; *or*, if seen as threatened, there are alternative *non*-linguistic salient dimensions deemed satisfactory for preserving ethnic identity;

(g) construe no cognitive alternatives to their subordinate status to the extent that it is attributed as legitimate and there is little likelihood of change; *or*, when aware of alternatives, these are realizable only through L2 acquisition;

(h)   perceive ingroup and outgroup boundaries to be soft and open;
(i)   identify with many other social categories, each of which pro-
      vides adequate group identities and a satisfactory intragroup
      status; and
(j)   perceive ingroup vitality as low and neglected relative to out-
      group vitality; *or*, it is judged that L2 acquisition will maintain or
      promote satisfying non-linguistic aspects of ingroup vitality.

In circumstances where (f)–(j) pertain, what kinds of *sociolin-guistic* climate will promote L2 acquisition? Beebe and Giles (1984) explored this issue and, along with several other conditions, sug-gested that learners might need, first, to promote the use of simplified L2 inputs from native speakers and others, and second, to attempt communicative strategies to compensate for their limited proficien-cy. As regards the former, included under the heading 'simplified codes' were 'foreigner talk', 'teacher talk' and 'interlanguage talk'. Some modification is required to this proposal, however, in the light of claims that such inputs may at times serve to *hinder* L2 acquisition (see, for example, Krashen 1985). Valdman (1981: 42) also suggests that foreigner talk 'is sometimes used to prevent foreign speakers acquiring the language', and this would actually be in accord with intergroup theory, and in line with Woolard's (1989) findings in Catalonia (see Chapter 3). Simplified talk from native speakers who experience a threat to their group distinctiveness can thus reduce or deny access to the target language for learners and thereby restrict them to simple codes, and these have traditionally been awarded low social prestige.

Some caution is also required with attempting communicative strategies to compensate for limited proficiency since it could be argued, after all, that the more effectively learners are able to compensate through L2 communicative strategies for the gap be-tween their communicative needs and their L2 linguistic competence, the less need they have for acquiring more of the L2. In turn, this could precipitate fossilization. To some extent, these complexities stem from a static/dynamic ambiguity in the term 'acquisition'. We may attempt to identify factors reflecting a particular stage in the process of acquisition, and therefore the quality of performance and capacity for accommodation at a given time. These, however, do not necessarily contribute to predicting *whether* acquisition to a level approaching native-like proficiency is more or less likely to occur over a given time period, and this was the question the IGM

Figure 5.4 The (revised) intergroup model of second language learning.

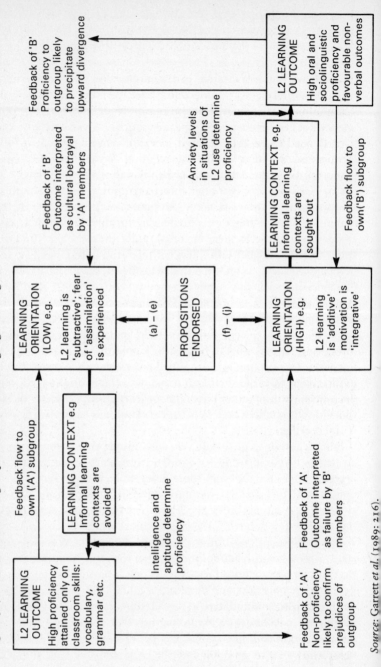

Source: Garrett *et al.* (1989: 216).

originally addressed. Apart from this, the very assumption that learners are capable of achieving 'native-like' proficiency is questionable; and precious few ever reach this level. More importantly, the concept of native-like proficiency begs at least three further questions. First, is the learner in fact aiming at any identifiable native variety, and if so, which? Second, what is meant by 'proficiency', 'communicative competence' and so on? Third, what level of proficiency does our model native speaker actually have? Such questions clearly need to be kept in mind as sociopsychological ideas on L2 acquisition are developed, even if it is beyond our immediate concerns to examine them in depth in this context.

The *learning contexts* characterized in our three sociolinguistic propositions, whether structurally constrained or open to creative construction, are therefore a further important component that the IGM needs to specify. Garrett *et al.* (1989) acknowledged them as such and gave them formal status in the revised model (Figure 5.4), which can function as a summary of the foregoing discussion.

Overall, we want to suggest that the IGM is a robust framework for considering the contexts of language learning, particularly now that it allows for greater variation in the possible relationships between language and cultural identity. The exploration of learner processes, cognitive mechanisms, pedagogical structures and their interaction with intergroup processes, including dimensions of political consciousness, still has far to go. Moreover, the IGM is still insufficiently clear about the interrelationships between its propositions, and about factors mediating group orientations and individual predispositions. While the essence of modelling is to discover *common* sociopsychological processes underlying different L2 acquisition contexts, each has its own particularities – a perspective apparent to us from Billig's (1987) recent work on prejudice among different social categories. So the IGM offers no more than a general template which must be filled out with the detail of historical, ideological and political forces particular to particular settings. Not only do different ethnic groups attach varying social meanings to their ingroup cultural identities, but they also attach different values to them in terms of importance, emotion and stability (Garza and Herringer 1987). That is, the multidimensional meanings associated with acquiring a second language will be highly variable. We are just beginning to isolate the complex factors which promote and impede L2 acquisition among minority groups. The evolving IGM model at least allows us to pinpoint how L2 acquisition is just as much a sociopsychological process as it is a linguistic or an educational one (see the quotation from Gardner at the outset of this chapter). The successes and failures of bilingual educational. programme, where they exist, cannot always be attributed to pedagogy alone.

The very survival of languages

The study of the conditions under which a language survives or erodes has been conducted in the main by sociologists of language (see Fishman 1989). Indeed, it was an analysis of the multiple social forces involved that led to the formulation of the objective vitality schema appearing in Figure 5.3. Following Bourhis (1984b), who led the first sociopsychological foray in this area, we now review the contribution social psychologists can make to understanding the maintenance of a language as a regular vehicle of communication. Let us first give a sense of the 'sociological' approach to language and ethnicity. In considering the influence of language contact on the erosion of a language, Lewis (1979) suggested there are primary (for instance, economic, demographic) and secondary (ideological, educational, and religious) factors operating. The former are the conditions which go towards producing language contact, while the latter factors do not do this but influence specific outcomes in different cases.

An important primary factor is industrialization. The rapid development of large-scale and labour-intensive industry is likely to lead to a saturation of the local area by immigrants as a supplement to the indigenous labour force. In Ireland, industrialization had little influence linguistically on the Irish-speaking areas since its industry was capital- rather than labour-intensive, and its development was phased to take account of the available local labour. In contrast, industrialization in Wales required large numbers of unskilled workers and produced a rapid influx of large numbers of English speakers. This led to increased contact with English and also meant that English became associated with economic advancement to a great extent. It seems, then, that one of the most decisive factors in language erosion is a revolutionary change in economic conditions, leading to a greater interaction between different language groups and to changes in the relative economic influence of one group over another. However, other primary factors have been considered crucial, particularly demographic ones such as fertility rates and intermarriage (Anderson 1979).

Following Giles, Leets and Coupland (1990), we shall shortly consider various limitations, as they appear from a social psychological perspective, within an influential sociological model, and suggest that recognizing cognitive and interactional processes extends that model's potential to explain minority-language survival or non-survival. In addition, we make reference to a diverse set of research efforts and theories in, on the one hand, the social psychology of language and intergroup behaviour and, on the other, intercultural communication. These literatures tackle a plethora of different issues and constitute, for the most part, independent areas of enquiry. We shall try to organize these areas into an integrative statement which has some predictive value.

Many research efforts are geared to the description – often historically and dynamically – of individual minority-language situations. We now need a consensually agreed set of principles that will permit us to address local concerns within the context of the larger-scale enterprise. It seems that scholars orientate to at least two clusters of issues. The first of these is the explanatory paradigm: what conditions give rise to language maintenance, survival, preservation, revival and death, when and why? The second is the interventionist paradigm: given emotional identification and often pragmatic involvement with minority-language survival in the context of widespread linguicism, what are the most appropriate means (educational, conflictual, or in terms of institutional support) of protecting which minority-language rights, and how? As Fishman (1982: 5) has noted, these two paradigms are often intertwined, the second predisposing many of us to work in the field and, defensibly, conditioning our moral positions on 'little peoples' and (hence) 'little languages'. What theory is available to model these integrating themes?

A fairly typical and relatively inclusive sociological model, proposed by de Vries (1984) (see Figure 5.5), neatly illustrates the direct and indirect influences demographic factors can have on language survival. As languages become dominant and spread, often because they give access to technology and modernity, they are often simultaneously contributing to the demise of minority or non-dominant languages. Fishman (1972) argues that language policy should ideally protect endangered languages; language planners would then be drawn towards particular kinds of sociostructural and political-legal enabling forces as a means of facilitating language maintenance.

Figure 5.5   De Vries's (1984) model

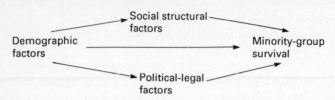

From a *sociopsychological* perspective, we should note a few caveats to de Vries's model. First, it beams into 'collective survival' as the ultimate dependent variable. It seems – and in fact this is acknowledged in other aspects of de Vries's (1987) conceptual work – that we also need to focus explicitly upon related outcome phenomena, including 'revitalization', 'reintroduction', 'conservation', 'maintenance', 'revival', 'expansion' and 'preservation'. These are *different* constructs to the extent that they presuppose different survival baselines. Contrary to general use, we need to operationalize terms in this area which prove to have contrastive value. The processes underlying them are likely to be qualitatively different, as will efforts at intervention and policy-making. Moreover, the focus on 'survival' needs to be balanced with systematic attention to 'non-survival' processes such as 'assimilation', 'atrophy', 'deterioration', 'decline', 'loss', 'contraction', 'death' and 'language suicide'. Again, it is likely that processes enabling non-survival are not simply the converse of those facilitating survival.

Second, minority-group survival is again being conceived of here in an intergroup vacuum. Fishman (1989) recognizes the importance of an intergroup perspective and has argued, for example, that ethnolinguistic diversity *per se* does not cause conflict. Rather, it may be the interaction of the various social identities of the groups involved, minority as well as majority groups. Thus, the *dominant* group's ideologies, strategies, and language status are an important and dynamic set of contributing forces. If language is an important aspect of dominant group identity, changes in the status of a minority language (through growth or decline) are likely to have direct implications for dominant language identity in ways that social identity theory and ethnolinguistic identity theory can articulate.

Third, the focus here is on group products and sociological antecedents. Those concerned with the development of the notion of 'vitality', discussed earlier, would argue that the potency of sociostructural and political-legal factors are necessarily mediated by individuals' subjective evaluations of languages and statuses in an *intergroup* context. In other words, the *cognitive representation* of these sociological forces is open to various interpretations at different historical times and, with regard to different ideologies, even among members of the same group. There are cognitive processes at work mediating group-level pressures towards maintenance and death (Giles and Johnson 1987) – what we shall shortly refer to as *intergroup cognitions*.

Fourth, the processes of influence as specified are abstracted from contexts of interaction. Yet the fates of languages, more obviously and directly then most social 'realities', can in crucial respects be worked out, defined and redefined in everyday discourse among members of the minority or majority language communities as well as in intergroup encounters (see also Collier and Thomas 1988). An insufficient number of studies have been conducted (see, however, Gorter 1987) into how the minority language is introduced as topic and talked about in context, managed and reacted to by ingroup and outgroup collectives. Such interactional experiences may well be compelling day-to-day fodder for sustaining or inhibiting language use at the group level over the longer term, and could usefully be set alongside sociolinguistic paradigms which investigate code switching and interlingual processes.

Integrating models of language survival

In the light of our commentary, a revised version of de Vries's model will appear later (in Figure 5.6) which calls attention to the intergroup fact that minority-language outcomes impinge upon, and in many ways are controlled by, *majority*-group interests; recognizes outcomes and processes apart from just survival; attends to 'cognitive climates' as a mediator of minority-language status; and emphasizes the interactional grounding of the entire process. Thus outcomes and climates are not 'frozen' states but reflexive, dynamic and transactive processes.

Far more energy so far has been devoted to defining the sociological climates of language maintenance and shift than to exploring any of their sociopsychological or interactional counterparts. Our goal here is merely to draw on some important – and for the most part surprisingly unrelated – areas of research which may well access cumulatively the kinds of sociopsychological climate implicated in minority-language survival and non-survival. For us, the separate research traditions of situational perceptions (Chapter 1), language attitudes (Chapter 2), accommodative strategies (Chapter 3), communication breakdown and language and ethnicity (Chapter 4), second language learning and vitality perceptions (this chapter) are intimately intertwined. In line with previous theorizing in this volume, we take intergroup cognitions to be a crucial force blending these – and many other – areas together. More particularly (and after Gallois *et al.* 1988), we consider dependence and solidarity as key integrating constructs here. Dependency relates to the extent to which one is dependent on one's ethnic group for identity definitions and so refers to the number of social group options available to one. Solidarity relates to the degree of identification and affect subjectively associated with membership of one's ingroup. Minority-group members are often heterogeneous in their construals of their social identity and here we identify two polar opposites: high dependency and solidarity, contrasted with low dependency and solidarity. We contend that the interactional or sociopsychological climates attending the former individuals are among those enabling the survival of an ingroup language while those attending the latter individuals can be instrumental in its demise.

What, then, is the flavour of these climates (see Giles, Leets and Coupland 1990, for further details)? We argue that those minority-group members who have *low* dependency and *low* solidarity are likely to see interactions with a (majority) outgroup member as low in intergroup but high in interpersonal terms, and will be less likely to see themselves as prototypical ingroup members, and this especially so for individuals with idiocentric orientations (that is, those who stress duty and obligations to their ingroups – see Triandis *et al.* 1988). They will be highly motivated to acquire the majority-group language but far less motivated to acquire or use extensively their own minority-group language. This will be particularly the case if they perceive relative vitality in favour of the majority-language speakers. In addition, they will be more likely to see their ingroup networks as relatively weak and loose (Yum 1988b). When evaluating minority speakers of a majority language (as overviewed in Chapter 2), then, the evaluative salience of non-ethnic cues (such as gender, age and context) will be quite high (see Gallois *et al.* 1984). The attitude profile emerging would be very favourably inclined towards majority outgroup speakers and especially on status traits where the context does not relate to minority-identity concerns, and when the outgroup culture and its institutions are valued highly (cf. Berry *et al.* 1987). In interethnic interactions, these speakers would be disposed towards attuning their language, discourse and non-verbal styles towards majority-group speakers (see Chapter 3) and in the event of interpersonal conflict would adopt more indirect and collaborative styles of engagement (Ting-Toomey 1988); the particular communicative competencies of the minority-group speaker (Hammer 1989) would be particularly important in accessing effective attuning and conflict strategies. Finally, and in such inter-group situations, these folk are likely to accommodate to the values of the majority community (see, for example, Bond 1983), and experience little anxiety (see Gudykunst 1988), high satisfaction (see Hecht, Ribeau and Alberts 1989) and communicational efficiency (Taylor and Simard 1975) when talking with members of the latter, thereby creating low potential for communication breakdown.

In contrast, those individuals who have high dependency and high solidarity are likely to see interactions with a (majority) outgroup member as high in intergroup but low in interpersonal terms, and to see themselves as prototypical ingroup members, and this especially so for individuals with allocentric orientations (that is, those who stress individual autonomy and personal goals). They will not be highly motivated to acquire the majority-group language but far more motivated to acquire or use extensively their own minority-group language. This will be particularly the case if they perceived relative vitality in favour of their own language community. In addition, they are more likely to see their ingroup networks as relatively strong and closely-knit. When evaluating minority speakers of a majority language, then, the evaluative salience of non-ethnic cues will be very low. The attitude profile emerging would be very favourably inclined towards minority-ingroup speakers, especially on solidarity traits where the context relates to their core identity concerns, and when the outgroup culture and its institutions are not valued highly. In interethnic interactions, these speakers would be disposed towards contra-attuning their language, discourse and non-verbal styles away from majority-group speakers and in the event of interpersonal conflict would adopt more direct and confrontational styles of engagement; the particular communicative competencies of the minority-group speaker are likely to be completely unimportant in their choice of language strategies. Finally, and in such intergroup situations, these folk are likely to

Figure 5.6   An interdisciplinary predictive model of minority-language survival

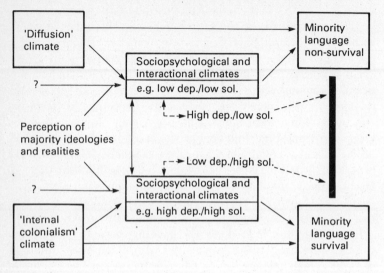

Source: Giles, Leets and Coupland (1990: 14)

affirm the values of their own culture, and to experience considerable anxiety, low satisfaction and communicational inefficiency when talking with members of the latter, thereby creating a high potential for communication breakdown.

Let us now unpack the implications of the above for a more comprehensive model of minority-language dynamics as in Figure 5.6. After de Vries (1984), we label the sociological climates promoting language survival (for example, large group numbers, politico-legal support) and non-survival as the 'internal colonial' and 'diffusion' climates, respectively. Although these climates may often operate in the ways mentioned, we would argue that they have the effects they do because of the manner in which they mould the sociopsychological, and within them interactional, climates. Group-level survival or non-survival is, therefore, effected through the minds and acts of individuals. We contend, then, that the kinds of intergroup cognition introduced above are potent subjective states, in that diffusion forces are likely to be associated with low dependency/low solidarity, and internal colonialism forces associated with high dependency/high solidarity. Sociopsychological climates should, therefore, be more precise predictors of survival or non-survival than the larger-scale sociological climates which, at least arguably, gave rise to them. It is also possible that (as the question-marks in Figure 5.6 are meant to indicate) particular sociopsychological or interactional climates – low dependency and solidarity in the case of non-survival, and high dependency and solidarity in the case of survival – may, at least in some contexts, be determined by *other* sociological forces thus far unspecified (such as enforced migration). Perceptions of the *dominant* group's states, beliefs and behaviours, also what other individuals within one's own minority-ingroup appear to have adopted as sociolinguistic norms and strategies (again, see Figure 5.6) are recognized herein as important influences. We are wary of dichotomizing survival from non-survival and it is inevitable that more sophisticated, and perhaps contexually sensitive, sociopsychological climates will be articulated than our two polar ones above; candidates would obviously include low dependency/high solidarity and high dependency/low solidarity. Indeed, we might speculate, as in the schematic model, that they would be differentially inclined towards points along the survival–non-survival continuum in its simplistic form as represented in Figure 5.6.

There are limitations inherent in the frameworks introduced here, though we think they do offer a basis for exchanging ideas across the disciplines, about applications as well as theory. While the kind of analysis we have suggested has seemingly more direct relevance to what we called the explanatory paradigm above – the who, when and why of 'survival' in its different forms – it also has significance for the interventionist effort – how we intervene effectively in the promotion of minority-language causes. For the first time in the language-planning literature, Bourhis (1984b) and colleagues tackle the sociopsychological climates in which language-planning efforts have emerged in Quebec at the governmental and community levels. In fact, the sociopsychological and interactional environments in which *planners themselves* operate need to find their way into our analyses of minority-language maintenance.

The world climate at the time of writing appears to be more amenable to minority-language survival than perhaps ever before. There are those who disagree; for instance, Edwards (1985) sees language shift and decline as a natural process, and languages to be valued only as long as the economic and social circumstances are conducive to it. Therefore, Edwards (1985: 117) finds pluralistic integration a much more 'reasonable' policy over the 'more militant forms of cultural pluralism'. Understandably, we recognize social change itself is inevitable and there are some repeated patterns of change recorded historically, but to see no alternative course of development besides an ineluctable and unopposed drift of minority-languages towards assimilation in all social contexts is unjustifiably pessimistic. More and more we are detecting the hint of a new spirit of worldliness evolving that is cutting across narrow, parochial boundaries. It may well that we need to harness such feelings if many of our linguistic minorities are to survive in what many now refer to as the 'global village'. As Cronen *et al.* (1988: 78) elegantly put it, 'probably the most important contribution that intercultural study can make is not reassurance of some underlying unity, but an idea of the range of possibilities for being human in different but productive ways'. People are likely to be more susceptible now to the message of the ecological human value of maintaining valued cultural institutions and recycling languages, along the same lines as they would condone preserving endangered species, raw and precious materials and localities, for the common global good. That said, it is critical to work for minority-language survival being endorsed more generally as an appropriate local facet of internationalism, and thereby counteracting any fallacy that internationalism requires international languages *and no others*.

Summary

In this chapter, the case was made that bilingualism is endemic to modern society in ways with which few non-Canadian social psychologists have come to terms. Two models of the social psychological climate conducive to proficient acquisition of a second language were reviewed and examined in the light of the thrust of the previous chapter. Despite the many obvious merits of these models, a more intergroup approach was advocated and articulated which attended to both outcomes of second language acquisition, in terms of competence and non-competence, and accorded language its proper role as an evolving system susceptible to changing sociopolitical and historical conditions. Moreover, this approach recognized the fact that language is not a core value of all ethnic groups and/or their numbers, and revisions to the model were thereby suggested. Some of the interactional factors facilitating those who had a positive motivational orientation to a second language were discussed. Having located potent social psychological forces propelling certain individuals towards learning another language, we then tried to integrate them with other processes, discussed in the study of intercultural communication, to provide a sociopsychological input to complement the sociological parameters of language survival and erosion. Such an approach not only extends the brief of social psychologists in societal issues involving the well-being of languages but also underscores the important point that languages share our mortality.

From linguistic survival in ethnic groups we now move to consider issues of *human* health and the roles played by language in relation to it across the lifespan. We take the position that the elderly, too, are a cultural group, and that the very same issues of context, accommodation, identity, stereotypes and breakdown, and even being 'intergenerationally bilingual', are no less integral to the process of ageing. That is, we shall be focusing on a subordinate group (in the West currently, anyway, despite changing conditions) in which most of us either now have or will have membership, accompanied by telling language experiences.

Suggestions for further reading

Asante, M. K. and Gudykunst, W. B. (eds) (1989). *Handbook of international and intercultural communication*. Newbury Park, CA: Sage. A wide-ranging volume authored in the main by communication scholars overviewing areas of significance for students of SPL in the intercultural domain.

Gass, S., Madden, C., Preston, D. and Selinker, L. (eds) (1989). *Variations in second language acquisition*, 2 volumes. Clevedon: Multilingual Matters. An extensive collection of largely data-based studies, on discourse/ pragmatic and psycholinguistic issues. An excellent entrée into the diversity of recent research in this area.

Gardner, R. C. (1985). *Social psychology and second language learning*. London: Edward Arnold. A comprehensive overview of social psychologically orientated research and theory in this area.

Fishman, J. A. (1989). *Language and ethnicity in minority sociolinguistic perspective*. Clevedon: Multilingual Matters. A selective but very large collection of the author's prolific and highly influential writing on the relationships between language and ethnicity, the revival of ethnicity, and sociological accounts of minority-language survival and death. A must for those concerned with these topics.

6 / LANGUAGE, AGEING AND HEALTH

It can be argued that much of the social psychology of language and sociolinguistics is ageist in its dominant emphases. Instances would include the tradition of using the voices of young adults as stimulus materials in matched-guise experiments, and certainly young listeners. Exceptions do, of course, occur and it may well be true that the middle-aged are studied to an even lesser extent. When older subjects do appear in our studies, they do so in relation to (undeniably important) health-related issues, such as coronary heart disease in men and role-loss problems in women. The young bias is also apparent in the media (Gerbner *et al.* 1980) where later life is all but invisible. It is as if the study of ageing has to be hived off as a speciality topic removed from mainstream social psychology. Specific issues relating to elderly communication are quite well documented (see, for example, Bayles and Kaszniak 1987). But, as Coupland and Coupland (1990) point out in their overview of this multidisciplinary area, the gerontological paradigm, in so far as it touches on non-disordered communication issues, is concerned with essentially cognitive psychological differences in skilled performance and decoding between young and old. And these differences are most often interpreted acontextually in terms of linguistic and communicative deficits, despite the fact that the majority of studies are conducted under constrained, task-related conditions. But our intention here is not to score ready-made gerontological points, but rather to suggest that ageing across the lifespan is a continuous *interculturing process*, with language playing some crucial sociopsychological roles as we adjust to the sociophysical consequences of ageing and a finite lifespan.

In the first part of this chapter, we shall suggest that intergenerational communication involves different (internally differentiated) cultural groups, who possess different values and beliefs about talk, different social and existential agendas and different language codes. Yet, few attempts at (as it were) 'bilingualism' between adult age groups are apparent. The discussion here will centre around studies which fall into what Coupland and Coupland (1990) term the 'anti-ageist paradigm' and little space will be accorded those which adhere to a decremental model. When young people do take the initiative and interact with the elderly, we shall see that it can often be misguided and have disturbing consequences, at both individual and collective levels. From this overview, we shall also see that much elderly talk centres around *health* issues. Currently, the role of social support as a means of bolstering psychological well-being and physical health, though not uncontroversially (see, for example, Ganster and Victor 1988) is a *Zeitgeist* in social psychology. Blazer (1982), for instance, has shown that there is a correlation between longevity and the receiving of social support. In the latter part of the chapter, we shall argue that *language* strategies such as accommodation are intricately involved in the process of providing and receiving social support, and hence in prolonging the quantity and quality of life, a perspective that is lamentably absent in current social psychological research and theory.

Intergenerational differences

Beliefs about talk

Before discussing actual communication differences between the generations, let us see whether they can be shown to have different beliefs about the functions and values of talk. In a British study reported in Giles, Coupland and Wiemann (in press), not only 'young' and 'elderly' people's beliefs about their own talk were studied but also both groups' stereotyped views first of their age-peers' talk and second of the other age-group's talk. In other words, the contention was that people have construals about how their belief profile relates to culturally similar and dissimilar others. Other data from group discussions with young and elderly participants suggested that each have quite distinct views of the sociolinguistic habits of the other.

Participants in this study were 75 members of a 'keep fit in retirement' club – the 'elderly' sample, averaging 70 years of age – and 75 higher education students, the 'young' sample, averaging 19 years of age. They were asked to respond based on how they felt (or how they thought members of the target groups felt) when conversing in general social situations. The 'beliefs about talk' instrument comprised 25 items. Two further versions of the instrument were produced to assess attributions about one's age-peer group's beliefs and those of the other group (for example, 'elderly people can talk for hours on end'). Each respondent was given a packet containing all three versions, with the self-report first, and one of the other two next, with their order of presentation counterbalanced. No one expressed difficulty with the task.

Up to now, responses to each of the three questionnaires by the two groups have been submitted to a principal components analysis with varimax rotation. Four factor solutions emerged in each case and *initial* interpretations of them are displayed in Table 6.1. Obviously, more stringent factor-analytical procedures are still necessary, and later statistical comparisons between the groups may require some interpretive modifications. While there is strong statistical evidence of significant communality in belief *dimensions* across experimental conditions in this study, some interesting differences between the groups seem apparent at this stage in the ways these belief dimensions are structured. We draw attention here to a few of these.

From the top band of Table 6.1, elderly informants appear to construe talk in more positive terms than young, although no less strategically. It is interesting to note also that 'silence' as a factor appears only in the self-ratings. Second, comparing the first and second bands, there are distinct qualitative differences in the way both groups report their own beliefs about talk in relation to their age-group peers. Young informants contended that *other* young people subscribe more to the social values of talk, though showing less initiative. The elderly, on the other hand, considered their peers to have more communication problems than they themselves. It is interesting to note the 'recreational' element common to both self- and peer-ratings of the elderly, a facet not appearing in the young's beliefs. Also, both young and elderly individuals downgrade their own age-peers' beliefs about talk relative to their own individual profiles. Third, moving down the table, young people appear to have negative stereotypical conceptions of the elderly's beliefs about talk.

Table 6.1 Factor structures of intergenerational beliefs about talk*

Young's self-ratings	Elderly's self-ratings
I: Negative evaluation (23%)	I: Recreation/assertive (15.8%)
II: (Enjoyable) Control (12%)	II: Silence avoidance/strategic (11.7%)
III: Assertive (7.3%)	III: Control (8%)
IV: Silence avoidance (6.6%)	IV: Values communication/cautious (7.9%)
Young's peer ratings	Elderly's peer ratings
I: Affiliative (18.1%)	I: Reticence (17.3%)
II: Non-assertive/strategic (10.7%)	II: Recreational (14.9%)
III: Control (8.3%)	III: Strategic (9.3%)
IV: Passive conversationalist (7.4%)	IV: Assertive/affiliative (7.8%)
Young's ratings of elderly	Elderly's ratings of young
I: Assertive/affiliative (19%)	I: Assertive (17.1%)
II: Strategic (11.5%)	II: Small talk valued (8.7%)
III: Small talk valued (8.3%)	III: Talk overrated (8.2%)
IV: Opinionated (6.7%)	IV: Dislike verbosity (7.5%)

Source: Giles, Coupland and Wiemann (in press)

* Factors listed had eigenvalues greater than 1.5 with figures in parentheses representing percentages of variance accounted.

They see the elderly placing great value on small-talk, with a strong tinge of egocentricism, and with an assertiveness not represented in the young's views of their own age-peers. This accords quite well with *interactive* data to be discussed shortly. The elderly's construals of young people's beliefs about talk suggest that they consider the young to be sceptical about the value of talk, yet believe they do see some strategic value in 'chit-chat'. Although a complex picture emerges here, it is possible that these beliefs about talk constitute important elements in age-groups' views of what is rule-governed and satisfying communication, intra- as well as intergenerationally.

Over- and underaccommodation

Accommodating to elderly beliefs about talk, their communicative needs and competences seems a laudable sentiment in many respects and there is some evidence of this in everyday settings. Caporael *et al.* (1983) have shown that some American nurses use a form of baby talk to institutionalized elderly people, irrespective of their functional autonomy. In other words, these nurses use a blanket speech register which linguistically depersonalizes those in their care; some institutionalized people, not surprisingly, find this distasteful, though others frame it more positively – as a nurturant. Other data suggest that the elderly in general – and those (the majority) outside of institutional and caring settings – are also the targets of what in Chapter 3 we called 'overaccommodation'. In some manifestations, this would appear as grammatical and ideational simplification, overly polite forms of language, and a slowed speech rate. Ryan *et al.* (1986) have noted that this might be mediated either by stereotypes of elderly's incompetence or sensory decrements and could also be encoded as a means of establishing social control.

Recent data to be reported by Ryan, Bourhis and Knops (pers. comm.) demonstrate that a cross-section of males visiting a Science Fair found such overaccommodative strategies disrespectful. Needless to say, it is not the sole prerogative of the elderly to be recipients of overaccommodation. Data show that the visually impaired (Klemz 1977) and the handicapped are spoken to in similar registers (Markova 1990), and undoubtedly the hospitalized young, too, in some settings. In any case, overaccommodation to elderly people can occur even when *avoidance* of such tactics has been vigorously and normatively prescribed – for example, in the training regimens of home-care assistants (Atkinson and Coupland 1988).

Coupland, Coupland, Giles, Henwood and Wiemann (1988) reported conversational data involving an upper-working-class sample of British women, aged 70–87 years, which showed that they spent, on average, one-sixth of their time in initial intergenerational encounters (with women in their thirties) disclosing personally painful information. In several cases, these accounts were given 'out of the blue', and more than half of all these 'painful self-disclosures' (PSDs) arose without having been directly or indirectly elicited. While these authors, in contrast to previous work, were keen to stress the interactional *process* of self-disclosure, the content of PSDs revolved largely around health issues, such as surgery undertaken, sensory impairments, immobility and so forth. Although elderly PSD is managed quite well by young interlocutors, at least in procedural terms, it is open to being evaluated by young people as 'underaccommodative', and attributed negatively as elderly egocentrism or social insensitivity. At the same time, and complementing the will to tell that is evident in many elderly PSDs, the younger interactants do a good deal of conversational work to elicit and sustain elderly PSD. As Coupland, Coupland, Giles and Henwood (in press (a)) comment:

> Goal consonance apparent in patterns of elderly self-disclosure and young elicitation, mutual tolerance of counter-normative and face-threatening intimacy, and the young's repertoire of sustaining and supporting moves may be possible only since young people access as well as construct such negative identities for the old, as depressed and depressing, and as dull, grouchy and unreliable conversationalists. Good procedural fit belies complex group-evaluative processes which are a barrier to healthy cross-generational relations ... Talking to the old is perceived as a time-consuming duty and a necessary therapy rather than as relational development and broadening.

At the same time, no doubt, this elderly lack of accommodation does allow some sorts of social control during the interaction, eliciting outwardly sympathetic, supportive and flattering responses from the young. The authors suggests it might also be viewed as self-handicapping as well as being, more poignantly, a rational reflection of many older people's life-circumstances.

Other features of discursive style

Another data set examining beliefs about talk, but this time *in talk*, through elderly-peer group discussions, also turned up some telling findings (Giles, Coupland and Wiemann, in press). Young interviewers raised questions about the values of talk with groups of elderly women from the same population as above (sometimes classified as 'old-old' in the gerontological literature). The procedural norms for such events, it was presumed, were to discuss the issues raised in a relatively orderly manner, making explicit and individuated disclosures about experiences and beliefs. Young-elderly participants (in identical group discussions) did indeed adhere to this kind of structure. But the old-old groups tolerated – or enjoyed – a looser topic frame. Throughout, selected facets of sub-topics were developed piecemeal by various participants as talk 'rolled' forward, in some respects tangential to the topic the researcher had established. Indeed, the interviewer's multiple attempts to reassert the topic were simply ignored by these groups, who seemed unprepared to fit her broader frame. Hence, on one occasion, 'talking to animals for company' apparently triggered 'coming to the Day Centre for company' which established a relevance for 'companionship with friends' which led to 'pen-friend communication', then to a '98 year-old writing aunt', ending up with a 'Scotland is lovely' theme. This pattern of topic flux with local coherence focus was well suited to developing personal narratives, as many elderly speakers did in this context. Admittedly the younger sample also sometimes used anecdotes, but they did so only to supplement and exemplify their direct responses to questions.

The groups also showed quite different patterns of co-ordinating speakers' contributions, and this was seen most obviously through simultaneous speech, which was more common with the old-old groups. There were points during the discussions where the researcher found it necessary to intrude and ask for this to be minimized. Interestingly, topic flux was often managed through simultaneous speech, and it was apparent that this was not judged as adversarial but rather in the construction of a *social cumulativity* where participants collaborated, and gave *credit* not blame for intrusions. Where simultaneous speech did occur with the younger groups, it appeared as part of a process of *thematic cumulativity*, where participants set out to support, explain, modify or reject others' lines of argument.

The style differences (which, of course, need to be explored in other and more extensive data sets) can very reasonably be traced to the participants' social contexts (Coupland and Coupland 1990). Speakers will predictably place a premium on talk when they are, like the old-old population in this study, relatively immobile, with restricted social contacts, and living alone. For them, talk was a valued commodity *in itself* and would have an autonomy as a fundamental life resource, above and beyond considerations of talking strictly to topic. For the younger group, however, talk in general was more accessible, and they were likely to find more value in the outcomes of, and discoveries from, talk rather than in the process of talk itself. Some old-old participants explicitly endorsed the view that talk *should* be 'light', and they even were heard to gloss the group discussions as 'nice little chats' and would congratulate themselves for having 'got on well'. This is understandable as part of a reaction to prolonged difficult (social, emotional and economic) circumstances and a self-imposed limit on the depth of interaction, possibly as a barrier against further painful or effortful experiences.

Telling age

Informal experience suggests that children and adolescents are often asked to tell their age by distant relatives or by other people with whom they are not familiar, or have their age revealed for them by parents or guardians. Inquiring about age in these situations seems to indicate an interest, in our society, in the maturation and development of young people. In the middle years of life, however, asking age surfaces only in more or less sarcastic comments, spoken or written, about time passing and birthdays. As Coupland *et al.* (1989: 129–30) argued:

> The admixture of fear, reticence and regret with which, facetiously or not, many middle-aged adults appear to represent their own ageing, and the consequent teasing and chiding of those whose ageing comes up for review, undoubtedly form part of the interactional means by which negative images of ageing and the elderly are reproduced.

The data they report suggests, however, that for the elderly, age-in-years resurfaces from its underground life. The propensity for asking and telling the ages of elderly people is at least initially surprising, given that other studies have shown that (old) age categories generally have pejorative overtones in our society (Covey 1988). But age-telling proves to be negotiated in rather complex ways involving the negotiation of age and health identities (see below).

Investigating the same getting-to-know-you intergenerational encounters referred to above, Coupland, Coupland, Giles and Henwood (in press (b)) identified two broad sets of discourse processes for marking elderly age identity. The first of these, 'age-categorization processes', subsumes direct and indirect references to the elderly's group membership, time of life, generational role, identification of frailty and age-associable problematic circumstances, and the disclosure of chronological age. The second set, 'temporal framing processes', refers to the adding of a time-past perspective to current issues with elderly people self-associating with the past and recognizing historical, cultural and/or social changes. Virtually every elderly person in this study projected an elderly identity by one or both of the above means, and 75% disclosed their actual chronological age. Young participants rarely did so, and when they did it was in response to an elderly speaker's age disclosure.

Coupland *et al.* (1989) confirmed these distributional findings in another data set, and analysed the process of disclosing chronological age (DCA) more closely. Essentially, they see DCA as an identity token whose value is determined to a large extent by its placement and timing in an interaction. In general, age proves to be intimately bound up with health and decrement. For instance, and not untypically, one participant remarked: 'I'm seventy . . . this October so I find I can't do it so good.' In terms of social attribution theory, age functions here as a category-based, stable, uncontrollable and external attribution (Hewstone 1989). The accounting can be done defensively and even aggressively, projecting frailty or ill health as a moral right in advancing years, to be explicitly conceded by a recipient rather than expressed with resignation by the teller. One elderly participant says 'at eight-four? I've got a right to be [a bit stiff] don't you think?'

DCA in this accounting pattern mitigates the negative associations

Figure 6.1   Subjective correlates of DCA management.

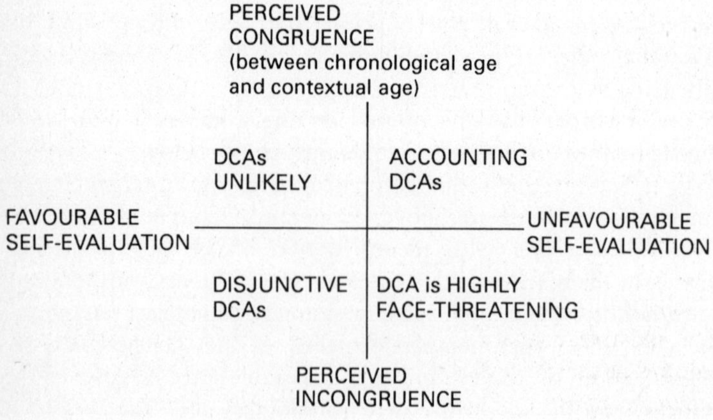

```
                        PERCEIVED
                        CONGRUENCE
                        (between chronological age
                        and contextual age)


                   DCAs          │ ACCOUNTING
                   UNLIKELY      │ DCAs
FAVOURABLE      ─────────────────┼───────────────── UNFAVOURABLE
SELF-EVALUATION                  │                  SELF-EVALUATION
                   DISJUNCTIVE   │ DCA is HIGHLY
                   DCAs          │ FACE-THREATENING

                        PERCEIVED
                        INCONGRUENCE
```

Source: Coupland *et al.* (1989: 139).

of actual frailty by appealing to decremental ageing as an extenuating circumstance. In a second, 'disjunctive' pattern of DCA, the discloser claims credit *against* normative expectations of frailty which are not (in fact or supposedly) realized. An example from the data was: 'mind I'm gone eighty I'm going eighty one! . . . and I think I'm pretty good.' While disclosing age carries very different identity potentials in these accounting and disjunctive patterns, they both find their meanings in the same underlying assumptions about the assumed nature of ageing itself in Western culture; that is, of sociophysical decrement. In both cases, chronological age is verbally established as one pole of a relational evaluation, the other pole being the subjectively experienced life position, or what can be called (after Rubin and Rubin 1982) *contextual age*. Ageing, then, is dually represented: first, in chronological terms, as a predictable, even eluctable progression along an incremental scale; second, in contextual terms, as a far less predictable ebbing and flowing, reflecting the arrival and passing of particular somatic, experiential and emotional circumstances (such as bereavement, illness, institutionalization). Coupland *et al.* (1989) located the two patterns of DCA in opposing quadrants of a two-dimensional model, as in Figure 6.1 above. The first dimension is a simple evaluative one reflecting the positivity or negativity of a person's self-appraised contextual ageing, while the other captures the degree to which the individual perceives his/her life position to be in or out of tune with contextual age. The model invites two further possibilities. The negative/incongruent configuration would clearly be face-threatening (Brown and Levinson 1987) – that is, 'I'm bad for my age' – and not surprisingly did not emerge in these data. The positive/congruent configuration (top left quadrant in Figure 6.1) was again not represented. People who tell age under these circumstances construe age as a salient aspect of their social identity (cf. Tajfel 1974) but disclosing age has no more significance than revealing any other piece of social data. Here we may find one explanation for the rarity of DCA in unmarked middle-age usage that we commented on earlier. In later life, this same configuration would be consistent only with the expectations held by a non-ageist society and individuals who had not been socialized into the norm of decremental ageing.

A crucial feature of the Coupland *et al.* analysis is highlighting the *negotiative* character of age-identity marking. For instance, a characteristic response to DCA (and especially the disjunctive type) by young recipients is surprise-at-age ('Oh! You're marvellous, aren't you?') with the prosodics of enthusiasm and disbelief. Such compliments and 'gifts' of praise mitigate or deny an interlocutor's supposedly predictable decrement, sometimes insistently. It is little wonder if DCA features in (perhaps quite rare) first acquaintances partly as a touchstone for older people to evaluate where they stand developmentally – and even existentially – and for modifying this self-conception if necessary. Age disclosure – rather like 'doing gender' (see Chapter 1) – is therefore one means for negotiating one's status as 'elderly' and one's projectable self.

Sustained supportive recipiency to DCA may, of course, be rewarding to an elderly's person's age identity. But, simultaneously, it may incur heavy costs, and this support may itself constrain elderly role opportunities and confirm age stereotypes. Motivated self-disclosure risks being construed as egocentricity, and fits well with the underaccommodative caricature of elderly communication painted above. Most strikingly, DCA appears to invite, in response, behaviours which are otherwise counternormative. Extended compliments and overtly expressed judgements of others on the basis of appearance are tabooed in most non-sexual and non-aggressive initial encounters beween young people, in Western culture anyway (Berger and Bradac 1982). These are processes which threaten negative face and ironically entail threats to the elderly identity it is designed to protect or enhance. Further risks are incurred in the assumption that some positive response will in fact be forthcoming; in the Coupland *et al.* data set, as it happens, the young women were experienced and sympathetic intergenerational talkers. Even where supportive feedback is obtained, there is no guarantee that the negotiative attempts by disclosers have been appreciated by recipients. There seems ample potential for age-telling–apparently so frequent in elderly talk to the young – to be misattributed and for elderly stereotypes to be confirmed (cf. the miscommunication model in Chapter 4).

Towards a lifespan communicative framework

There is another potential process intruding in the studies reported above and this derives theoretically from Turner's (1987) self-stereotyping theory. When group identity (in this case, elderliness) becomes salient for whatever contextual reason, people not only depersonalize and stereotype a relevant outgroup, they also stereotype themselves, as mentioned in Chapters 1 and 4. In other words, they take on characteristics they believe (rightly or wrongly) to be prototypical of the social group to which they themselves belong. Given that age was made salient in the above-mentioned intergenerational encounters, painful self-disclosures and telling age may well be facets of elderly speakers 'acting their age'. We could hypothesize that when age is made salient (in the contexts of overaccommodating talk being used to the elderly, or when decremental portrayals of old age appear in the media), older people will, compared to a non-age-salient condition, look, move, sound, think, talk and account 'older', a self-stereotyping process termed 'instant ageing' (Giles and Coupland 1991). And of course, there is no shortage of societal cues, beyond interactional ones, to make age salient for elderly people in Western societies, as analyses of literature, humour, magazine fiction, television drama and commercials attest (see, for example, Berman and Sobkowska-Ashcroft 1986).

By the time we reach retirement age, many of us will have been well primed to accept the 'reality' of decremental ageing that discourse strategies endorse. As Baker's (1985) data show, young people (in the United States) feel that a person's social status decreases linearly from 30 years until the mid-eighties; and patterns of seeking information from others have also been shown to be linearly related to a person's age (Franklyn-Stokes, Harriman, Giles, and Coupland 1988). Stereotypes of the middle-aged also impute negative competence, and in a recent study, Adja Henzel at Bristol found that young British undergraduates had a tremendous reservoir of stereotypes of middle age, the majority pertaining to sensory and physical decrement, with a keen desire to look younger than they were! But ageist assumptions about energy and competence are also not infrequent among the over-thirties, and many of us collude in propagating such myths through humour, accounting for others' and our own disappointments, failures and so forth in age-related terms. This collusion is doubtless an important element in the construction of our physical and psychological decline. The ageing process is, then, a developmental one to the extent that beliefs about ageing, health and the relationships between them are socialized early in life and significant foundations laid for the quality of elderly life (cf. Peterson, Seligman and Vaillant 1988).

In line with the above, and as Figure 6.2 schematizes, language attitudes mediate young people's conceptions of the elderly's interpretive and cognitive competences as well as the elderly's construals

Figure 6.2 Revised interactive model for the communicative predicament of ageing

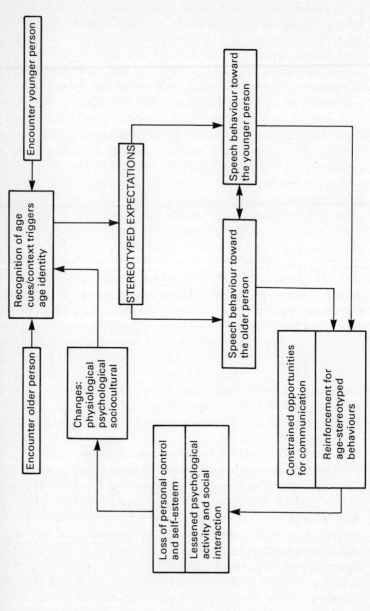

Source: Coupland, Coupland, Giles and Henwood (1988: 34).

of their own capacities. Younger people's communication may include overaccommodation, the sociolinguistic meanings of which can fuel elderly helplessness, a negative personal and social identity, and perceived, actual and 'instant' ageing. In these cases, and in the spontaneous evocation of elderly painful self-disclosure, socio-linguistic stereotypes are a potent force not only in miscommunication, as we argued in Chapter 4, but also in the construction and acceleration of ageing. We need to acknowledge the cultural distinctiveness of different generation groups, and that ageing is development, not ineluctable decline. Elderly people do not only inhabit different historical cohorts, often associated with different values and predispositions (communicative as well as non-communicative), but also have different problems (some existential) to which to adjust, somatically and life-historically. Developmental adaptation, and ultimately a positive personal identity, is likely to be achieved through being exposed to more enlightened values and interactional stances by younger people. An acknowledgement of biculturalism should put us on the path towards effective 'bilingualism'. We must learn from the history of other traditions of research into language and social categories (such as social class and gender) and move swiftly beyond the documentation of intercategory language and communicative differences towards an analysis of the communicative processes of ageism.

Language, health and social support

Theoretical and applied research into the communication correlates of elderly health is a rather recent and exciting research enterprise (see, for example, Shadden 1988). It is built on the old adage that health is not the sole prerogative of medical science but must embrace developments in social – and therefore language and communication – studies. At the same time, research on social support has taken a gerontological turn. For instance, it is now widely held that the ageing process is, in part, socially constructed and that social relationships (medical and non-medical) affect our physical health in important and very complex ways (Heller and Mansbach 1984). Nussbaum et al. (1989) find that survivability among the institutionalized elderly is associated with the level of intimacy in friendships formed with nursing staff. Revenson (1990) shows that reciprocity of support exchanges – either in amount or kind – is necessary for life satisfaction, and Rook (1990) argues that support, as manifest in positive social control, may be necessary to mediate good health outcomes. So, it may be disturbing to learn that perceived social support *declines* over the lifespan (Field and Mikler 1988). However, ever since Rook (1984) demonstrated that *negative* social relations could mediate *positive* elderly psychological well-being, there has been an appreciation that the relationship between support and health outcomes is an exceedingly complex one. More recently, Rotenberg and Hamel (1988: 315–16) argued, on the basis of their study of depression in elderly women, that social contacts may in fact exacerbate their clinical condition:

> It may be that elderly individuals become depressed, not because they lack frequent social interaction *per se*, as has often been proposed, but more specifically because they lack frequent social contacts in which they can *converse* . . . It may be that depression initially causes the elderly individual to form reciprocally intimate relationships because of the need to share feelings. It may be the case, though, that the social relationship serves to maintain depression because of the negativity of the exchange.

Regrettably, the social support literature has had little recourse to methods, analyses and theories in the language and communication sciences. This is rather surprising given that the key parameters of social support (for example, emotional, informational) are usually manifest interactionally.

As argued by Giles, Williams and Coupland (1990), communication forms the linchpin to understanding the complex and controversial interrelationships of social support practices, various measures of psychological well-being, and physical health. Communication is central to providing effective care, enabling valued independence to be fostered among the elderly, promoting health-educational practices and a positive sense of elderly identity, as well as enhancing the effectiveness of interactions between physician or carer and the elderly patient. Yet, talk to, from and about the elderly is perhaps the area in which we are least well informed. Much of the existing empirical work on elderly health is gleaned via self-reports; and these are, in actuality, cross-generation communication episodes. Self-reports in any case tend to gloss over interactional and network experiences producing *Gestalten* (for instance, 'support', 'caring') which probably relate poorly to the minute-to-minute contextual realities of any one social situation. Hence, proposed interventionist strategies and policies can often be very insensitive to the communicative demands of particular elderly people in specified sociolinguistic settings, as witnessed in recent discussions and policy recommendations in this area (see, for example, Heller, Price and McNeill, in press).

Research on the social psychology of health in general was summarized by Stephenson (1988: 427), in a recent text, as having

> concentrated on elucidating the characteristics of the victim who requires assistance, the characteristics of the potential benefactor, and the situational cues which make it more or less likely that help will be given. In addition, the emphasis in research has been on those situations in which help is urgently required, like assisting someone who has collapsed dramatically in public.

The elderly health literatures can be similarly caricatured: they also perhaps have overinvested in stress and coping mechanisms. In fact, there are data to show that the elderly experience fewer problems and stresses than younger people (Folkman *et al.* 1987) and suffer less *Angst* from supposed loneliness (Schultz and Moore 1988). What may be more significant to understanding the quality of life for the elderly, as we argued above, is the elderly's negotiation of their age identities and subjective health in everyday social contacts. Indeed, Cartwright and Smith (1988: 52) reported that three-fifths of elderly people regarded their health as 'good for their age'. In other words, and in line with our own data, age is being used here as a yardstick against which to construe expectations about normative health. We know a great deal about the who, when and where of providing good and bad support, diagnosis and caring, and sometimes even the why, but far less about the *how* of its interactional management.

This may be particularly true when we consider the *inter-relationships* between the elderly, talk, and health more carefully. Generally in the literature, these constructs are treated as wholly distinct, and this has obvious advantages in terms of conceptualization and measurement. Yet they are sociopsychologically interdependent, in ways that need to be confronted in future research and theory:

For instance, in the data we discussed above, age is explicitly identified when elderly talk addresses health issues; the structure and functions of talk are age-dependent; and construals of health are often age-related and determined by socially comparative exchanges. Moreover, Hall *et al.* (in press) have found that the meanings of health for the elderly are multidimensional and significantly bound up with the nature of their social relationships. In a gerontological frame, we cannot really conceive of any one element of the communication–health–ageing triad without invoking the other two:

Talk to/from elderly	← age- and health-dependent
Felt elderliness	← communicative and health experiences
Health-identity	← age expectations and communicative experiences

So, when we analyse, traditionally, so-called 'elderly well-being or non-well-being' we cannot avoid considering situated communicative acts about and enacting social and health practices. Furthermore, shifts in one of the three dimensions will probably entail changes in the others – such as when sudden ill health limits the nature and quality of elderly social contact and reinforces an (elderly, frail) age identity.

Therefore, we should question the assumption that psychological and physical well-being versus non-well-being are bipolar extremes of two continua. In our quantitative studies, we tend to assume that variables either load positively or negatively with it. We are very sensitive to the likelihood that different forms of social support have different antecedents and consequences (Dunkel-Schetter *et al.* 1987), but is it not possible – as we argued analogously in the last chapter – that we should be considering well-being and non-well-being as causally determined by quite *different* processes? For instance, what we are beginning to visualize as the sociolinguistic route to ill health and dissatisfaction seems to be underpinned by a decremental lifespan ideology – with all its developmental triggers in terms of social clocks, 'cultural' transitions and attributional styles – that rests on biological individualism. The sociolinguistic route to good health and a younger contextual age for some may build on a quite contrastive ideology and social attributional style – one that acknowledges the social constructive process of ageing and seriously (and perhaps assertively) questions the often illegitimate consequences of being a member of a stigmatized social group. Ageing individuals here would discursively *resist* elderly identity roles and styles and *deny* stereotypic attributions in their own and in others' talk; generally, they would 'de-depersonalize' and become politically active at the level of interpersonal interaction.

While individual differences such as locus of control and self-esteem are implicated in studies of social support, we would advocate also drawing on more *social* measures which reflect the multidimensional structure of age identity (Oglivie 1987) as well as the elderly's cognitive representations of the social structure along age- and power-related lines. (The notion of 'ethnolinguistic vitality', in Chapter 5, therefore seems to transfer well to intergenerational contexts). Indeed, one might propose that social support factors may operate not by bolstering locus of control and self-esteem directly but by providing a communicative atmosphere which allows elderly people to negotiate their social identities successfully; locus of control and self-esteem may actually be enhanced as a *personal identity* byproduct of this process (Tajfel and Turner 1979).

A language perspective on health and social support

Can we devise a theoretical model which can embrace these notions more concretely? In view of the considerations we have introduced above (social identity of the elderly, the interdependence of health, ageing and communication, cultural differences and values) it would seem that present theory in the sociopsychology of health (see, for example, Spacapan and Oskamp 1989) cannot cope with the complex dynamics involved. An interactionally grounded model is thus proposed here (Williams, Giles, Coupland, Dalby and Manasse 1990) in the hope of stimulating, on the one hand, more sophisticated discursive analyses in the study of social support processes and, on the other, a social psychology of language which was alert to the broader health implications of within- and across-generation interaction. Even so, it seems to us that the perspective we introduce below is relevant to supportive encounters at all ages.

The model will take as its starting point Albrecht and Adelman's

(1987) framework of 'communicating social support'. Indeed, this is, the first interpersonal, language-related system to be applied to the area of health, and as such is an important advance. Albrecht and Adelman's model invokes Berger's (1979) uncertainty reduction theory (UCR) for understanding initial relationships, in which it is argued that individuals engage in communication in order to describe, predict and explain others' behaviour; as the relationship proceeds, their uncertainty is reduced by a mutual exchange of information. Notwithstanding the general benefits of Albrecht and Adelman's explicit communicative focus and the way they conceptualize network communication systems as the most salient facet of social support, their information-based model seems unnecessarily limited as an explanation of the subtle, shifting, differentiated, multi-level and subjective variable that support undoubtedly is in the contexts of its delivery and reception. Indeed, it may be that what Brown and Rogers (1991) denigrate as 'the epistemology of objects' in discussions of relational development (including UCR) is sustained through the reification of support-as-product, when a perspective on support-as-*process* is a prerequisite for dynamic explanation and intervention. Certainly, as our highlighting of identity issues above would indicate, UCR language strategies (modification of amount of verbal communication, non-verbal affiliative expressiveness, information seeking, intimacy level and reciprocity rate) are not the only ones used in supportive encounters. The model below, then, acknowledges the impetus provided by Albrecht and Adelman but has at its core communication accommodation theory (CAT), as overviewed in Chapter 3.

CAT can be important to elderly health in the sense that high attuning may be a core component of many supportive encounters – not only productively but also receptively in terms of active listening to the elderly. Indeed, *feeling* supported may to some extent be a function of the degree of attuning one receives, so that those who are known or perceived to possess high attuning skills may be preferentially sought out as supporters. Harvey, Orbuch and Weber's (1990) sequential model of account-making in response to severe stress posits various psychosomatic and negative affective consequences arising from failures of the stressed to engage in a completion of 'their story' of the events. Seeking out accommodative partners and providing them with the necessary verbal and non-verbal feedback are obviously integral processes in successful support exchanges. But as Figure 6.3 suggests, high attuning and supportiveness are not intrinsically positive correlates, and attuning may not always be a sufficient criterion for support. There can be occasions (see cell B) where encounters designed to be supportive are discursively managed by *low* attuning, where supporters may challenge recipients' assumptions and identities, predictably through interruptions, repeated clarification requests, subverting discourse and generally *contra*-attuning. In this vein, Arntson and Droge (1987) have shown, from observing epileptic support groups, that positive self-images, healthier attitudes and lifestyles are fostered when the group *discourages* indulgent 'victim narratives'. Nor are we arguing that support is a property of a single interaction itself – although it could be – as low support from any one localized interaction can be instrumental in the provision of longer-term support programmes. On occasions, the seeds of *non*-supportive encounters can also be sown by *high* attuning (cell G), where familial security, empathy and understanding shown (with perhaps the best of motives) can encourage dependency and a sick-role. In this way, negatively valenced perceptions can be validated which may *not* boost the individual's own psychosocial resourcefulness and capacities to adapt to some conditions of ageing and ill health.

Lehman *et al.* (1986) point to some supposedly empathic comments made by supporters in a bereavement context ('I know exactly how you feel') which can actually be evaluated by the recipient in our model's terms as exceedingly *underaccommodative*. These scholars have suggested that rather than reflecting misunderstandings or upset, failed support attempts may be related to anxiety caused by extreme sensitivity to the listener's vulnerability and heightened awareness that a negative outcome may result from saying the wrong

Figure 6.3 A three-dimensional model of the interrelationships among attuning, support and health outcomes

	SUPPORT			
	High		Low	
	ATTUNING			
	High	Low	High	Low
LONG-TERM HEALTH OUTCOMES				
Positive	A	B	C	D
Negative	E	F	G	H

Source: Williams *et al.* (1990: 128)

Figure 6.4   An interactional model of elderly health communication

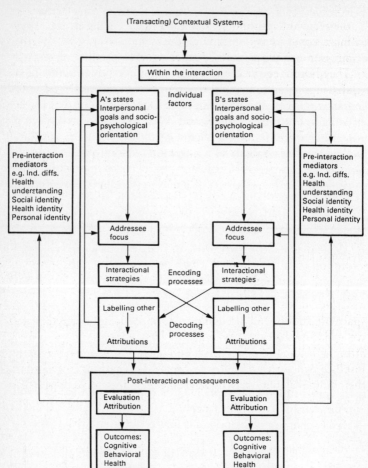

Source: Williams *et al.* (1990: 130)

thing (see also Dunkel-Schetter and Wortman 1982). In Brown and Levinson's (1987) terms, support providers are anxious about their facility to threaten the negative face of their recipients. Gottlieb (in press) provides a further valuable perspective, pointing out that support providers are often exposed to some of the same stresses experienced by support recipients. Generally, expressing and receiving support can then be a collaborative effort, as Gottlieb contends:

both the supporter and the would-be recipient become involved in the process of comparing their emotional reactions to
the event and responding to one another's coping efforts. They
must concurrently deal with the demands imposed by the
stressor and those imposed by each other's coping responses.
They both face the challenge of modulating their adjustment
strivings so as to avoid disrupting the coping efforts of their
partner while gaining his/her support. At the same time, as
providers of support, they must be careful not to extend types
of support that are more instrumental in helping to regulate
their own emotions than in meeting the needs of the recipient.

As real outcomes in the interactional model, we are concerned
about promoting good health habits, social relations, and a positive
sense of age identity among the elderly. Indeed, this research area in
general needs to lay down some priorities regarding the dependent
variables we should focus upon. At the moment, they vary from
study to study and include happiness, life satisfaction, emotional
well-being and so forth, making cross-study comparisons and generalizations difficult. An important element in our three-dimensional
model in Figure 6.3 is 'long-term health outcomes'. Here – although
space precludes a full discussion of each of the eight cells depicted –
we conceptualize the feasibility of high social support and high
attuning leading to poor health outcomes in the long term – as, for
instance, when two close friends depend on each other to promote
their mutual alcohol or drug abuses (cell E). In sum, each pair of our
three dimensions in Figure 6.3 is orthogonally related, as contra-
attuning and low (or ultimately withdrawn) support could in some
circumstances (for example, airing certain interpersonal grievances
in the context of a loving relationship) eventuate in significant
cognitive reappraisals and positive health outcomes (cell D).

Contextual dimensions

The interactive model, schematically represented in Figure 6.4, is
built around the interchangeable roles of support seeker and support
provider – individuals A and B. As in Albrecht and Adelman's (1987)
approach, communication network systems form a crucial backdrop, consisting of family, friends, weak ties, work relationships,
culture, etc., although Bronfenbrenner's (1979) contextual model of

networks as *transacting* systems allows further distinctions to be made (as outlined in Chapter 1). In his terms, contexts have a nested structure; an individual's relationship with the environment is trans-actional and contexts are conceptualized as evolving systems which are undergoing constant change. In this way the model can reflect how elderly people may perceive different social episodes along dimensions salient to them; perhaps health explicit–implicit and caring high–low, formal–informal, and so forth. In addition, and in line with the discussion in Chapter 1, how they construe social norms, interactional goals and relational rules will doubtless have an impact on the interactional process. But this schematization also acknowledges that the full range of contextual influences and predis-positions may be *variably* salient during face-to-face interaction, and that the sequential constraints of talk itself may play a part in determining which contextual dimensions are in fact accessed, when and why. Unfortunately, little focused empirical work exists in any of these areas (for example, the extent to which norms and rules are salient in elderly interactions, agreed upon by elderly peers, and strictly or tolerantly applied) for us to develop precise hypotheses about the situated phenomenology of the elderly.

Pre-interactional mediators

Following Gallois *et al.* (1988) and, of course, Patterson (1983), the model in Figure 6.4 highlights the psychosociolinguistic armoury individuals bring to different situations; our so-called 'pre-interactional mediators'. A host of individual differences might be important here, but one prime set for our purposes is the extent of people's interpersonal sensitivities and communicative competences. Taking a transactional approach again, the seeker of support needs to provide sufficient cues to supporters to enable them to come to a shared definition of the situation and for the latter to access what is required in response (see Dunkel-Schetter *et al.* 1987). Sociodemo-graphic factors such as age (psychological as well as chronological) and gender are inevitably also important. For example, in elderly patient–young provider interactions, it has been found that gender matching decreases interpersonal distance, and increases disclosure and rapport (Davis 1988). Interestingly, Cartwright and Smith (1988) found that British women doctors differ from men, not in their attitudes towards the elderly or in their prescribing practices, but in the way they are regarded and used by patients. More specifically, women doctors are seen as more understanding and good at explaining and are consulted more frequently (probably as a consequence). These authors claim that such patterns make no difference to actual care. From the present theoretical perspective, this seems counterintuitive and Cartwright and Smith's position may be a function of their 'sociological survey' techniques which were probably not sensitive enough to detect these differences. Patients may feel freer to interrupt, to ask more questions of, even perhaps to challenge, a female doctor (West 1990). This may be due to patients' perceptions of smaller power and status differentials between themselves and a female as opposed to a male doctor. Thus the question of whether women doctors elicit quite different discursive styles from their patients – and the sociomedical consequences of this – are worth pursuing.

Adopting Pendleton's (1983) terminology, the 'health understanding' of *both* participants (see Figure 6.4) can be crucial in *all* social contexts, whether health concerns are explicit or not and whether care is or is not a recognized interactional function. Interlocutors bring to the interaction certain information and expectations, schemata, attributions and constructs of health which are often ageist. Folk models of health and illness are a case in point: they may differ between historical cohorts (for example, pre- and post-antibiotics) and thus lead to misunderstandings of cause and cure between interlocutors of different ages (see also Arntson 1989). Medical personnel must therefore tread a careful path between collusion with or accommodation to folk beliefs that may lead to erroneous modes of treatment on the one hand, and misunderstandings caused by overinvestment in (underaccommodative use of) biomedical explanations on the other. If interlocutors' health understandings are at odds, this can lead to miscommunication and negative evaluations and attributions of the encounter (West and Frankel 1991). Hall *et al.* (in press) showed just such mismatches between physicians' and the elderly's conceptions of health. While elderly construals of physical and mental health incorporated emotional health, physicians' ratings did not.

We would also wish to invoke the notion of *health identity*, which we take to refer not only to a person's cognitive construction of own health status, but also to constructions of it by others. Subjective health identity will affect interactional strategies (for instance, *vis-à-vis* self-disclosure) and will in turn (see Figure 6.4) result from local evaluations and attributions made during interaction. Since being elderly is at least perceptually associated with declining health (so much so that assumptions of decremental decline have come to dominate the language- and communication-gerontological litera-tures – see Coupland and Coupland 1990), other people may be treated communicatively in a stigmatized and unhealthy fashion, irrespective of the older person's actual subjective health identity. Individuals may have or may develop a health identity – and also a social identity – as 'aged' that leads them to seek out particular types of supportive interaction that reinforce that identity. For example, those elderly who view and project themselves as 'old and of declining health' – and from the above studies this appears not uncommon – may seek out and cue sympathetic and attuned responses from their conversational partners.

The model allows for the possibility (which we cannot substanti-ate in the above instance) that local support of this kind can be *non*-supportive in the longer term to the extent that it may reinforce ill and ageing identities leading, by means of the self-fulfilling prophecy, to ill health. Hence, institutions, such as community care, nursing homes and so forth, will set agendas for talk and social action based on health identities they themselves construct for their elderly carees. In fact, a recent analysis of carer–elderly resident interaction in long-stay nursing homes (Grainger *et al.* 1990) shows how, probably in response to institutional, task-orientated pressures, nurses regularly adopt a range of deflective strategies in talk to elderly care recipients. In one characteristic instance, nurses reject an elderly resident's perception of the bathing routine: it is 'a lovely bath', 'nice' and 'beautiful', conversationally constituted as a brief penance, even a treat, despite the elderly person's protestations to the contrary. Grainger *et al.* interpret such acts of deflection as the moulding of circumstantial realities to fit institutional priorities.

Though data such as the above are among the most challenging to social support theorists and to policy-makers alike, we would not want to underestimate the constructivist potential of individuals themselves, where they do have role discretion, in determining their own social support recipiency. Not only do we construct our own development transactionally across the lifespan (Lerner and Busch-Rossnagel 1981), but by choosing who we confide in, and when, amounts of self-disclosure, the variety of sociolinguistic cues we provide, and so forth, we also participate in actively constructing our own social support (see Reardon and Buck 1989). If we do not confide in friends, or do not provide medical personnel with an adequate symptomatic context, we of course seriously constrain their ability to provide support and care. Conceivably, older patients may in some ways contribute to miscommunicative exchanges with their doctors because of their lesser desire to make or assist in making medical decisions, and their greater acceptance of medical 'authority'. Such considerations are a necessary antidote to what is arguably a 'provider-heavy' tradition of research into the characteristics, motivations and modes of social support.

Goals and strategies

The range of pre-interactional mediators we have considered – including social and personal identities – feeds directly into any encounter, potentially influencing the communicative goals and motivational orientations of the participants. These in turn set the tone for the particular addressee focus and interactional strategies adopted.

In some cases, the interactional goals of provider and seeker (A and B in Figure 6.4) are congruent or complementary whereas in others they may be discordant. The motivation to seek support, to provide support, or to avoid helping will depend on the personal goals of the interactants. Albrecht and Adelman (1987) describe a variety of motives for providing support such as altruism, personal satisfaction, social manipulation and so forth. We would also wish to recognize that support can be dictated by institutional regimens and ideologies which can sometimes at least *defer* personal goals. Albrecht and Adelman do not, however, articulate how these motives are tied to the particular sociolinguistic strategies of interactants. We would invoke links with the attuning strategies introduced in Chapter 4, but with the proviso that accommodation would be guided by addressee foci that involve *perceptual* processes. Hence, as we noted above, inadvertently misdirected high attuning on certain dimensions of talk can be quite unsuccessful; likewise, cell B of Figure 6.3 indicates that support (as well as long-term positive health outcomes) can sometimes best be achieved through *low* attuning, for example in dismissing false worries. Given the plethora of verbal and non-verbal (proxemic, kinesic, paralinguistic, prosodic), symbolic as well as referential, dimensions of possible variation that our encoding options subsume, the notion of 'mixed-attuning' is endemic in the accommodation model. Quite conceivably, then, some of the anxiety often experienced by supporters may be located in their desire to achieve competing projected outcomes, and their need to compromise in the face of accommodative dilemmas. Gottlieb (in press) provides a compelling analysis of implicitly incongruent and mixed goals of married couples coping with children diagnosed as having serious illnesses. In providing a content analysis of the various language strategies spouses claimed they used in an interview study, Gottlieb shows how support transactions are a *contingent process*:

> wives will gain suppport only by shielding their husbands from the tensions surrounding the child's illness and by concentrating on the instrumental demands of the illness regimen and the routines of caregiving. To maintain their emotional equilibrium, the husbands need their wives' reassurance, expressions of hopefulness, dedication to the caregiving role, and recognition of their main contribution as breadwinners. In turn, the wives' bids for needed emotional support, expressed by venting their anxiety and fearfulness, go unanswered because they disrupt their husbands' reliance on a posture of stoic acceptance, their preoccupation with the managerial dimension of the illness, and their denial.

In the spirit of CAT, identifying motives for *not* providing effective support would seem an important pursuit, and these would include the desire to communicate a contrastive self- or group image, to avoid threats to face (of giver), and/or to maintain or achieve an alternative role definition. Finally here, it can be speculated that persons will be motivated to *seek* support when they find themselves in stressful situations with high uncertainty, including definitions of *themselves* in terms of personal, social and health identities; when they need an increasing sense of control and empathy; and when they desire reassurance about their (sometimes changing) identities and outcomes, thereby yearning for a period of 'stability' to adjust to new threats. Although it could be suggested that they might often seek high attuning and signal cues in this regard, it could also be that on occasions they desire support through non-attuning. An instance might be when elderly people desire younger interlocutors to communicate with them in terms of their *personal* identities and not to depersonalize them and treat them as undifferentiated members of an (aged) social category.

Decoding

Cognitive responding, social evaluations and attributions during the interaction can feedback to influence sociolinguistic adjustment throughout conversation as recognized by the 'decoding processes' element of our model. But it is clear that speakers sometimes mindfully reflect on conversations and weigh up what has been said after the event; they can summarize how they feel about it and their partner. Pendleton's (1983) doctor–patient communication model gives status to outcomes that may result *from* the interaction and this is clearly important to us, too, within a more general health context. Hence, built into the model are two post-communication phases (see Figure 6.4): the first involving immediate evaluations and attributions; the second involving 'outcomes' – cognitive, affective and behavioural – which have health consequences as a direct result of an interaction *or* an *accumulation* of them.

Post-interactional consequences

Albrecht and Adelman contend that people will feel supported if uncertainty is reduced and when the support they receive results in increased feelings of personal control. This perspective refers primarily to cognitive/emotional criteria and we would wish to access more of the sociolinguistic parameters of suppport encounters. For instance, the perception of increased control is likely to occur if the (supportive) listener takes the other's perspective and explicitly acknowledges, elaborates and legitimizes the other's feelings. Such features align well with research and theory into the process of empathy. For instance, Yeoman's eight-stage model of empathy (cited in MacLean and Gould 1988) describes how (in a counselling context) a client's sense of control is facilitated through self-knowledge brought about by the counsellor's sensitivity, identification and ability accurately to reflect and elaborate the client's feelings. More specifically, this would come about by engendering receptivity to extended self-disclosure, overriding topic taboos where appropriate, and propounding a reciprocal climate of openness and trust. This would be achieved discursively through extending others' turns, back channelling, by multiplying clarification requests, creating summary glosses in order negotiatively to structure or restructure the problem which can be confirmed or denied, and so forth. Finally, collaborative work with the stressed person is undertaken to work out action plans for change and giving support for such changes. In the context of Figure 6.4, we should be wary of overstressing high attuning, when such accommodation can sometimes perpetuate negative social and health identities. Also, while the implicit emphasis here has been on 'stress situations', effective attuning is probably just as important to maintenance of psychological well-being when it is responsive to everyday difficulties and annoyances which, as it happens, are arguably more predictive of depression than major life event crises (Argyle and Henderson 1985).

According to a recent review (Turnquist *et al.* 1988), attributions of any type are related to physical and psychological *outcomes*. Unfortunately, research is patchy and findings have been equivocal. Yet, we can suggest that when social and personal identities for an elderly person are unfavourable and few other sources of support are available, low attuning will probably be evaluated negatively. And if such evaluations, or affective reactions, are attributed as internal, stable and global, then psychological well-being and physical health will suffer. Alternatively, internal, stable and global attributions in response to well-attuned interactions may be more likely to result in positive health outcomes. These straightforward hypotheses will, needless to say, need to be refined and further specified in the wake of empirical studies. Relatedly, the attributional style of participants may interact in diverse and complex ways to influence both evaluations and outcomes (Brenders 1989).

As highlighted by others (see, for example, Stoller and Pugliesi 1989), communicating support and in our terms *successful attuning* (be it high or low) can be beneficial for the *provider* as well as for the recipient. This would be particularly so when providers believe they have been effective agents of redefinition and change (Albrecht and Adelman 1987) and such positive sentiments are attributed internally. Certainly, the provision of emotional support via language is beneficial to the affective state of the provider, too. Notarius and Herrick (1988) showed that those informants (in a role-playing task) who were able to express empathy, to listen supportively and to offer encouragement to a supposedly depressed confederate were much less depressed themselves after the event than those who were able only to offer concrete behavioural advice or who attempted to distract the depressed other from this mood state. In this way, attuning skills may be reinforced and the relationship would be likely to develop or at the very least be maintained, and even health gains for the provider could result. Some of the ways in which attuning, combined with various evaluations and attributions, might predispose certain long-term outcomes, such as reinforced and improved attuning skills, changes in esteem, health and social identity, and changes in physical and emotional health, have been illustrated. Hence, a person who receives an attuned reaction (high or low) which leads to effective cognitive responding will be more inclined to seek out support (within probable limits) from the same source. If health is explicitly salient, s/he will be more likely to comply with health-related advice. Conversely, if the supported is attuned in a manner which leads either to minimal cognitive responding or more potently to negatively valenced thought elaboration, then compliance would be less likely and future interaction with that source may be avoided. But if contact was unavoidable then low-quality care would predictably be consolidated and spiral downwards over repeated interactions.

In some cases, demands made by seekers may be greater than the experiential and sociolinguistic resources held by providers or *allowed* to them by institutional regimens. Negative evaluations will follow if providers see themselves as having coped badly with the situation and attribute their low attuning to lack of ability rather than effort. Also, if this experience is consistently felt over different kinds of interaction, interpersonal and attuning skills may fail to improve and learned helplessness and communication avoidance can result.

Clearly, the predictive force of the model at this stage is limited, and several of its constructs and theoretical links remain to be sharpened in the context of relevant data. We also need to look to the negotiative complexities of the attuning *process* in terms of how it is introduced, managed, reacted to, and concluded in discourse. Nevertheless, a unique feature of this model is that it highlights dynamic *language* strategies as a *core* element within sequential interactional processes which are themselves embedded within transacting levels of context. This is crucial as it allows us ultimately to take on board aspects of the relationships between culture and communication; is amenable to exploring the *heterogeneity* of elderly phenomenology as it relates to different health and communication styles; and elevates communication processes to their rightful place as potential determinants of health status. However, the emphasis on context makes us well aware of the pitfalls inherent in focusing upon (let alone intervening in) interpersonal communication processes without taking into account the contemporary social structures and policies in which they are embedded; that would be to pluck off the heads of weeds and let them remain standing. But the issues we have been addressing go some way towards explaining how social, political and economic biases are engendered and sustained. Our objective has been to establish language as a core process in health aspects of social gerontology, and the elderly as a poorly understood cultural group in social psychology, sociolinguistics and communication studies in general. Such an enterprise may be the springboard to developing a truly interdisciplinary framework for the study of health issues in lifespan communication.

Summary

In this chapter, we looked at some of the language-related differences between elderly and younger interlocutors in terms of beliefs about talk, aspects of discursive style and self-disclosure. Not only do the dynamics of young-elderly conversations appear to involve a mutually disturbing imbalance, identified by the concepts of over- and underaccommodation, but there are sufficient data to suggest unwitting collusion by younger people in drawing out 'problematical' interactional behaviours from the elderly. We argued that the origins of these interactional predispositions are established quite early in the lifespan, and that they function to the ultimate disadvantage of us all. Rather than approach elderly discourse from the traditional decremental perspective, we interpreted it as a series of coping strategies, given the life circumstances of the elderly people involved. In the constructivist spirit of previous chapters, our analysis of the role of language in the ageing process was one which underlined the mutual interdependence of talk and elderliness, as well as health. Examining social contexts of language use which were to varying degrees health-related, we proposed models which argued for a sophisticated blend of attuning and social support processes which, in the long term, could facilitate the health of supporter, supportee, their relationship, and the strength of the networks which they share. This perspective seems fundamental to understanding not only health care for the elderly but also the linguistic mechanics of social support exchange at any age. We end, then, with the claim that everyday language can at best be a life-support system, and at worst a magnet to physical demise.

Suggestions for further reading

Albrecht, A., Adelman, M. B. and associates (eds) (1987). *Communication and social support*. Newbury Park: Sage. The first, and thus far the only, important collection of essays and research investigating the interrelationships between social support and communicative behaviours.

Gravell, R. (1988). *Communication problems in elderly people: Practical approaches to management*. London: Croom Helm. A very lively and more pragmatically orientated book dealing with interaction patterns and the elderly.

Nussbaum, J. F., Thompson, T. and Robinson, J. D. (1989). *Communication and ageing*. New York: Harper and Row. An authoritative and well-written book overviewing communicative and linguistic patterns of the elderly.

Stewart, M. and Roter, D. (eds) (1989). *Communicating with medical patients*. Newbury Park. CA: Sage. An important set of essays examining the interrelationships between medical care, communication and language behaviours.

7 / EPILOGUE

Speech and expression are a function of the contexts in which they are produced. Such contexts can be analysed objectively as well as construed by communicators themselves in terms of the immediate situational factors operating at a given time and relevant macro-societal forces in which they are embedded. Interaction itself recycles meaning into its context. An important dimension of situational construals which resurfaces throughout this book has been the 'interindividual' – 'intergroup' distinction. Sometimes we think of a situation as archetypally inter*personal* – such as a romantic encounter. Yet very often this can shift into, or simultaneously be, an intergroup (between-gender) situation. The long history of male and female relations is thereby a set of macro-societal forces impinging on the way conversations are negotiated by particular interactants. Reciprocally, we also noted that people's continual choices of language forms for representing others, events and themselves can have dramatic effects on how we construe them. Those we believe to be socially influential, whether media or authority figures or friends, can therefore shape and transform our understanding of how the world is, why it is, and what we believe can and cannot be done with it. Various elite groups, then, can impose a discourse on how other relevant groups have been, are, and/or will be performing on, say, vitality dimensions – and their choice of language to so do can significantly affect how we account for the status quo and what we believe may feasibly be accomplished in many or different spheres.

We also saw that for at least some groups, or rather certain members within them, language behaviours are a vital symbolic resource representing their distinctiveness. If people orientate politically, economically or ideologically to an outgroup, then very often it is mandatory that the outgroup's code and/or style are adopted. If they are more concerned with the preservation of ingroup identities and habits, they are likely to resist acquiring that group's pattern of usage and will strive to maintain as well as create new forms of differentiated language use. Language, then, is a crucial factor in intergroup relations to the extent that the social meanings of its many, and sometimes very subtle, forms are salient, complex and diverse. Our own and others' choices of linguistic styles and variables significantly affect the nature of the perceived context, how we feel about ourselves and how others respond to us. Language is not divorced from contexts; it can be the very *essence* of that situation in ways that have probably been underappreciated by many cognitively orientated social psychologists up to now. The emotional *Angst*, ambiguities, contradictions and legitimate conflicts which have their life not only in cognitive experiences but also widely and vividly in talk seem to us to be woefully missing from many social psychological paradigms.

The unfolding of language as social discourse finds us, as often frail social beings, engaging in providing and seeking forms of support, in ways that are only just beginning to be appreciated. But we are somewhat impotent in addressing the alluring concept of social support, and attempting to measure and implement it, if we do not access the complex discursive processes which dynamically achieve the experience of being supported. We cannot provide convincing theory or intervene effectively in support encounters without this. That some elderly people – as a cultural group – engage in talk which is imbued with affairs of the heart, lungs, and limbs also leads us to claim that language is a critical component of health identity and health itself. Growing evidence that younger people can collude in this process by soliciting 'unhealthy talk' is instructive of the ways in which we contribute to others', and in the long run our own, personal growth or decline.

Future priorities

Let us consider what the future should hold for the social psychology of language (SPL), against the background assumption that SPL is already generating significant interdisciplinary findings and theory. SPL's richness is evident in the recent growth of middle-range theories and in its ability to sustain an emergent eclecticism in methodological and epistemological stances and a delightful tendency to draw on the riches of other language-orientated disciplines and data bases (see, for example, Brown and Gilman 1989). Throughout the book, we have proposed concrete suggestions for specific new directions and drawn attention to particular processes and phenomena in need of closer examination. We would now like to air a manageable number of concerns for future directions. These concerns (the choice is no doubt idiosyncratic) are the relationship between miscommunication and communication, the unit of analysis in SPL, and the epistemological dilemma of entertaining a positivistic as well as a constructivistic stance.

The status of miscommunication

The study of language and communication phenomena and processes has currently favoured understandings in terms of competence, effectiveness, efficiency and satisfaction. Yet, it is equally plausible, as Coupland, Wiemann and Giles (1991) contend, to construe communication as an intrinsically problematic activity, demanding 'work' from those who sustain it. Such a perspective naturally invites analysis of those exceptional *and routine* miscommunicative instances when communication is noteworthy for its *lack of* satisfaction, *in*efficiency, *un*desirability, and so on, to one or more participant and/or observer, whether consciously or not, intentionally or not. When attention has been given to such problems across social groups, social situations, and communicative modes (and this, interestingly enough, appears to be growing), there is widespread conceptual confusion regarding the meaning, boundaries and types of 'miscommunication', 'communication breakdown', 'problematic talk', and 'fault-finding'.

When 'miscommunication' has been identified in sociolinguistics (Milroy 1984), it has been taken to relate to mismatching of intended and comprehended referential meanings. Milroy (1984: 15) makes a useful preliminary distinction between dialect miscommunications which are 'misunderstandings' (involving simple disparity between speakers' and hearers' referential semantic analyses of a given utterance) and 'communicative breakdown' (when one or more participants perceives that something has gone wrong). Nevertheless, this linguistically focused work lacks the complexity of theoretical apparatus needed to begin to understand the attributional, evaluative and broader social consequences of these categories of miscommunication. Again, an assumption seems to be made that such miscommunications are self-generating sociolinguistic behaviours, since no consideration is given to interpersonal or intergroup factors operating in the contexts of their production. In his work on interethnic talk, Gumperz (1982) takes a broader, but still linguistically based, view of communication difficulties where 'even an odd word or turn of phrase, or a misunderstood tone of voice, can seriously affect trust among participants' (1982: 8). Here we have a seemingly amorphous set of miscommunications which are neither misunderstanding nor breakdown in Milroy's terms and may be felt as awkwardness, unfocused dissatisfaction and the unexplained wish to avoid future contact. As with Milroy's work, there is much to be gained here, we would argue, from richer sociopsychological analyses of these events.

Communication science has also for its part emphasized positive, desirable communicative behaviour, although attention is now being focused on negativity in social interaction (Kellerman 1989). Research and particularly theory is couched in pro-social terms with little regard for the fact that most communicators are, quite routinely, sceptical and crafty and less than veracious (Friedman and Tucker 1990). Indeed, Hopper and Bell (1984) cluster-analysed respondents' judgements of deception-related terms suggesting a preliminary typology of no less than six types (in Western culture anyway). The structure they obtained was: *fictions*: irony, tall tales, make-believe, etc.; *playings:* jokes, teasing, bluffs, etc.; *lies:* dishonesty, fibs, cheating, etc.; *crimes:* disguises, cons, counterfeits, etc.; *masks:* masking, backstabbing, two-facedness, etc.; *unlies:* distortion, misleading, false implications, and misrepresenting. Communicators also evade difficult questions by a range of linguistic devices (see Bavelas 1990 for a discussion of equivocation); they keep secrets and second-guess the lies, evasions and secrets of others (Hewes *et al.* 1989). As argued elsewhere, communication can sometimes be complex and exhausting work as we attempt to 'pull the wool over the ears of others' while debugging their messages at one and the same time (Giles and Wiemann 1987). Even those who steadfastly peddle the supposed truth interpersonally, do not deceive, account accurately, and express intentions and credentials as they see them, may still from an intergroup perspective embellish their own valued ingroups' capabilities, attributes and potentials.

But those writing about communicative competence focus on how interactants can display competence by being open, honest, friendly, and the like. The more one displays such qualities, the 'better' communicator one is thought to be. Intentionally negative messages are seen as the product of unskilled individuals, and in the extreme as symptoms of psychopathology. Several workers have begun to point out limitations of this view. Competence, for example, is more appropriately seen as the ability to avoid problems, to conduct encounters and relationships in a manner which is adequate in context, rather than excellent or perfect (Wiemann and Kelly 1981). Much of what is said is neither clearly true nor false, but rather is constructed to appear to address issues at hand while saying little. In fact, we argued in Chapter 1 that speakers and hearers sometimes co-operate in constructing messages that are ambiguous, that omit as much as they reveal; certainly we should be more alert theoretically to issues of what is *not* said (and/or tabooed) as this can often be as interpretively rich as what is said, and hence traditionally analysed (Cronen *et al.* 1988). Redding (1972) has shown that in organization, clear, concise, honest communication is as frequently the *cause* of difficulties as it is the solution to them. From this view, then, the idea of 'communication' loses much of its meaning while 'miscommunication' is seen as a theoretically rich but underexplored concept with should fall squarely within the precincts of normal language behaviour, and not be compartmentalized, in SPL, as an aberration from it.

Units of analysis

The unit of most language study analyses is the individual. This is understandable given the psychological base of SPL, but the attention paid by discourse analysts and others to idiosyncracy (Cronen *et al.* 1988) and interindividual variability in the qualitative use of language forms is sadly neglected – most clearly in studies which aggregate numerical means and merely provide statements of standard deviation (see also Potter and Wetherell 1987). As important as this is to address, we should also be alert to relational and network systems operating. For instance, Giles and Fitzpatrick (1984) showed that when rating a married couple talking on audiotape, listeners (in a way that contrasts vividly with the individualistic bias inherent in research that we discussed in Chapter 2) formed cogent cognitive representations of the couple's marital type on the basis of language cues in the dialogue. In other words, we use language diagnostically to tap into relational meanings and in ways that doubtless mediate couple presentations in language usage. Fitzpatrick (1990) has discussed the ways in which spouses form marital schemata (sometimes divergently) to guide and interpret each others' language behaviours. Indeed, her use of such notions where individuals define themselves in terms of a couple or spousal unit has much in common with our position on ethnic identity in Chapter 4. Similarly, Wiemann and Bradac (1987) also conceive of communicative competence not as an individual skill but rather as a capacity to achieve, negotiatively with others, a satisfactory level of relational communication, which is, of course, more than the sum of the language contributions of the two individuals analysed separately.

This facet of communication would then be well complemented by attention to the *networks* in which communicators are involved, as modelled in Chapter 5, inherent in Chapter 6, and explicitly documented in Milroy's (1980) compelling analysis of sociolinguistic variation in Northern Ireland. Bourhis (1989) has recently been exploring what he terms the 'linguistic work environments' of speakers in Canada. He shows that the number of one's co-workers who are Francophone or Anglophone, and bilingual or not, can have important effects on whether one, as a bilingual Anglophone, accommodates or not to the mother tongue of an individual Francophone. Yet the work environment of a Francophone – and even the status of the co-workers (for example, as subordinate or superior) – had very little effect on whether s/he converged to an Anglophone; the overriding tendency here was that Francophone did converge.

This kind of linguistic network analysis is begging for implementation, with appropriate transformations, in other communicative spheres, including support and caring as we have just discussed them. The job environment is one rarely investigated in SPL studies, but how language patterns operate there can have a significant knock-on effect in other domains, as pointed out by Fenstermaker *et al.* (in press) in the context of 'doing gender' work. Relatedly, we considered Gottlieb's (in press) analysis of how professional males' work environments continually reinforce certain emotional expressions and sanction others, and how this can have a detrimental effect on their attempts at supportive responses to their wive's affective ventilations. The domestic scene itself is often a system of intergenerational networks, the rewards and tensions of which can again influence the reception and production of language behaviours outside this system. The point is that relational schemata, network characteristics and their perceptions are integral to everyday communication in ways that have yet to be reflected in the largely individualistic tradition of SPL.

Epistemological dilemmas

Throughout this book, two broad philosophies of research and knowledge have been reported which are, frankly, uneasy bedfellows. On the one hand, we have studies which treat, say, social identities as given to the extent that these are manipulated under laboratory-like conditions and their effects measured sociopsycholinguistically. On the other hand, we have another, more subjectivist, orientation which disavows itself of this tradition and sees identities and contexts as evolving organically out of communication practices (see Gudykunst and Nishida 1989, for a consideration of the objectivist versus subjectivist debate). Representing this second perspective, Potter and Wetherell (1987) deconstructed many sociopsychological concepts which have tended to be treated as frozen, immutable entities, and reconceptualized them as discursively constituted processes. These insights have in fact seen the light of day previously within many traditions, including symbolic interactionism, though the current revival of enthusiasm for qualitative and constructivist approaches is intellectually (and intuitively) very appealing. What is required now is an empirical fleshing-out of this epistemology so that we have far more data to examine the processes that its rhetoric refers to. Herbert Clark and associates offer a model of this kind of programmatic research (see Chapter 3) with respect to the amorphous and alluring notions of 'negotiative talk' and 'speaker–hearer collaborations'.

The discursive perspective is a vital one for SPL, and much of our own work in gerontology and language attitudes has been orientated in this direction. On the other hand, Potter and Wetherell's tendency to dichotomize cognition and discourse seems unnecessary. In fact, analyses of language in context *require* the integration of the two. To the extent that discourse is projected by its proponents in revolutionary terms, and reacted to by 'traditionalists' as 'unscientific' and 'soft', it will be an ever-increasing problem for SPL. Internal conflicts may marr SPL's potential to impact even more strongly on mainstream social psychology. Learning to appreciate a diversity of approaches, and attempting to integrate wherever possible is a worthwhile first step, because there is already evidence of different factions distancing from each other's insights. But this epistemological dilemma (confronting the social and human sciences generally) will not be breached easily, if at all. We must engage the problematic, and the following is nothing more than a brief and preliminary attempt in this direction, illustrated with respect to language and social identity.

It may be useful to shift the debate away from methodological dogma (what is or is not permissible by way of analysis and interpretation) on to interactants' cognitions (what is or is not cognitively represented regarding language behaviour). This can give us the two (admittedly gross) orthogonal dimensions in Figure 7.1. Some theorists discuss pre-interactional psychological states (such as moods, or feelings of ethnic belongingness) affecting language behaviours (see Chapter 6). These can, it is argued, guide us sociolinguistically through the entirety of a long interactional engagement, where our preconceptions may be substantiated or may, of course, be severely redressed. Either way, it seems entirely plausible that some of us have identities that are fairly clearly represented and which we can call upon recurringly on different occasions. These are certainly not immutable, but it is not theoretically unreasonable to investigate them (or seek their existence) in positivistically orientated methodologies such as the laboratory. On other occasions, it is certainly more apposite to view identities as emergent, being socially constructed or radically transformed in real time. Such identities are probably less well representable and are less likely to shepherd language choices in ways we can empirically recover (lower left-hand quadrant, Figure 7.1).

The left pole of the horizontal axis in Figure 7.1 would be the domain of constructivism *par excellence*. The cognitive perspective on this dimension (as well as on the vertical) is an attempt to dilute any dichotomy between discourse and cognition itself. But since interactants both plan and retrospectively review identity aspects of their interactions on occasions, the upper pole of the vertical axis is also identifiable. Certainly, it is possible to find intuitive instances where the upper left-hand quadrant will provide the best fit to the cognitive realities of language in context. Speakers may confidently access a firm identity based on being socialized into pre-existing, prototypical categories and meanings of group identity, but be

Figure 7.1   Dimensions relevant to understanding constructivist and positivistic views of language and identity

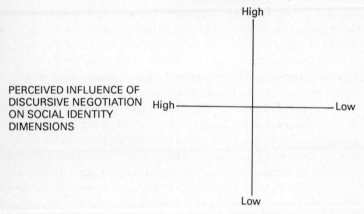

working avidly and creatively on its constitution in many other domains, privately as well as interactionally. Many elderly people discussed in Chapter 6 might well fall into this quadrant. The upper right-hand quadrant would include those strident and perhaps vocal ingroup supporters whose group boundaries (and their social meanings) are not up for negotiation.

Interestingly, Billig (1989) provides us with a case study of an individual expressing supposedly strong views which, on closer examination, are not only rhetorically variable but are dependent on (presumably fluctuating) views of the opposition. In other words, real extremes may in actuality be hard to find, despite the unwavering hard line espoused by different proponents. The lower right-hand quadrant could be accommodated by those who are categorized by *others* (for example, as 'old') but who do not self-define in this way (cf. Table 4.1 in Chapter 4). They may have no need to work through an identity, and have not succumbed to a core aspect of an (elderly) identity that they can firmly represent. In terms of this heuristic, constructivism and positivism are variable properties of participants' cognitions, not self-selected sets of analytical blinkers. Neither extreme ideological position seems wholly tenable, and therefore the challenge will be to maintain a dialogue, rather than further to problematize the conflict.

In conclusion

The thrust of this book, then, has been that language, languages and language behaviours are social constructions which are integral to evolving attitudes, contexts, identities and health, to name but a few. Our social lives are built around the symbolic functioning of language; in our language we give life, meaning and value to our relationships, allegiances, institutions and, of course, ourselves; the social conditions that structure all of these again find their shape in the language we use. Sustained attention to linguistic issues is one of the newer elements of social psychology, but a dimension in which social psychology can make a significant, distinctive contribution to social science generally. The social psychology of language has far to travel, but we hope the contextual, intergroup, cultural, and lifespan perspectives in this book have forged some connections between apparently disparate areas of study, and in ways that are helpful to future developments, both for interdisciplinary language scholars and for social psychologists new to language research. We also hope to have stimulated further reading in literatures we have not sufficiently represented here. An emerging generation of committed language researchers involved in the theoretics of attitude formation and change, relational development and decline, intergroup relations of all sorts, social support, selfhood, personality and so forth would be a major asset. In this way, as social psychologists and social scientists generally, we would be able to function more effectively in applied programmes and interventions, in areas to do with health, the environment, peace and social equality, as well as in counselling projects with individuals, couples, communities, organizations and institutions. This will be so because we will have the resources to explore and explain the complex but ubiquitous intersection of cognition, language and society. To our minds, the state of the art is already such that we should be more involved in policy and action at national and international levels, in areas like language planning, care for the elderly, diplomacy, medicine and information technologies.

BIBLIOGRAPHY

Aboud, F. E. (1976). Social developmental aspects of language. *Papers in Linguistics*, 9, 15–37.

Aboud, F. E., Clément, R. and Taylor D. M. (1974). Evaluational reactions to discrepancies between social class and language. *Sociometry*, 37, 239–50.

Abrams, D. and Hogg, M. A. (1987). Language attitudes, frames of reference and social identity: A Scottish dimension. *Journal of Language and Social Psychology*, 6, 201–14.

Adorno, W. (1973). The attitudes of selected Mexican and Mexican-American parents in regards to bilingual/bicultural attitudes. Dissertation, US International University.

Albert, R. D. (1986). Communication and attributional differences between Hispanics and Anglo-Americans. In Y. Y. Kim (ed.), *Interethnic communication: Current research*. Beverly Hills, CA: Sage, pp. 42–59.

Albo, X. (1979). The future of the oppressed languages in the Andes. In W. C. McCormack and S. A. Wurm (eds), *Language and society: Anthropological issues*. The Hague: Mouton, pp. 309–30.

Albrecht, T. L. Adelman, M. B. and associates (eds) (1987). *Communicating social support*. Newbury Park, CA: Sage.

Allard, R. and Landry, R. (1986). Subjective ethnolinguistic vitality viewed as a belief system. *Journal of Multilingual and Multicultural Development*, 7, 1–12.

Allport, G. (1954). *The nature of prejudice*. Reading, MA: Addison-Wesley.

Anderson, A. and Garrod, S. C. (1987). The dynamics of referential meaning in spontaneous conversation: Some preliminary studies. In R. G. Reilly (ed.), *Communication failure in dialogue and discourse, detection and repair processes*. Amsterdam: North Holland.

Anderson, A. B. (1979). The survival of ethnolinguistic minorities: Canadian and comparative research. In H. Giles and B. Saint-Jacques (eds), *Language and ethnic relations*. Oxford: Pergamon, pp. 67–86.

Antaki, C. (1985). Ordinary explanation in conversation: Causal structures and their defence. *European Journal of Social Psychology*, **15**, 213–30.

Argyle, M. and Crossland, J. (1987). The dimensions of positive emotions. *British Journal of Social Psychology*, **26**, 127–37.

Argyle, M., Furnham, A. and Graham, J. A. (eds) (1981). *Social situations*. Cambridge: Cambridge University Press.

Argyle, M. and Henderson, M. (1985). *The anatomy of relationships*. Harmondsworth: Penguin.

Arntson, P. (1989). Improving citizens' health competencies. *Health Communication*, **1**, 29–34.

Arntson, P. and Droge, D. (1987). Social support in self-help groups: The role of communication in enabling perceptions of control. In T. L. Albrecht, M. B. Adelman and associates (eds), *Communicating social support*. Newbury Park, CA: Sage, pp. 148–70.

Aronson, E. and Linder, D. (1965). Gain and loss of esteem as determinants of interpersonal attractiveness. *Journal of Experimental Social Psychology*, **1**, 156–71.

Atkinson, K. and Coupland, N. (1988). Accommodation as ideology. *Language and Communication*, **8**, 821–8.

Baker, C. (1988). *Key issues in bilingualism and bilingual education*. Clevedon: Multilingual Matters.

Baker, P. M. (1985). The status of age: Preliminary results. *Journal of Gerontology*, **40**, 506–8.

Banks, S. P. (1987). Achieving 'unmarkedness' in organizational discourse: A praxis perspective on ethnolinguistic identity. *Journal of Language and Social Psychology*, **6**, 171–90.

Barth, F. (1969). *Ethnic groups and boundaries: The social organization of culture differences*. Boston: Little, Brown and Company.

Baskauskas, L. (1977). Multiple identities: Adjusted Lithuanian refugees in Los Angeles. *Urban Anthropology*, **6**, 141–54.

Basso, K. H. (1979). *Portraits of 'the whiteman'*. Cambridge: Cambridge University Press.

Bavelas, J. (1990). *Equivocation*. Newbury Park, CA: Sage.

Baxter, L. A. (1984). Trajectories of relationship disengagment. *Journal of Social and Clinical Psychology*, **2**, 29–48.

Baxter, L. A. (1985). Accomplishing relationship disengagement. In S. Duck and D. Perlmann (eds), *Understanding personal relationships*. Beverly Hills, CA: Sage.

Bayles, K. A. and Kaszniak, A. W. (1987). *Communication and cognition in normal aging and dementia*. London: Taylor and Francis.

Beebe, L. (1981). Social and situational factors affecting communicative strategy of dialect code-switching. *International Journal of the Sociology of Language*, 32, 139–49.

Beebe, L. and Giles, H. (1984). Speech accommodation theories: A discussion in terms of second language acquisition. *International Journal of the Sociology of Language*, 46, 5–32.

Bell, A. (1984). Language style as audience design. *Language in Society*, 13, 145–204.

Berger, C. R. (1979) Beyond initial interaction: Uncertainty, understanding, and the development of interpersonal relationships. In H. Giles and R. St Clair (eds), *Language and social psychology*. Oxford: Blackwell, pp. 122–44.

Berger, C. R. and Bradac, J. J. (1982). *Language and social knowledge*. London: Edward Arnold.

Berger, C. R. and Roloff, M. E. (1980). Social cognition, self-awareness and interpersonal communication. In B. Dervin and M. J. Wright (eds), *Progress in communication science, Vol. 2*. Norwood, NJ: Ablex, pp. 1–50.

Berk-Seligson, S. (1984). Subjective reactions to phonological variation in Costa Rican Spanish. *Journal of Psycholinguistic Research*, 13, 415–42.

Berk-Seligson, S. (1988). The impact of politeness in witness testimony: The influence of the court interpreter. *Multilingua*, 7, 411–39.

Berman, L. and Sobkowska-Ashcroft, I. (1986). The old in language and literature. *Language and Communication*, 6, 139–44.

Berry, J. W., Kim, U. and Boski, P. (1987). Psychological acculturation of immigrants. In Y. Y. Kim and W. B. Gudykunst (eds), *Cross-cultural adaptation: Current approaches*. Newbury Park, CA: Sage, pp. 62–89.

Billig, M. (1976). *Social psychology and intergroup relations*. London: Academic Press.

Billig, M. (1987). *Arguing and thinking: A rhetorical approach to social psychology*. Cambridge: Cambridge University Press.

Billig, M. (1989). The argumentative nature of holding strong views: A case study. *European Journal of Social Psychology*, 19, 203–24.

Bilous, F. R. and Krauss, R. M. (1988). Dominance and accommodation in the conversational behaviours of same- and mixed-gender dyads. *Language and Communication*, 8, 183–94.

Blazer, D. G. (1982). Social support and mortality in an elderly community population. *American Journal of Epidemiology*, 115, 684–94.

Bond, M. H. (1983). How language variation affects inter-cultural differentiation of values by Hong Kong bilinguals. *Journal of Language and Social Psychology*, 2, 57–66.

Bond, M. H. and King, A. Y. C. (1985). Coping with the threat of Westernization in Hong Kong. *International Journal of Intercultural Relations*, 9, 351–64.

Bones, J. (1986). Language and Rastafari. In D. Sutcliffe and A. Wong (eds), *The language of black experience*. Oxford: Blackwell.

Booth-Butterfield, M. and Jordan, F. (1989). Communication adaptation among racially homogeneous and heterogeneous groups. *The Southern Communication Journal*, 54, 253–72.

Bourhis, R. Y. (1979). Language in ethnic interaction. A social psychological approach. In H. Giles and B. Saint-Jacques (eds), *Language and ethnic relations*. Oxford, Pergamon, pp. 117–41.

Bourhis, R. Y. (1983). Language attitudes and self-reports of French-English language usage in Quebec. *Journal of Multilingual and Multicultural Development*, 4, 163–80.

Bourhis, R. Y. (1984a). Cross-cultural communication in Montreal: Two field studies since Bill 101. *International Journal of the Sociology of Language*, 46, 13–16.

Bourhis, R. Y. (Ed.) (1984b). *Conflict and language planning in Quebec*. Clevedon: Multilingual Matters.

Bourhis, R. Y. (1985). The sequential nature of language choice in cross-cultural communication. In R. L. Street, Jr. and J. N. Cappella (eds), *Sequence and pattern in communicative behaviour*. London: Arnold, pp. 120–41.

Bourhis. R. Y. (1989). Bilingual communication in organizational settings: Aspects of the Canadian case. In S. Ting-Toomey and F. Korzenny (eds), *Language, communication, and culture*. Newbury Park, CA: Sage, pp. 244–64.

Bourhis, R. Y. and Giles, H. (1976). The language of co-operation in Wales: A field study. *Language Sciences*, 42, 13–16.

Bourhis, R. Y. and Giles, H. (1977). The language of intergroup distinctiveness. In H. Giles (ed.), *Language, ethnicity and intergroup relations*. London: Academic Press, pp. 119–35.

Bourhis, R. Y., Giles, H. and Lambert, W. E. (1975). Social consequences of accommodating one's style of speech: A cross-national investigation. *International Journal of the Sociology of Language*, 6, 55–72.

Bourhis, R. Y., Giles, H., Leyens, J. P. and Tajfel, H. (1979). Psycholinguistic distinctiveness: Language divergence in Belgium. In H. Giles and R. St Clair (eds), *Language and social psychology*. Oxford: Blackwell, pp. 158–85.

Bourhis, R. Y., Giles, H. and Rosenthal, D. (1981). Notes on the construction of a 'Subjective Vitality Questionnaire' for ethnolinguistic groups. *Journal of Multilingual and Multicultural Development*, 2, 144–55.

Bourhis, R. Y., Giles, H. and Tajfel, H. (1973). Language as a determinant of Welsh identity. *European Journal of Social Psychology*, 3, 447–60.

Bourhis, R. Y., Roth, S. and MacQueen, G. (1988). Communication in the hospital setting: A survey of medical and everyday language use amongst patients, nurses and doctors. *Social Science and Medicine*, **24**, 1–8.

Bourhis, R. Y. and Sachdev, I (1984). Vitality perceptions and language attitudes. *Journal of Language and Social Psychology*, **3**, 97–126.

Boyer, P. (1984). From activism to apathy: the American people and nuclear weapons. *Journal of American History*, **70**, 821–44.

Bradac, J. J. (1990). Language attitudes and impression formation. In H. Giles and W. P. Robinson (eds), *Handbook of language and social psychology*. Chichester: Wiley, pp. 387–412.

Bradac, J. J., Mulac, A. and House, A. (1988). Lexical diversity and magnitude of convergent versus divergent style-shifting: Perceptual and evaluative consequences. *Language and Communication*, **8**, 213–28.

Bradac, J. and Wisegarver, R. (1984). Ascribed status, lexical diversity, and accent: Determinants of perceived status, solidarity, and control of speech style. *Journal of Language and Social Psychology*, **3**, 239–56.

Brenders, D. A. (1989). Perceived control and the interpersonal dimension of health care. *Health Communication*, **1**, 117–35.

Brennan, E. M., Ryan, E. B. and Dawson, W. E. (1975). Scaling of apparent accentedness by magnitude estimation and sensory modality matching. *Journal of Psycholinguistic Research*, **4**, 27–36.

Bronfenbrenner, U. (1979). *The ecology of human development: Experiments by nature and design*. Cambridge, MA: Harvard University Press.

Brown, J. R. and Rogers, L. E. (1991). Problem talk and problem contexts. In N. Coupland, H. Giles and J. Wiemann (eds), *'Miscommunication' and problematic talk*. Newbury Park, CA: Sage.

Brown, P. and Fraser, C. (1979). Speech as a marker of situation. In K. R. Scherer and H. Giles (eds), *Social markers in speech*. Cambridge: Cambridge University Press, pp. 33–108.

Brown, P. and Levinson, S. (1987). *Politeness: Some universals in language usage*. Cambridge: Cambridge University Press.

Brown, P. M. and Dell, G. S. (1987). Adapting production to comprehension: The explicit mention of instruments. *Cognitive Psychology*, **19**, 441–72.

Brown, R. and Gilman, A. (1989). Politeness theory and Shakespeare's four major tragedies. *Language in Society*, **18**, 159–212.

Brown, R. J. (1978). Divided we fall: An analysis of relations between sections of a factory workforce. In H. Tajfel (ed.), *Differentiation between social groups*, London: Academic Press, pp. 395–430.

Buller, D. B. and Aune, R. K. (1988). The effects of vocalics and nonverbal sensitivity on compliance: A speech accommodation theory explanation. *Human Communication Research*, **14**, 301–32.

Burgoon, M. (1983). Argument from Aristotle to analysis of variance: A modest reinterpretation. *Journal of Language and Social Psychology*, **2**, 105–22.

Byrne, D. (1971). *The attraction paradigm.* New York: Academic Press.

Cairns, E. and Dubiez, B. (1976). The influence of speaker's accent on recall by Catholic and Protestant schoolchildren in Northern Ireland. *British Journal of Social and Clinical Psychology,* 15, 441–2.

Caporael, L. R., Lukaszewski, M. P. and Culbertson, G. H. (1983). Secondary baby talk: Judgments by institutionalized elderly and their caregivers. *Journal of Personality and Social Psychology,* 44, 746–54.

Cappella, J. N. and Greene, J. (1982). A discrepancy-arousal explanation of mutual influence in expressive behaviour for adult–adult and infant–adult interaction. *Communication Monographs,* 49, 89–114.

Carranza, M. A. and Ryan, E. B. (1975). Evaluative reactions of bilingual Anglo and Mexican-American adolescents towards speakers of English and Spanish. *International Journal of the Sociology of Language,* 6, 83–104.

Cartwright, A. and Smith, C. (1988). *Elderly people, their medicines, and their doctors.* London: Routledge & Kegan Paul.

Chaffee, S. and Berger, C. R. (eds) 1987). *Handbook of communication science.* Newbury Park, CA: Sage.

Cheung, Y.-W. and New, P. K.-M. (1984). The magic of the 'foreign devils': The missionary doctor–Chinese patient relationship in early twentieth century China. In *Proceedings of the 6th. International Symposium on Asian Studies.* Hong Kong: Asian Research Service, pp. 95–108.

Chomsky, N. (1965). *Aspects of the theory of syntax.* Cambridge, MA: MIT Press.

Choy, S. and Dodd, D. (1976). Standard-English speaking and non-standard Hawaiian-English-speaking children: Comprehension of both dialects and teachers' evaluations. *Journal of Educational Psychology,* 68, 184–93.

Clark, H. H. and Wilkes-Gibbs, D. (1986). Referring as a collaborative process. *Cognition,* 22, 1–39.

Clark, R. A. (1984). *Persuasive messages.* New York: Harper and Row.

Clément, R. (1980). Ethnicity, contact and communicative competence in a second language. In H. Giles. W. P. Robinson and P. M. Smith (eds), *Language: Social psychological perspectives.* Oxford: Pergamon, pp. 147–54.

Cody, M. J. and McLaughlin, M. (1990). Interpersonal accounting. In H. Giles and W. P. Robinson (eds), *Handbook of language and social psychology.* Chichester: Wiley, pp. 227–57.

Cohen, E. and Cooper, R. L. (1986). Language and tourism. *Annals of Tourism Research,* 13, 535–63.

Cohen, R. (1987). Problems of intercultural communication in Egyptian–American diplomatic relations. *International Journal of Intercultural Relations,* 11, 29–47.

Collier, M. J. and Thomas, M. (1988). Cultural identity: An interpretive perspective. In Y. Y. Kim and W. B. Gudykunst (eds), *Theories in Intercultural Communication*. Newbury Park, CA: Sage, pp. 99–122.

Coupland, N. (1984). Accommodation at work: Some phonological data and their implications. *International Journal of the Sociology of Language*, 46, 49–70.

Coupland, N. (1985). 'Hark, hark the lark': Social motivations for phonological style shifting. *Language and communication*, 5, 153–71.

Coupland, N. (1988). *Dialect in use*. Cardiff: University of Wales Press.

Coupland, N. and Coupland J. (1990). Language and later life. In H. Giles and W. P. Robinson (eds), *Handbook of language and social psychology*. Chichester: Wiley, pp. 451–70.

Coupland, N., Coupland, J. and Giles, H. (1989). Telling age in later life: Identity and face implications. *Text*, 9, 129–51.

Coupland, N., Coupland, J., Giles, H. and Henwood, K. (1988). Accommodating the elderly: Invoking and extending a theory. *Language in Society*, 17, 1–41.

Coupland, N., Coupland, J., Giles H. and Henwood, K. (in press (a)). Intergenerational talk: Goal consonance and intergroup dissonance. In K. Tracy (ed.), *Understanding face-to-face interaction: Issues linking goals and discourse*. Hillsdale, NJ, Erlbaum.

Coupland, J., Coupland, N., Giles, H. and Henwood, K. (in press (b)). Formulating age: Dimensions of age-identity in elderly talk. *Discourse Processes*.

Coupland, N., Coupland, J., Giles, H., Henwood, K. and Wiemann, J. (1988). Elderly self-disclosure: Interactional and intergroup issues. *Language and Communication*, 8, 109–33.

Coupland, N. and Giles, H. (1988). Introduction: The communicative contexts of accommodation. *Language and Communication*, 8, 175–82.

Coupland, N., Giles, H. and Wiemann, J. M. (Eds) (1991). *'Miscommunication' and problematic talk*. Newbury Park, CA: Sage.

Coupland, N., Wiemann, J. M. and Giles, H. (1991). Talk as 'problem' and communication as 'miscommunication': An integrative analysis. In N. Coupland, H. Giles and J. M. Wiemann (eds), *'Miscommunication' and problematic talk*. Newbury Park, CA: Sage.

Covey, H. C., (1988). Historical terminology used to represent older people. *Gerontologist*, 28, 291–7.

Creber, C. and Giles, H. (1983). Social context and language attitudes: The role of formality–informality of the setting. *Language Sciences*, 5, 155–62.

Cronen, V. E., Chen, V. and Pearce W. B. (1988). Coordinated management of meaning: A critical theory. In Y. Y. Kim and W. B. Gudykunst (eds), *Theories in intercultural communication*. Newbury Park, CA: Sage pp. 66–98.

Davis, K. (1988). Paternalism under the microscope. In A. D. Todd and S. Fisher (eds), *Gender and discourse: The power of talk*. Norwood, NJ: Ablex, pp. 19–54.

De Vos, G. (1975). Ethnic pluralism: Conflict and accommodation. In G. de Vos and K. Romanucci-Ross (eds), *Ethnic identity: Cultural continuity and change*. Palo Alto, CA: Mayfield.

de Vries, J. (1984). Factors affecting the survival of linguistic minorities: A preliminary comparative analysis of data for western Europe. *Journal of Multilingual and Multicultural Development*, 5, 207–16.

de Vries, J. (1987). Problems of measurement in the study of linguistic minorities. *Journal of Multilingual and Multicultural Development*, 8, 23–31.

Denison, N. (1977). Language death or language suicide? *International Journal of the Sociology of Language*, 12, 13–22.

Dijker, A. J. M. (1987). Emotional reactions to ethnic minorities. *European Journal of Social Psychology*, 17, 305–25.

Doise, W., Sinclair, A. and Bourhis, R. Y. (1976). Evaluation of accent convergence and divergence in cooperative and competitive intergroup situations. *British Journal of Social and Clinical Psychology*, 15, 247–52.

Dubé-Simard, L. (1983). Genesis of social categorization, threat to identity, and perceptions of social injustice: Their role in intergroup communication breakdown. *Journal of Language and Social Psychology*, 2, 183–206.

Duck, S. (1982). A topography of relationship disengagement and dissolution. In S. Duck (ed.), *Personal relationships, Vol. 2*. London: Academic Press.

Duck, S. (ed.) (1984). *Personal relationships, Vol. 5*. London: Academic Press.

Dunkel-Schetter, C., Folkman, S. and Lazarus, R. S. (1987). Correlates of social support receipt. *Journal of Personality and Social Psychology*, 53, 71–80.

Dunkel-Schetter, C. and Wortman, C. B. (1982). The interpersonal dynamics of cancer: Problems in social relationships and their impact on the patient. In H. S. Friedman and M. R. DiMatteo (eds), *Interpersonal issues in health care*. New York: Academic Press, pp. 69–100.

Edwards, J. R. (1977). Ethnic identity and bilingual education. In H. Giles (ed.), *Language, ethnicity and intergroup relations*. London: Academic Press, pp. 253–82.

Edwards, J. R. (1982). Language attitudes and their implications among English speakers. In E. B. Ryan and H. Giles (eds), *Attitudes towards language variation*. London: Edward Arnold, pp. 20–33.

Edwards, J. R. (1985). *Language, society and identity*. Oxford: Basil Blackwell.

Edwards, J. R. and Jacobsen, M. (1987). Standard and regional standard speech: Distinctions and similarities. *Language in Society*, 16, 369–80.

Eiser, J. R. (1980). *Cognitive social psychology*. London: McGraw-Hill.

Elwell, C. M., Brown, R. J. and Rutter, D. R. (1984). Effects of accent and visual information on impression formation. *Journal of Language and Social Psychology*, 3, 297–9.

Emry, R. and Wiseman, R. L. (1987). An intercultural understanding of ablebodied and disabled persons' communication. *International Journal of Intercultural Relations*, 11, 7–27.

Ervin-Tripp, S. M. (1969). Sociolinguistics. *Advances in Experimental Social Psychology*, 4, 91–165.

Ervin-Tripp, S. M. (1980). Speech acts, social meaning and social learning. In H. Giles, W. P. Robinson and P. M. Smith (eds), *Language: Social psychological perspectives*. Oxford: Pergamon, pp. 389–96.

Fanon, F. (1961). *Black skin, white masks*. New York: Grove Press.

Fasold, R. W. (1984). *The sociolinguistics of society*. Oxford: Blackwell.

Fenstermaker, S., West, C. and Zimmerman, D. (in press). In R. Blumberg (ed.), *Gender, family, and economy: The triple overlap*. Newbury Park, CA: Sage.

Ferrara, K. (in press). Accommodation in therapy. In H. Giles, J. Coupland and N. Coupland (eds), *Contexts of accommodation: Developments in applied sociolinguistics*. Cambridge: Cambridge University Press.

Field, D. and Mikler, M. (1988). Continuity and change in social support between young-old and old-old and very-old age. *Journal of Gerontology*, 43, 100–106.

Fielder, K., Semin, G. R. and Bolten, S. (1989). Language use and reification of social information: Top-down and bottom-up processing in person cognition. *European Journal of Social Psychology*, 19, 271–95.

Fielding, G. and Evered, C. (1980). The influence of patients' speech upon doctors. In R. N. St. Clair and H. Giles (eds), *The social and psychological contexts of language*. Hillsdale, NJ: Erlbaum, pp. 51–72.

Fishbein, M. and Ajzen, I. (1975). *Beliefs, attitude, intention and behaviour*. Reading, MA: Addison-Wesley.

Fisher, S. and Todd, A. (1986). Introduction: Communication in institutional contexts, social interaction and social structure. In S. Fisher and A. Todd (eds), *Discourse and institutional authority, medicine, education and law*. Norwood, NJ, Ablex, pp. ix–xvii.

Fishman, J. A. (1968). Nationality-nationalism and nation-nationism. In J. A. Fishman, C. A. Ferguson and J. Das Gupta (eds), *Language problems of developing nations*, New York: Wiley, pp. 39–52.

Fishman, J. A. (1971). *Sociolinguistics: A brief introduction*. Rowley: Newbury House.

Fishman, J. A. (1972). *Language and nationalism*. Rowley, MA: Newbury House.

Fishman, J. A. (1977). Language and ethnicity. In H. Giles (ed.), *Language, ethnicity and intergroup relations*. London: Academic Press, pp. 15–58.

Fishman, J. A. (1982). Whorfianism of the third kind: Ethnolinguistic diversity as a worldwide societal asset (The Whorfian hypothesis: Varieties of validation, confirmation, and disconfirmation II). *Language in Society*, 33, 1–14.

Fishman, J. A. (1989). *Language and ethnicity in minority sociolinguistic perspective*. Clevedon: Multilingual Matters.

Fishman, P. (1980). Conversational insecurity. In H. Giles, W. P. Robinson and P. M. Smith (eds), *Language: Social psychological perspectives*, Oxford: Pergamon, pp. 127–32.

Fitzpatrick, M. A. (1990). Models of marital interaction. In H. Giles and W. P. Robinson (eds), *Handbook of language and social psychology*. Chichester: Wiley, pp. 433–50.

Flores, N. and Hopper, R. (1975). If you speak Spanish they'll think you are a German: Attitudes towards language choice in multilingual environments. *Journal of Multilingual and Multicultural Development*, 4, 115–28.

Folkman, S., Lazarus, R. S., Pimley, S. and Novacek, J. (1987). Age differences in stress and coping processes. *Psychology and Ageing*, 2, 171–84.

Forgas, J. P. (1979). Multidimensional scaling of social episodes: A new method in social psychology. In G. P. Ginsburg (ed.), *Emerging strategies in social psychology*. London: Wiley.

Forgas, J. P. (1988). Episode representations in intercultural communication. In Y. Y. Kim and W. B. Gudykunst (eds), *Theories in intercultural communication*. Newbury Park, CA: Sage, pp. 186–212.

Franklyn-Stokes, A., Harriman, J., Giles, H. and Coupland, N. (1988). Information-seeking across the lifespan. *Journal of Social Psychology*, 128, 419–21.

Friedman, H. S., Riggio, R. E. and Casella, D. F. (1988) Non verbal skill, personal charisma, and initial attraction. *Personality and Social Psychology Bulletin*, 14, 203–11.

Friedman, H. S. and Tucker, J. S. (1990). Language and deception. In H. Giles and W. P. Robinson (eds), *Handbook of language and social psychology*. Chichester: Wiley, pp. 257–70.

Frye, M. (1983). *The politics of reality: Essays in feminist theory*. Trumansburg, NY: Crossing Press.

Furnham, A. (1986). Situational determinants of intergroup communication. In W. B. Gudykunst (ed.), *Intergroup communication*. London: Edward Arnold, pp. 96–113.

Gallois, C. and Callan, V. J. (1988). Communication accommodation and the prototypical speaker: Predicting evaluations of status solidarity. *Language and Communication*, 8, 271–84.

Gallois, C. and Callan, V. J. (in press). Interethnic accommodation: The role of norms. In H. Giles, J. Coupland and N. Coupland (eds), *Contexts of accommodation: Developments in applied sociolinguistics*. Cambridge: Cambridge University Press.

Gallois, C., Callan, V. and Johnstone, M. (1984). Personality judgements of Australian Aborigine and white speakers: Ethnicity, sex and context. *Journal of Language and Social Psychology*, 3, 39–57.

Gallois, C., Franklyn-Stokes, A., Giles, H. and Coupland, N. (1988). Communication accommodation theory and intercultural encounters: Intergroup and interpersonal considerations. In Y. Y. Kim and W. B. Gudykunst (eds), *Theories in Intercultural Communication*. Newbury Park, CA: Sage, pp. 157–85.

Ganster, D. C. and Victor, B. (1988). The impact of social support on mental and physical health. *British Journal of Medical Psychology*, 61, 17–36.

Gardner, R. C. (1979). Social psychological aspects of second language acquisition. In H. Giles and R. St Clair (eds), *Language and social psychology*. Oxford: Basil Blackwell, pp. 193–220.

Gardner, R. C. (1985). *Social psychology and second language learning: The role of attitudes and motivation*. London: Edward Arnold.

Gardner, R. C. and Lambert, W. E. (1972). *Attitudes and motivation in second language learning*. Rowley, MA: Newbury House.

Garrett, P., Giles, H. and Coupland, N. (1989). The contexts of language learning: Extending the intergroup model of second language acquisition. In S. Ting-Toomey and F. Korzenny (eds), *Language, communication, and culture*. Newbury Park, CA: Sage, pp. 201–21.

Garza, R. T. and Herringer, L. G. (1987). Social identity: A multidimensional approach. *Journal of Social Psychology*, 127, 299–308.

Genesee, F. (1984). The social-psychological significance of code-switching for children. *Applied Psycholinguistics*, 5, 3–20.

Genesee, F. and Bourhis, R. Y. (1988). Evaluative reactions to language choice strategies: The role of sociostructural factors. *Language and Communication*, 8, 229–50.

Genesee, F. and Holobow, N. E. (1989). Change and stability in intergroup perceptions. *Journal of Language and Social Psychology*, 8, 17–38.

Genesee, F., Rogers, P. and Holobow, N. (1983). The social psychology of second language learning: Another point of view. *Language Learning*, 33, 209–24.

Gerbner, G., Gross, L., Signorielli, N. and Morgan, N. (1980). Ageing with television: Images on television drama and conceptions of social reality. *Journal of Communication*, 30, 37–47.

Gilbert, D. T., Krull, D. S. and Pelham, B. W. (1988). Of thoughts unspoken: Social influence and the self-regulation of behaviour. *Journal of Personality and Social Psychology*, 55, 685–94.

Giles, H. (1973). Accent mobility, A model and some data. *Anthropological Linguistics*, 15, 87–105.

Giles, H. (1978). Linguistic differentiation between ethnic groups. In H. Tajfel (ed.), *Differentiation between social groups*. London: Academic Press, pp. 361–93.

Giles, H. (1979). Ethnicity markers in speech. In K. R. Scherer and H. Giles (eds), *Social markers in speech*. Cambridge: Cambridge University Press, pp. 251–90.

Giles, H. Baker, S. and Fielding, G. (1975). Communication length as a behavioural index of accent prejudice. *International Journal of the Sociology of Language*, 6, 73–81.

Giles, H. and Bourhis, R. Y. (1975). Linguistic assimilation: West Indians in Cardiff. *Language Sciences*, 38, 9–12.

Giles, H. and Bourhis, R. Y. (1976). Black speakers with white speech–a real problem? In G. Nickel (ed.), *Proceedings of the 4th. International Congress on Applied Linguistics*, Vol. 1. Stuttgart: Hochschul-Verlag, pp. 575–84.

Giles, H., Bourhis, R. Y. and Taylor, D. M. (1977). Towards a theory of language in ethnic group relations. In H. Giles (ed.), *Language, ethnicity, and intergroup relations*. London, Academic Press, pp. 307–48.

Giles, H. and Byrne, J. L. (1982). The intergroup model of second language acquisition. *Journal of Multilingual and Multicultural Development*, 3, 17–40.

Giles, H. and Coupland, N. (1991). Language attitudes: Discursive, contextual and gerontological considerations. In A. G. Reynolds (ed.), *Bilingualism, multiculturalism, and second language learning*. Hillsdale, NJ: Erlbaum.

Giles, H., Coupland, J. and Coupland, N. (eds) (in press). *Contexts of accommodation: Developments in applied sociolinguistics*. Cambridge: Cambridge University Press.

Giles, H., Coupland, N., Henwood, K., Harriman, J. and Coupland, J. (1990). The social meaning of RP: A intergenerational perspective. In S. Ramsaran (ed.), *Studies in the pronunciation of English: A commemorative volume in honour of A. C. Gimson*. London: Routledge.

Giles H. Coupland, N. and Wiemann, J. (in press) 'Talk is cheap . . .' but 'my word is my bond': Beliefs about talk. In K. Bolton and H. Kwok (eds) *Sociolinguistics today: Eastern and Western perspectives*. London: Routledge.

Giles, H. and Farrar, K. (1979). Some behavioural consequences of speech and dress styles. *British Journal of Social and Clinical Psychology*, 18, 209–10.

Giles, H., and Fitzpatrick, M. A. (1984). Personal, group and couple identities: Towards a relational context for the study of language attitudes and linguistic forms. In D. Schiffrin (ed.), *Meaning, form and use in context: Linguistic applications*. Washington, DC: Georgetown University Press, pp. 253–77.

Giles, H., Harrison, C., Creber, C., Smith, P. M. and Freeman, N. H. (1983). Developmental and contextual aspects of British children's language attitudes. *Language and Communication*, 3, 1–6.

Giles, H. and Hewstone, M. (1982). Cognitive structures, speech and social situations: Two integrative models. *Language Sciences*, 4, 187–219.

Giles, H., and Johnson, P. (1981). The role of language in ethnic group relations. In J. C. Turner and H. Giles (eds), *Intergroup behaviour*. Oxford: Blackwell, pp. 199–243.

Giles, H. and Johnson, P. (1986). Perceived threat, ethnic commitment and interethnic language behaviour. In Y. Kim (ed.), *Interethnic communication: Current research*. Beverley Hills, CA: Sage, pp. 91–116.

Giles, H. and Johnson, P. (1987). Ethnolinguistic identity theory: a social psychological approach to language maintenance. *International Journal of the Sociology of Language*, 68, 66–99.

Giles, H., Leets, L. and Coupland, N. (1990). Minority language group status: A theoretical conspexus. *Journal of Multilingual and Multicultural Development*, 11, 1–19.

Giles, H., Mulac, A., Bradac, J. J. and Johnson, P. (1987). Speech accommodation theory: The next decade and beyond. In *Communication Yearbook, Vol. 10*. Newbury Park, CA: Sage, pp. 13–48.

Giles, H. and Powesland, P. F. (1975). *Speech style and social evaluation*. London: Academic Press.

Giles, H. and Robinson, W. P. (eds) (1990). *Handbook of language and social psychology*. Chichester: Wiley.

Giles, H., Rosenthal, R. and Young, L. (1985). Perceived ethnolinguistic vitality: The Anglo- and Greek-Australian setting. *Journal of Multilingual and Multicultural Development*, 6, 253–69.

Giles, H. and Ryan, E. B. (1982). Prolegomena for developing a social psychological theory of language attitudes. In E. B. Ryan and H. Giles (eds), *Attitudes towards language variation*. London: Edward Arnold, pp. 208–23.

Giles, H. and Sassoon, C. (1983). The effects of speakers' accent, social class, background and message style on British listeners' social judgements. *Language and Communication*, 3, 305–13.

Giles, H., Scherer, K. R. and Taylor, D. M. (1979). Speech markers in social interaction. In K. R. Scherer and H. Giles (eds), *Social markers in speech*. Cambridge, Cambridge University Press, pp. 343–81.

Giles, H. and Smith, P. M. (1979). Accommodation theory: Optimal levels of convergence. In H. Giles and R. St Clair (eds), *Language and social psychology*. Oxford: Blackwell, pp. 45–65.

Giles, H., Smith, P. M., Ford, B., Condor, S. and Thakerar, J. N. (1980).

Speech styles and the fluctuating saliency of sex. *Language Sciences*, 2, 260–82.

Giles, H. and Street, R. (1985). Communicator characteristics and behaviour. In M. L. Knapp and G. R. Miller (eds), *Handbook of interpersonal communication*. Beverly Hills, CA: Sage, pp. 205–61.

Giles, H., Taylor, D. M., and Bourhis, R. Y. (1973). Towards a theory of interpersonal accommodation through language: Some Canadian data. *Language in Society*, 2, 177–92.

Giles, H. and Wiemann, J. (1987). Language, social comparison, and power. In S. Chaffee and C. R. Berger (eds), *Handbook of communication science*. Newbury Park, CA: Sage, pp. 350–84.

Giles, H., Williams, A. and Coupland, N. (1990). Communication, health and the elderly: Frameworks, agenda and a model. In H. Giles, N. Coupland, and J. M. Wiemann (eds), *Communication, health and the elderly*. Manchester: Manchester University Press, pp. 1–28.

Giles, H., Wilson, P. and Conway, A. (1981). Accent and lexical diversity as determinants of impression formation and employment selection. *Language Sciences*, 3, 92–103.

Goffman, E. (1967). *The presentation of self in everyday life*. Harmondsworth: Penguin.

Good, C. (1979). Language as social activity: Negotiating conversation. *Journal of Pragmatics*, 3, 151–67.

Gorter, D. (1987). Aspects of language choice in the Frisian–Dutch bilingual context: Neutrality and asymmetry. *Journal of Multilingual and Multicultural Development*, 8, 121–32.

Gottlieb, B. H. (in press). The contingent nature of social support. In J. Eckenrode (ed.), *Social context of stress*. New York: Plenum.

Gottman, J. (1982). Emotional responsiveness in marital conversations. *Journal of Communication*, 32, 108–20.

Grainger, K., Atkinson, K. and Coupland, N. (1990). Responding to the elderly: Troubles talk in the caring context. In H. Giles, N. Coupland and J. M. Wiemann (eds), *Communication, health and the elderly*. Manchester: Manchester University Press, pp. 192–212.

Grice, H. P. (1971). Meaning. In D. D. Steinberg and L. A. Jakobovitz (eds), *Semantics: An interdisciplinary reader*. Cambridge: Cambridge University Press, pp. 53–9.

Gudykunst, W. B. (1988). Uncertainty and anxiety. In Y. Y. Kim and W. B. Gudykunst (eds), *Theories in intercultural communication*. Newbury Park, CA: Sage, pp. 123–56.

Gudykunst, W. B. and Kim, Y. Y. (1984). *Communicating with strangers: An approach to intercultural communication*. New York: Random House.

Gudykunst, W. B. and Nishida, T. (1989). Theoretical perspectives for studying intercultural communication. In M. K. Asante and W. B.

Gudykunst (eds), *Handbook of international and intercultural communication*. Newbury Park, CA: Sage, pp. 17–46.

Gudykunst, W. B. and Ting-Toomey, S. (1990). Ethnic identity, language, and communication breakdowns. In H. Giles and W. P. Robinson (eds), *Handbook of language and social psychology*. Chichester: Wiley, pp. 309–23.

Gudykunst, W. B., Yoon, Y. C. and Nishida, T. (1987). The influence of individualism–collectivism on perceptions of communication in ingroup and outgroup relationships. *Communication Monographs*, 54, 295–306.

Gumperz, J. J. (ed.) (1982). *Language and social identity*. Cambridge: Cambridge University Press.

Gurin, P., Miller, H. and Gurin, G. (1980). Stratum identification and consciousness. *Social Psychology Quarterly*, 43, 30–47.

Gurr, T. R. (1970). *Why men rebel*. Princeton, NJ: Princeton University Press.

Hakuta, K. (1986). *Mirror of language: The debate on bilingualism*. New York: Basic Books.

Hall, A. A., Epstein, A. M. and McNeill, B. J. (in press). Multidimensionality of health status in an elderly population: Construct validity of a measurement battery. *Medical Care*.

Hall, B. J. and Gudykunst, W. B. (1986). The intergroup theory of second language ability. *Journal of Language and Social Psychology*, 5, 291–302.

Hammer, M. R. (1989). Intercultural communication competence. In M. K. Asante and W. B. Gudykunst (eds), *Handbook of international and intercultural communication*. Newbury Park, CA: Sage.

Hancock, I. F. (1974). Identity, equality and standard language. *Florida FL Reporter*, **Spring/Fall**, 49–52, 101–2.

Hart, R. P., Carlson, R. E. and Eadie, W. F. (1980). Attitudes toward communication and the assessment of rhetorical sensitivity. *Communication Monographs*, 47, 1–22.

Harvey, J. H., Orbuch, T. L. and Weber, A. L. (1990). *Interpersonal accounts*. Oxford: Blackwell.

Haslett, B. (1990). Social class, social status and communicative behaviour. In H. Giles and W. P. Robinson (eds), *Handbook of language and social psychology*. Chichester: Wiley, pp. 329–44.

Hecht, M., Boster, F. J. and LaMer, S. (1989). The effect of extroversion and differentiation on listener-adapted communication. *Communication Reports*, 2, 1–8.

Hecht, M., Ribeau, S. and Alberts, J. K. (1989). An Afro-American perspective on interethnic communication. *Communication Monographs*, 56, 385–410.

Heller, K. and Mansbach, W. E. (1984). The multifaceted nature of social support in a community sample of elderly women. *Journal of Social Issues*, 40, 99–112.

Heller, K., Price, R. H. and McNeill, J. R. (in press). The role of social support in community and clinical intervention. In I. G. Sarason, B. R. Sarason and G. R. Pierce (eds), *Social support: An interactional view*. New York: Wiley.

Hermann, T. (1982). Language and situation: The pars pro toto principle. In C. Fraser and K. R. Scherer (eds), *Advances in the social psychology of language*. Cambridge: Cambridge University Press, pp. 123–58.

Hewes, D. E. Graham, M. L., Monsour, M. and Doelger, J. A. (1989). Cognition and social information-gathering strategies. *Human Communication Research*, 16, 297–320.

Hewstone, M. (1989). *Causal attribution*. Oxford: Blackwell.

Hewstone, M., and Giles, H. (1986). Social groups and social stereotypes in intergroup communication: A review and model of intergroup communication breakdown. In W. B. Gudykunst (ed.) *Intergroup communication*. London: Edward Arnold, pp. 10–26.

Higgins, E. T. and McCann, D. (1984). Social encoding and subsequent attitudes, impressions and memory: 'Context-decision' and motivational aspects of processing. *Journal of Personality and Social Psychology*, 47, 26–39.

Hofstede, G. (1983). Dimensions of national cultures in fifty countries and three regions. In J. B. Derogowski, S. Dziurawiec and R. C. Annis (eds), *Expiscations in cross-cultural psychology*. Lisse:Swets and Zeitlinger, pp. 335–55.

Hogg, M., Joyce, N. and Abrams, D. (1984). Diglossia in Switzerland? A social identity analysis of speaker evaluations. *Journal of Language and Social Psychology*, 3, 185–96.

Holtgraves, T. (1990). The language of self-disclosure. In H. Giles and W. P. Robinson (eds), *Handbook of language and social psychology*. Chichester: Wiley, pp. 191–210.

Hopper, R. (1981). The taken-for-granted. *Human Communication Research*, 7, 195–211.

Hopper, R. (1986). Speech evaluation of intergroup dialect differences: The shibboleth schema. In W. B. Gudykunst (ed.), *Intergroup communication*. London: Edward Arnold, pp. 126–36.

Hopper, R. and Bell, R. A. (1984). Broadening the deception construct. *Quarterly Journal of Speech*, 70, 287–302.

Hopper, R. and Williams, F. (1973). Speech characteristics and employability. *Speech Monographs*, 46, 296–302.

Hurtado, A. and Arce, C. H. (1987). Mexicans, Chicanos, Mexican Americans, or Pochos . . . ? Qué somos? The impact of language and nativity on ethnic labelling. *Aztlan*, 17, 103–29.

Hurtado, A. and Rodriguez, R. (1989). Language as a social problem: The repression of Spanish in south Texas. *Journal of Multilingual and Multicultural Development*, 10, 401–20.

Husband, C. (1977). News media, language and race relations: A case study in identity maintenance. In H. Giles (ed.), *Language, ethnicity and intergroup relations*. London: Academic Press, pp. 211–40.

Huspek, M. R. (1986). Linguistic variation, context and meanings: A case of -ing/in' variation in North American workers' speech. *Language in Society*, 15, 149–64.

Hymes, D. (1972). Models of the interaction of language and social setting. In J. J. Gumperz and D. Hymes (eds), *Directions in sociolinguistics: The ethnography of communication*. New York: Holt, Rinehart and Winston, pp. 35–71.

Ickes, W., Patterson M. L., Rajecki, D. W. and Tanford, S. (1982). Behavioural and cognitive consequences of reciprocal and compensatory responses to preinteraction expectancies. *Social Cognition*, 1, 160–90.

Isaacs, E. A. and Clark, H. H. (1987). References in conversation between experts and novices. *Journal of Experimental Psychology: General*, 116, 26–37.

Jaccard, J. (1981). Attitudes and behaviour: Implications of attitudes toward behavioural alternatives. *Journal of Experimental Social Psychology*, 17, 286–307.

Jefferson, G. (1984). On the organisation of laughter in talk about troubles. In J. Atkinson and J. Heritage (eds), *Structures of social action*. Cambridge: Cambridge University Press, pp. 346–69.

Johnson, P., Giles, H. and Bourhis, R. Y. (1983). The viability of ethnolinguistic vitality: A reply to Husband and Khan. *Journal of Multilingual and Multicultural Development*, 4, 255–69.

Kalin, R. and Rayko, D. (1980). The social significance of speech in the job interview. In R. N. St Clair and H. Giles (eds), *The social and psychological contexts of language*. London: Edward Arnold, pp. 39–50.

Kauffman, C. (1989). Names and weapons. *Communication Monographs*, 56, 273–85.

Kellerman, K. (1989). The negativity effect in interaction. *Human Communication Research*, 16, 147–83.

Klemz, A. (1977). *Blindness and partial sight*. Cambridge: Woodhead-Faulkner.

Kline, S. L. (in press). Construct differentiation, legitimate authority, and features of regulative messages. *Journal of Language and Social Psychology*.

Knapp, M. L. (1983). Dyadic relationship development, In J. M. Wiemann and R. P. Harrison (eds), *Nonverbal interaction*. Beverly Hills: Sage, pp. 179–208.

Kochman, T. (1976). Perceptions along the power axis: A cognitive residue of inter-racial encounters. *Anthropological Linguistics*, 18, 261–73.

Kochman, T. (1986). Black verbal dualing strategies in interethnic communication. In Y. Y. Kim (ed.), *Interethnic communication: Recent research*. Newbury Park, CA: Sage, pp. 136–57.

Kraemer, R. and Olshtain, E. (1989). Perceived ethnolinguistic vitality and language attitudes: The Israel setting. *Journal of Multilingual and Multicultural Development*, 10, 197–212.

Kramarae, C. (1990). Changing the complexion of gender in language research. In H. Giles and W. P. Robinson (eds), *Handbook of language and social psychology*. Chichester: Wiley, pp. 345–62.

Krashen, S. D. (1982). *Principles and practice in second language acquisition*. Oxford: Pergamon.

Krashen, S. D. (1985). *The input hypothesis: Issues and implication*. London: Longman.

Krauss, R. M. (1987). The role of the listener: Addressee influences on message formulation. *Journal of Language and Social Psychology*, 6, 81–97.

Krauss, R. M. and Fussell, S. R. (1988). Other-relatedness in language processing, discussion and comments. *Journal of Language and Social Psychology*, 7, 263–79.

Kristiansen, T. (1989). A case for language attitudes. Mimeo: Dialectology, University of Copenhagen.

Labov, W. (1964). Phonological correlates of social stratification. In Supplement to *American Anthropologist*, 66, 164–76.

Labov, W. (1966). *The social stratification of English in New York City*. Washington, DC: Center for Applied Linguistics.

Labov, W. (1969). The logic of nonstandard English. *Georgetown Monographs on Language and Linguistics*, 22, 1–31.

Labrie, N. and Clément, R. (1986). Ethnolinguistic vitality, self-confidence and second language proficiency: An investigation. *Journal of Multilingual and Multicultural Development*, 7, 269–82.

LaFrance, M. (1985). Postural mirroring and intergroup relations. *Personality and Social Psychology Bulletin*, 11, 207–17.

Lakoff, R. (1973). Language and women's place. *Language in Society*, 2, 45–80.

Lambert, W. E. (1967). A social psychology of bilingualism. *Journal of Social Issues*, 23, 91–109.

Lambert, W. E. (1974). Culture and language as factors in learning and education. In F. E. Aboud and R. D. Meade (eds), *Cultural factors in learning and education*. Bellingham, WA: Western Washington College Press.

Lambert, W. E. (1980). The social psychology of language: A perspective for the 1980s. In H. Giles, W. P. Robinson and P. M. Smith (eds), *Language: Social psychological perspectives*. Oxford: Pergamon, pp. 415–24.

Lambert, W. E. Hodgson, R., Gardner, R. C. and Fillenbaum, S. (1960). Evaluational reactions to spoken languages. *Journal of Abnormal and Social Psychology*, 60, 44–51.

Lambert, W. E., Mermigis, L. and Taylor, D. M. (1986). Greek Canadians' attitudes toward own group and other Canadian ethnic groups: A test of the multiculturalism hypothesis. *Canadian Journal of Behavioural Science*, 18, 35–51.

Lambert, W. E. and Tucker, G. R. (1972). *Bilingual education of children: The St Lambert experiment*. Rowley, MA: Newbury House.

Langer, E. J. (1978). Rethinking the role of thought in social interaction. In J. H. Harvey, W. J. Ickes and R. F. Kidd (eds), *New directions in attribution research, Vol. 2*. Hillsdale, NJ: Erlbaum, pp. 36–58.

Larsen, K., Martin, H. J. and Giles, H. (1977). Anticipated social cost and interpersonal accommodation. *Human Communication Research*, 3, 303–8.

Laver, J. and Trudgill, P. (1979). Phonetic and linguistic markers in speech. In K. R. Scherer and H. Giles (eds), *Social markers in speech*. Cambridge: Cambridge University Press, pp. 1–32.

Lehmann, D. R., Ellard, J. H. and Wortman, C. B. (1986). Social support for the bereaved: Recipients' and providers' perspectives on what is helpful. *Journal of Counseling and Clinical Psychology*, 54, 438–46.

Lerner, R. and Busch-Rossnagel, N., (1981). *Individuals as producers of their development: A life span perspective*. New York: Academic Press.

Levin, H. and Lin, T. (1988). An accommodating witness. *Language and Communications*, 8, 195–8.

Lewis, G. (1979). A comparative study of language contact: The influence of demographic factors in Wales and the Soviet Union. In W. C. McCormack and S. A. Wurm (eds), *Language and society: Anthropological issues*. The Hague: Mouton, pp. 331–58.

Louw, J., Louw-Potgieter, J., Bokhurst, F. and Patel, C. (in press). Subjective vitality ratings of three Indian languages in South Africa. *Journal of South African Linguistics*.

Louw-Potgieter, J. and Giles, H. (1987). Imposed identity and linguistic strategies. *Journal of Language and Social Psychology*, 6, 261–86.

Luhman, R. (1990). Appalachian English stereotypes: Language attitudes in Kentucky. *Language in Society*, 19, 331–48.

Lukens, J. (1979). Interethnic conflict and communicative distance. In H. Giles and R. Saint-Jacques (eds), *Language and ethnic group relations*. Oxford: Pergamon Press.

Maas, A., Salvi, D., Arcuri, L. and Semin, G. (1989). Language use in intergroup contexts: The linguistic intergroup bias. *Journal of Personality and Social Psychology*, 57, 981–93.

MacLean, D. and Gould, S. (1988). *The helping process: An introduction*. New York: Croom Helm.

McKirnan, D. and Hamayan, E. V. (1984). Speech norms and attitudes toward outgroup members: a test of a model in a bicultural context. *Journal of Language and Social Psychology*, 3, 21–38.

McNabb, S. L. (1986). Stereotypes and interaction conventions of Eskimos and non-Eskimos. In Y. Y. Kim (ed.), *Interethnic communication: Recent research*. Newbury Park, CA: Sage, pp. 21–41.

McNamara, T. F. (1987). Language and social identity: Israelis abroad. *Journal of Language and Social Psychology*, 6, 215–28.

Maltz, D. N. and Borker, R. (1982). A cultural approach to male–female communication. In J. J. Gumperz (ed.), *Language and social identity*. Cambridge: Cambridge University Press, pp. 195–216.

Markova, I. (1990). Language and communication in mental handicap. In H. Giles and W. P. Robinson (eds), *Handbook of language and social psychology*. Chichester: Wiley, pp. 363–82.

Mercer, N., Mercer, E. and Mears, R. (1979). Linguistic and cultural affiliation amongst young Asian people in Leicester. In H. Giles and B. Saint-Jacques (eds), *Language and ethnic relations*. Oxford: Pergamon, pp. 15–26.

Miller, G. R. and Steinberg, M. (1975). *Between people: A new analysis of interpersonal communication*. Chicago: Science Research Associate.

Miller, R. A. (1982). *The Japanese language: The myth and beyond*. Tokyo: Weatherhill Inc.

Milroy, L. (1980). *Language and social networks*. Oxford: Blackwell.

Milroy, L. (1984). Comprehension and context: Successful communication and communication breakdown. In P. Trudgill (ed.), *Applied Sociolinguistics*. London: Academic Press, pp. 7–32.

Montepare, J. M. and Vega, C. (1988). Women's vocal reactions to intimate and casual male friends. *Personality and Social Psychology Bulletin*, 14, 103–12.

Mulac, A. and Lundell, T. (1986). Linguistic contributions to the gender-linked language effect. *Journal of Language and Social Psychology*, 5, 81–101.

Mulac, A. Studley, L. B., Wiemann, J. M. and Bradac, J. J. (1987). Male/female gaze in same-sex and mixed-sex dyads: Gender-linked differences and mutual influence. *Human Communication Research*, 13, 323–43.

Mulac, A., Wiemann, J. M., Widenmann, S. and Gibson, T. W. (1988). Male/female language differences and effects in same-sex and mixed-sex dyads: The gender-linked language effect. *Communication Monographs*, 55, 315–35.

Murphy, T. M. and Street, R. L., Jr (1987). Interpersonal orientation and speech behaviour. *Communication Monographs*, 54, 42–62.

Muthiani, J. (1979). Sociopsychological bases of language choice and use: The case of Swahili vernaculars and English in Kenya. In W. C.

McCormack and S. A. Wurm (eds), *Language and society: Anthropological issues*. The Hague: Mouton, pp. 377–88.

Natalé, M. (1975a). Convergence of mean vocal intensity in dyadic communications as a function of social desirability. *Journal of Personality and Social Psychology*, 32, 790–804.

Natalé, M. (1975b). Social desirability as related to convergence of temporal speech patterns. *Perceptual and Motor Skills*, 40, 827–30.

Ng, S. H. (1990). Language and control. In H. Giles and W. P. Robinson (eds), *Handbook of language and social psychology*. Chichester: Wiley, pp. 271–88.

Noller, P. and Fitzpatrick, M. A. (eds) (1988). *Perspectives on marital interaction*. Clevedon: Multilingual Matters.

Notarius, C. I. and Herrick, L. R. (1988). Listener response strategies to a distressed other. *Journal of Social and Personal Relationships*, 5, 97–108.

Nussbaum, J., Thompson, T. and Robinson, J. D. (1989). *Communication and Aging*. New York: Harper and Row.

Oglivie, D. M. (1987). Life satisfaction and identity structure in late middle-aged men and women. *Psychology and Ageing*, 2, 217–24.

O'Keefe, B. J., and Delia, J. G. (1985). Psychological and interactional dimensions of communicative development. In H. Giles and R. N. St Clair (eds), *Recent advances in language, communication and social psychology*. London: Erlbaum, pp. 41–85.

Paltridge, J. and Giles, H. (1984). Attitudes towards speakers of regional accents of French: Effects of regionality, age and sex of listeners. *Linguistische Berichte*, 90, 71–85.

Patterson, M. (1983). *Nonverbal behavior: A functional perspective*. New York: Springer-Verlag.

Paulhus, D. L. and Martin, C. L. (1988). Functional flexibility: A new conception of interpersonal flexibility. *Journal of Personality and Social Psychology*, 55, 88–101.

Pear, T. H. (1931). *Voice and personality*. London: Wiley.

Pedersen, P. (1983). Learning about the Chinese culture through the Chinese language. *Communication and Cognition*, 16, 403–12.

Pellowe, J. (1990). Who is context? In G. McGregor and R. S. White (eds), *Reception and response*. London: Routledge, pp. 69–96.

Pendleton, D. (1983). Doctor–patient communication: A review. In D. Pendleton and D. Hasler (eds), *Doctor–patient communication*. London: Academic Press, pp. 5–53.

Pendleton, D. and Bochner, S. (1980). The communication of medical information in general practice consultations as a function of patients' social class. *Social Science and Medicine*, 14, 669–73.

Penman, R. (1991). Facework and politeness: Multiple goals in courtroom discourse. *Journal of Language and Social Psychology*, 9.

Peterson, C., Seligman, M. E. P. and Vaillant, G. E. (1988). Pessimistic explanatory style as a risk factor of physical illness: A thirty-five-year longitudinal study. *Journal of Personality and Social Psychology*, 55, 23–7.

Pierson, H. D. and Bond, M. H. (1982). How do Chinese bilinguals respond to variations of interviewer language and ethnicity? *Journal of Language and Social Psychology*, 1, 123–40.

Pierson, H., Giles, H. and Young, L. (1987). Intergroup vitality perceptions during a period of political uncertainty: The case of Hong Kong. *Journal of Multilingual and Multicultural Development*, 8, 451–60.

Platt, J. (1977). A model of polyglossia and multilingualism. *Language in Society*, 6, 361–78.

Platt, J. and Weber, H. (1984). Speech convergence miscarried: An investigation into inappropriate accommodation strategies. *International Journal of the Sociology of Language*, 46, 131–46.

Potter, J. and Reicher, S. (1987). Discourses of community and conflict: The organization of social categories in accounts of a 'riot'. *British Journal of Social Psychology*, 26, 25–40.

Potter, J. and Wetherell, M. (1987). *Discourse and social psychology: Beyond attitudes and behaviour*. London: Sage.

Powesland, P. and Giles, H. (1975). Persuasiveness and accent–message incompatibility. *Human Relations*, 28, 85–93.

Price, S., Fluck, M. and Giles, H. (1983). The effects of testing bilingual preadolescents' attitudes towards Welsh and varieties of English. *Journal of Multilingual and Multicultural Development*, 4, 149–62.

Purcell, A. K. (1984). Code shifting in Hawaiian style: Children's accommodation along a decreolizing continuum. *International Journal of the Sociology of Language*, 46, 71–86.

Putnam, W. and Street, R. (1984). The conception and perception of noncontent speech performance: Implications for speech accommodation theory. *International Journal of the Sociology of Language*, 46, 97–114.

Rabbie, J. M., Schot, J. C. and Visser, L. (1989). Social identity theory: A conceptual and empirical critique from the perspective of a behavioural interaction model. *European Journal of Social Psychology*, 19, 171–202.

Ragan, S. L. and Hopper, R. (1984). Ways to leave your lover: A conversational analysis of literature. *Communication Quarterly*, 32, 318–27.

Reardon, K. and Buck, R. (1989). Emotion, reason and communication in coping with cancer. *Health Communication*, 1, 41–54.

Redding, W. C. (1972). *Communication within organizations*. New York: Industrial Communication Council.

Revenson, T. A. (1990). Social support among chronically ill elders: Patient and provider perspectives. In H. Giles, N. Coupland and J. M.

Wiemann (eds), *Communication, health and the elderly*. Manchester: Manchester University Press, pp. 92–113.

Rivera, C. (1984). *Communicative competence approaches to language proficiency assessment: Research and application*. Clevedon: Multilingual Matters.

Robinson, W. P. (1972). *Language and social behaviour*. Harmondsworth: Penguin.

Rommetveit, R. (1979). On the architecture of intersubjectivity. In R. Rommetveit and R. M. Blakar (eds), *Studies of language, thought, and communication*. London: Academic Press, pp. 93–107.

Rook, K. (1984). The negative side of social interaction. *Journal of Personality and Social Psychology*, 46, 1097–1108.

Rook, K. (1990). Social networks as a source of social control in older adults' lives. In H. Giles, N. Coupland and J. M. Wiemann (eds), *Communication, health and the elderly*. Manchester: Manchester University Press pp. 45–63.

Ros, M., Cano, J. I. and Huici, C. (1987). Language and intergroup perception in Spain. *Journal of Language and Social Psychology*, 6, 243–59.

Rosenthal, M. (1974). The magic boxes: Pre-school children's attitudes toward black and standard English. *The Florida FL Reporter*, 12, 55–62, 92–3.

Ross, H. H. (1984). Speaking the unspeakable: The language of civil defense research. In J. Learing and L. Keyes (eds), *The counterfeit ark: Crisis relocation for nuclear war*. Cambridge MA: Ballinger.

Ross, J. (1979). Language and the mobilization of ethnic identity. In H. Giles and B. Saint-Jacques (eds), *Language and ethnic relations*. Oxford: Pergamon, pp. 1–14.

Ross, S. and Shortreed, I. (1990). Japanese foreigner talk: Convergence or divergence? *Journal of Asian Pacific Communication*, 1, 135–46.

Rotenberg, K. and Hamel, J. (1988). Social interaction and depression in elderly individuals. *International Journal of Ageing and Human Development*, 27, 305–18.

Rubin, A. M. and Rubin, R. B. (1982). Contextual age and television use. *Human Communication Research*, 9, 287–313.

Rubin, D. L. (1986). 'Nobody play by the rule he know': Ethnic interference in classroom questioning events. In Y. Y. Kim (ed.), *Interethnic communication: Recent research*. Newbury Park, CA: Sage, pp. 158–75.

Rubin, J. (1962). Bilingualism in Paraguay. *Anthropological Linguistics*, 4, 52–8.

Ryan, E. B., Carranza, M. A. and Moffie, R. W. (1977). Reactions towards varying degrees of accentedness in the speech of Spanish-English. *Language and Speech*, 20, 267–73.

Ryan, E. B., Giles, H., Bartolucci, G. and Henwood, K. (1986). Psycholinguistic and social psychological components of communication by and with the elderly. *Language and Communication*, 6, 1–24.

Ryan, E. B. and Sebastian, R. J. (1980). The effects of speech style and social class background on social judgements of speakers. *British Journal of Social and Clinical Psychology*, 19, 229–33.

Ryan, E. B., Giles, H. and Sebastian, R. (1982). An integrative perspective for the study of attitudes toward language variation. In E. B. Ryan and H. Giles (eds), *Attitudes towards language variation*. London: Edward Arnold, pp. 1–19.

Ryan, E. B., Hewstone, M. and Giles, H. (1984). Language and intergroup attitudes. In J. R. Eiser (ed.), *Attitudinal judgement*. New York: Springer-Verlag.

Sachdev, I. and Bourhis, R. Y. (1990). Bilinguality and multilinguality. In H. Giles and W. P. Robinson (eds), *Handbook of language and social psychology*. Chichester: Wiley, pp. 293–308.

Saint-Blancat, C. (1985). The effect of minority group vitality upon its sociopsychological behaviour and strategies. *Journal of Multilingual and Multicultural Development*, 6, 31–44.

San Antonio, P. M. (1987). Social mobility and language use in an American company in Japan. *Journal of Language and Social Psychology*, 6, 191–200.

Schaffer, D. R., Smith, J. E. and Tomarelli, M. (1982). Self-monitoring as a determinant of self-disclosure reciprocity during the acquaintance process. *Journal of Personality and Social Psychology*, 43, 163–75.

Schegloff, E. and Sacks, H. (1973). Openings and closings. *Semiotica*, 8, 289–327.

Scherer, K. R. (1979). Personality markets in speech. In K. R. Scherer and H. Giles (eds), *Social markers in speech*. Cambridge: Cambridge University Press, pp. 147–210.

Scherer, K. R. (1988). On the symbolic functions of vocal affect expression. *Journal of Language and Social Psychology*, 7, 79–100.

Schiappa, E. (1989). The rhetoric of nukespeak. *Communication Monographs*, 56, 253–72.

Schober, M. F. and Clark, H. H. (1989). Understanding by addressees and overhearers. *Cognitive Psychology*, 21, 211–32.

Schultz, N. R. and Moore, D. (1988). Loneliness: Differences across three age levels. *Journal of Social and Personal Relationships*, 5, 275–84.

Schumann, J. H. (1986). Research on the acculturation model for second language acquisition. *Journal of Multilingual and Multicultural Development*, 7, 379–92.

Scotton, C. M. (1979). Codeswitching as a 'safe choice' in choosing a lingua franca. In W. C. McCormack and S. Wurm (eds), *Language and society: Anthropological issues*. The Hague: Mouton, pp. 71–83.

Scotton, C. M. (1985). What the heck, sir: Style shifting and lexical colouring as features of powerful language. In R. L. Street, Jr and J. N. Cappella (eds), *Sequence and pattern in communicative behaviour*. London, Edward Arnold, pp. 103–19.

Seggie, I. (1983). Attribution of guilt as a function of ethnic accent and type of crime. *Journal of Multilingual and Multicultural Development*, 4, 197–206.

Seggie, I., Smith, N. and Hodgins, P. (1986). Evaluations of employment suitability based on accent alone: An Australian case study. *Language Sciences*, 8, 129–40.

Seligman, C., Tucker, G. R. and Lambert, W. E. (1972). The effects of speech style and other attributes on teachers' attitudes toward pupils. *Language in Society*, 1, 131–42.

Seltig, M. (1985). Levels of style-shifting exemplified in the interaction strategies of a moderator in a listener participation programme. *Journal of Pragmatics*, 9, 179–97.

Semin, G. R. (1989). The contribution of linguistic factors to attribute inferences and semantic judgements. *European Journal of Social Psychology*, 19, 85–100.

Semin, G. R. and Fielder, K. (1989). Relocating attributional phenomena within a language–cognition interface: The case of actors' and observers' perspectives. *European Journal of Social Psychology*, 19, 491–508.

Shadden, B. B. (ed.) (1988). *Communication behaviour and ageing: A sourcebook for clinicians*. Baltimore, MD: Williams and Wilkins.

Shuy, R., Baratz, J. and Wolfram, W. (1969). *Sociolinguistic factors in speech identification*. National Institute of Mental Health Research Project No. MH-15048-01. Washington, DC: Centre for Applied Linguistics.

Simard, L., Taylor, D. M. and Giles, H. (1976). Attribution processes and interpersonal accommodation in a bilingual setting. *Language and Speech*, 19, 374–87.

Smith, P. M., Giles, H. and Hewstone, M. (1980). Sociolinguistics: A social psychological perspective. In R. St Clair and H. Giles (eds), *The social and psychological contexts of language*. Hillsdale, NJ: Erlbaum, pp. 283–98.

Smolicz, J. J. (1984). Minority languages and the core values of culture: Changing policies and ethnic response in Australia. *Journal of Multilingual and Multicultural Development*, 5, 23–41.

Snyder, M. (1981). On the self-perpetuating nature of social stereotypes. In D. L. Hamilton (ed.), *Cognitive processes in stereotyping and intergroup behaviour*. Hillsdale, NJ: Lawrence Erlbaum.

Spacapan, S. and Oskamp, S. (1989). *The social psychology of ageing*. Newbury Park, CA: Sage.

Stephenson, G. M. (1988). Applied social psychology. In M. Hewstone, W.

Stroebe, J. P. Codol, and G. M. Stephenson (eds), *Introduction to Social Psychology*, pp. 413–44. Oxford: Blackwell.

Stewart, M. A., Ryan, E. B. and Giles, H. (1985). Accent and social class effects on status and solidarity evaluations. *Personality and Social Psychology Bulletin*, 11, 98–105.

Stoller, E. P. and Pugliesi, K. L. (1989). The transition to the caregiving role: A panel study of helpers of elderly people. *Research on Ageing*, 11, 312–30.

Street, R. L., Jr. (1982). Evaluation of noncontent speech accommodation. *Language and Communication*, 2, 13–31.

Street, R. L., Jr. (1984). Speech convergence and speech evaluation in fact-finding interviews. *Human Communication Research*, 11, 139–69.

Street, R. L., Jr. (in press). Accommodation in medical consultations. In H. Giles, J. Coupland and N. Coupland (eds), *Contexts of accommodation: Developments in applied sociolinguistics*. Cambridge: Cambridge University Press.

Street, R. L., Brady, R. M. and Lee, R. M. (1983). Evaluative responses to communications: The effects of speech rate, sex and interaction context. *Western Journal of Speech Communication*, 48, 14–27.

Street, R. L., Jr. and Hopper, R. (1982). A model of speech style evaluation. In E. B. Ryan and H. Giles (eds), *Attitudes towards language variation*. London: Edward Arnold, pp. 175–88.

Street, R. L., Jr., Street, N. J. and Van Kleeck, A. (1983). Speech convergence among talkative and reticent three-year-olds. *Language Sciences*, 5, 79–86.

Swain, M. (in press). Additive bilingualism and French immersion education: The roles of language proficiency and literacy. In A. G. Reynolds (ed.), *Bilingualism, multiculturalism, and second language learning*. Hillsdale: NJ: Erlbaum.

Tajfel, H. (1959). A note on Lambert's 'Evaluational reactions to spoken language'. *Canadian Journal of Psychology*, 13, 86–92.

Tajfel, H. (1974). Social identity and intergroup behaviour. *Social Science Information*, 13, 65–93.

Tajfel, H. (ed.) (1978). *Differentiation between social groups*. London: Academic Press.

Tajfel, H. (1981). Social stereotypes and social groups. In J. C. Turner and H. Giles (eds), *Intergroup behaviour*. Oxford: Blackwell, pp. 144–65.

Tajfel, H., and Turner, J. C. (1979). An integrative theory of intergroup conflict. In W. C. Austin and S. Worchel (eds), *The social psychology of intergroup relations*. Monterey, CA: Brooks/Cole, pp. 33–53.

Taylor, D. M., Bassili, J. N. and Aboud, F. (1973). Dimensions of ethnic identiy: An example from Quebec. *Journal of Social Psychology*, 89, 185–92.

Taylor, D. M., Delain, M., Pearson, P. D. and Anderson, R. C. (1985). Reading comprehension and creativity in black language use: You stand to gain by playing the sounding game! *American Educational Research Journal*, 22, 155–73.

Taylor, D. M. and McKirnan, D. J. (1984). A five-stage theory of intergroup behaviour. *British Journal of Social Psychology*, 23, 291–300.

Taylor, D. M. and Royer, E. (1980). Group processes affecting anticipated language choice in intergroup relations. In H. Giles, W. P. Robinson and P. M. Smith (eds), *Language: Social psychological perspectives*. Oxford: Pergamon, pp. 185–92.

Taylor, D. M. and Simard, L. (1975). Social interaction in a bilingual setting. *Canadian Psychological Review*, 16, 240–54.

Taylor, D. M., Simard, L. and Papineau, D. (1978). Perceptions of cultural differences and language use: A field study in a bilingual environment. *Canadian Journal of Behaviour Science*, 10, 181–91.

Thakerar, J. N., Giles, H., and Cheshire, J. (1982). Psychological and linguistic parameters of speech accommodation theory. In C. Fraser and K. R. Scherer (eds), *Advances in the social psychology of language*. Cambridge, Cambridge University Press, pp. 205–55.

Ting-Toomey, S. (1988). Intercultural conflict styles: A face-negotiation theory. In Y. Y. Kim, and W. B. Gudykunst (eds), *Theories in intercultural communication*. Newbury Park, CA: Sage, pp. 213–38.

Tracy, K. and Coupland, N. (eds) (1991). Multiple goals in discourse. *Journal of Language and Social Psychology*, 9.

Triandis, H. (1972). *The analysis of subjective culture*, New York: Wiley.

Triandis, H. (1985). Commentary. *Journal of Multilingual and Multicultural Development*, 6, 313–23.

Triandis, H. C., Bontempo, R., Villarcal, M. J., Asai, M. and Lucca, N. (1988). Individualism–collectivism: Cross-cultural perspectives on self–group relationships. *Journal of Personality and Social Psychology*, 54, 323–38.

Tromel-Plötz, S. (1981). Review article: The languages of oppression. *Journal of Pragmatics*, 5, 67–80.

Trudgill, P. (1974). *Sociolinguistics*. Harmondsworth: Penguin.

Trudgill, P. (1986). *Dialects in contact*. Oxford: Blackwell.

Trudgill, P. and Giles, H. (1978). Sociolinguistics and linguistic value judgements: Correctness, adequacy and aesthetics. In F. Coppiertiers and D. Goyvaerts (eds), *The functions of language and literature studies*. Ghent: Storia Scientia.

Turner, J. C., with Hogg, M. A. *et al.* (1987). *Rediscovering the social group: A self-categorization theory*. Oxford, Blackwell.

Turner, J. C., Hogg, M., Turner, P. J. and Smith, P. M. (1984). Failure and defeat as determinants of group cohesiveness. *British Journal of Social Psychology*, 23, 97–112.

Turnquist, D., Harvey, J. H. and Anderson, B. L. (1988). Attributions and adjustment to life threatening illness. *British Journal of Clinical Psychology*, 27, 53–65.

Ullrich, H. E. (1971). Linguistic aspects of antiquity: A dialect study. *Anthropological Linguistics*, 13, 106–13.

Valdman, A. (1981). Sociolinguistic aspects of foreigner talk. *International Journal of the Sociology of Language*, 28, 41–52.

van den Berg, M. E., (1985). *Language planning and language use in Taiwan*. Dordrecht: ICG Printing.

van Dijk, T. A. (1987). *Communicating racism*. Newbury Park, CA: Sage.

Watzlawick, P., Beavin, J. H. and Jackson, D. (1967). *Pragmatics of human communication*. New York: Norton.

Weary, G. and Arkin, R. M. (1981). Attributional self-presentation. In J. H. Harvey, M. J. Ickes and R. Kidd (eds), *New directions in attribution theory and research, Vol. 3*. Hillsdale, NJ: Erlbaum.

Weiner, B., Perry, R. P. and Magnusson, J. (1988). An attributional analysis of reactions to stigmas. *Journal of Personality and Social Psychology*, 55, 738–48.

Welkowitz, J. G., Cariffe, G. and Feldstein, S. (1976) Conversational congruence as a criterion of socialisation in children. *Child Development*, 47, 269–72.

Welkowitz, J. and Feldstein, S. (1970). Relation of experimentally-manipulated interpersonal perception and psychological differentiation to the temporal patterning of conversation. *Proceedings of the 78th Annual Convention of the American Psychological Association*, 5, 387–8.

Welkowtiz, J., Feldstein, S., Finklestein, M. and Aylesworth, L. (1972). Changes in vocal intensity as a function of interspeaker influence. *Perceptual and Motor Skills*, 35, 715–18.

West, C. (1990). Not just 'doctors' orders': Directive-response sequences in patients' visits to women and men physicians. *Discourse and Society*, 1, 85–112.

West, C. and Frankel, R. (1991). Miscommunication in medicine. In N. Coupland, H. Giles and J. M. Wiemann (eds), *'Miscommunication' and problematic talk*. Newbury Park, CA: Sage.

West, C. and Garcia, A. (1988). Conversational shift work: A study of topical transitions between women and men. *Social Problems*, 35, 551–75.

West, C. and Zimmerman, D. H. (1987). Doing gender. *Gender and Society*, 1, 125–51.

White, S. (1989). Backchannels across cultures: A study of Americans and Japanese. *Language in Society*, 18, 59–76.

Whorf, B. (1941). The relationship of habitual thought and behaviour to language. In L. Sapir (ed.), *Language, culture and personality: Essays in memory of Edward Sapir*. Menasha, WI: Sapir Memorial Publication Fund, pp. 75–93.

Wiemann, J. M. and Bradac, J. J. (1987). Meta-theoretical issues in the study of communicative competence: Structural and functional approaches. *Progress in Communication Sciences*, 9, 261–84.

Wiemann, J. M. and Giles, H. (1988). Interpersonal communication. In M. Hewstone, W. Stroebe, J. P. London and G. M. Stephenson (eds), *Introducing social psychology*. Oxford: Blackwell, pp. 199–221.

Wiemann, J. M. and Kelly, C. W. (1981). Pragmatics of interpersonal competence. In C. Wilder-Mott and J. H. Weakland (eds), *Rigour and imagination: Essays from the legacy of Gregory Bateson*. New York: Praeger, pp. 283–97.

Williams, A., Giles, H., Coupland, N., Dalby, M. and Manasse, H. (1990). The communicative contexts of elderly social support and health: A theoretical model. *Health Communication*, 2, 123–43.

Williams, F. (1976). *Explorations of the linguistic attitudes of teachers*. Rowley, MA: Newbury House.

Wilmot, W. W. and Shellen, W. N. (1990). Language in friendships. In H. Giles and W. P. Robinson (eds), *Handbook of language and social psychology*. Chichester: Wiley, pp. 413–32.

Wish, M. and Kaplan, S. (1977). Toward an implicit theory of interpersonal communication. *Sociometry*, 40, 234–46.

Wolfram, W. (1973). Sociolinguistic aspects of assimilation: Puerto Rican English in Easter Harlem. In R. W. Shuy and R. W. Fasold (eds), *Language attitudes: Current trends and prospects*. Washington, DC: Centre for Applied Linguistics.

Woolard, K. A. (1989). *Double talk: Bilingualism and the politics of ethnicity in Catalonia*. Stanford, CA: Stanford University Press.

Woolard, K. A. and Gahng, T-J. (1990). Changing language policies and attitudes in autonomous Catalonia. *Language in Society*, 19, 311–30.

Yaeger-Dror, M. (1988). The influence of changing vitality on convergence toward a dominant linguistic norm: An Israeli example. *Language and Communication*, 8, 285–306.

Young, L., Bell, N. and Giles, H. (1988). Perceived vitality and context: A national majority in a minority setting. *Journal of Multilingual and Multicultural Development*, 9, 285–9.

Young, L., Giles, H. and Pierson, H. D. (1986). Sociopolitical change and perceived vitality. *International Journal of Intercultural Relations*, 10, 459–69.

Yum, J. O. (1988a). The impact of Confucianism on interpersonal relationships and communication patterns in East Asia. *Communication Monographs*, 55, 374–88.

Yum, J. O. (1988b). Network theory in intercultural communication. In Y.

Y. Kim and W. B. Gudykunst (eds), *Theories in intercultural communication*. Newbury Park, CA: Sage, pp. 239–58.

Zimmerman, D. H. and West, C. (1975). Sex roles, interruptions and silences in conversation. In B. Thorne and N. Henley (eds), *Language and sex: Difference and dominance*. Rowley, MA: Newbury House, pp. 105–29.

AUTHOR INDEX

SUBJECT INDEX